SOCIAL WORK AND THE THIRD WAY
Tough Love as Social Policy

SOCIAL WORK
AND THE THIRD WAY

Tough Love as Social Policy

BILL JORDAN

with
CHARLIE JORDAN

SAGE Publications
London • Thousand Oaks • New Delhi

First published in 2000

SAGE Publications Ltd
1 Oliver's Yard
55 City Road
London EC1Y 1SP

SAGE Publications Inc.
2455 Teller Road
Thousand Oaks, California 91320

SAGE Publications India Pvt Ltd
B-42, Panchsheel Enclave
Post Box 4109
New Delhi 110 017

British Library Cataloguing in Publication data

A catalogue record for this book is available from the British Library

C 978-0-7619-6720-0   P 978-0-7619-6721-7

Library of Congress catalog record available

Typeset by SIVA Math Setters, Chennai, India
Printed in Great Britain by The Cromwell Press Ltd, Trowbridge, Wiltshire

Contents

Acknowledgements

This book is the result of a long collaboration between brothers, largely conducted through telephone calls and (more recently) e-mails. We have, since the
late 1960s, been working mainly in adjacent fields – Bill in public-sector social
work and training, Charlie in youth and community work, the voluntary and community sectors – only to a limited extent crossing into each other's territories.
Although we have shared many ideas and inspirations, and often subscribed to the
same causes, the advent of the New Labour government has led to us working
together on a number of projects of common commitment. This book arises from
the recognition that the divisions between our fields of action make less and less
sense in the present context.

We would like to pay individual and joint tribute to a number of friends and
colleagues who helped in the preparation of the text, especially Andrew Travers
and Nigel Parton, who gave detailed comments and suggestions on the whole of
the first draft; and to the late Gerry Smale, whose work informed so much of it.
The book reflects many discussions and much direct borrowing from the thoughts
of others, notably Mita Castle-Kanerova, Franck Düvell, Phil Agulnik, Stuart
Duffin, Duncan Burbidge and Barry Hulyer. Bob Holman inspired much of
the optimism in it.

We are grateful to several colleagues and friends who provided material for the
case studies and examples, especially Jo Pass and Jeff Townsend; and to those
anonymised in the other examples for their permission to use these in the book.

Finally, Bill Jordan would like to thank his colleagues at Exeter, Huddersfield
and North London Universities, at the Max-Planck Institute for the Study of
Societies in Cologne (where he did much of his writing), and in Budapest,
Bratislava and Prague, for many of the arguments, analyses and topics of the
book. Special thanks are due to Gill Watson and Diana Cooper for expert work
in preparing the typescript.

Introduction: The Central Themes of the Book

This book is about the implementation of New Labour's programme of reforms of the welfare state. The UK government is strong on values, aspirations, goals and targets, but weaker on how to implement them. We will show that weaknesses in the implementation process reveal muddles, inconsistencies and gaps in the reform programme itself. Using a series of real-life case examples and case studies, we will illustrate the damaging unintended consequences of new policies, and suggest alternative methods. This introduction provides an overall orientation, context and summary of our main themes.

Throughout the book, we will try to balance our account between appreciation of the strengths of New Labour's approach, and criticism of the weaknesses it conceals. There can be no doubting the political skill with which the government has mobilized a new reformist coalition of electoral support, or the energy it has brought to the task. The strategy of promising mainstream voters that welfare spending will be used to build a new system that promotes employment and independence has been highly successful, and has created a wonderful opportunity for radical change. It has also instigated a stream of new interactions between government agencies (often themselves revamped or newly established) and civil society organizations.

But we will argue that the present directions of change are not sustainable, either in economic terms, or as culture shifts. It is not too late to modify or transform them, if the government is willing to listen to those involved in trying to make its policies work. Unless it does so, it risks losing its momentum and sacrificing gains already achieved.

As a way of analysing New Labour's implementation dilemmas, the book focuses on *social work* as an instrument for realizing the programme:

1 because New Labour is surprisingly reliant on methods involving face-to-face interventions by officials (often called 'counsellors' or 'advisers') to achieve changes in behaviour and culture it seeks;
2 yet existing public social work agencies are seldom its chosen vehicles for implementation – it prefers to create new agencies and roles, often with a specifically enforcement emphasis;
3 this symbolizes New Labour's suspicion of the public sector in general, and local authorities in particular, which it regards as harbouring Old Labour values and interests, and hence being part of 'the forces of conservatism';
4 yet New Labour's policies, especially those for economic and social regeneration, spawn masses of new projects, community groups and informal

associations, all of which – like its new public agencies – are involved in 'social work' (in its broadest sense) and whose success is crucial for the reform programme;

5 therefore it is important to understand the nature, potential and limitations of these methods and activities, and their wider implications for the economy and the polity – for the longer-term evolution of labour markets, social relations and democratic governance.

The first thesis of this book is that reform of the welfare state is an even more important part of New Labour's overall programme than the government claims it to be. In breaking out of the impasse over public spending (which the Conservative governments of the 1980s and 1990s had ultimately failed to reduce) and the 'underclass' (defying Thatcherism and its successor regime by various unorthodox and deviant means) the Blair administration has solved one set of problems, but will soon be confronted with another. It has adopted as a central principle the idea of a welfare system which demands more of those who receive assistance – 'no rights without responsibilities' – and which in exchange improves their incentives and opportunities. But this in turn faces it with new issues about the nature of the *work* around which it aims to build the welfare system, and the kinds of *security* and inclusion it offers them as a reward. These questions are not separate from the ones about social work and implementation already raised. They are two sides of the same coin.

The Third Way

Throughout the book, we use the term 'Third Way' to indicate the broad philosophy and principles behind the programme of the New Labour government. These have been set out by Tony Blair himself (Blair, 1998a) and by his sociological guru Tony Giddens (Giddens, 1998) in works bearing that title; the common elements in their accounts are summarized in Box 2 on p. 20. But despite the sometimes grandiose claims on its behalf, the Third Way is a specifically British solution to a set of issues which – in one form or another – confront all welfare states. Because its course has been set largely by the opportunities and problems it inherited from Margaret Thatcher's free-market policies, it has limited application to other countries. Our concern is to examine how its claim to reconcile the liberty of market relations with equality and community stand up at the implementation stage of the reform process, and why quasi-social-work methods are part of that programme. This theme will be explored in Part I.

In all the OECD countries, reform of welfare systems has been forced on governments by the erosion of collective institutions for protecting employment, redistributing income and providing social services (Scharpf, 1999). It was possible to establish these institutions in the postwar period because national governments were able to control their economic boundaries; levels of transnational trade were low because of the war, and capital movements were limited by law. The rapid growth in trade and the breakdown of restrictions on the free movement of capital have brought about the international integration of markets known as 'globalization', which undermines nation states' capacities to manage demand and employment, raise revenue and protect living standards.

What was distinctive about the responses of governments in the Anglo-Saxon or liberal welfare states to this challenge was that they *embraced* the disciplines of global economic forces, imposing new regimes of market austerity on their public services, and economic competition on their citizens. Whereas Continental European and Scandinavian countries chose to increase social insurance contributions as a response to rising unemployment, and to protect wage levels and job security, Anglo-Saxon states spread the net of taxes on personal incomes (Scharpf, 1999, table 5), shifted further towards means-tested benefit systems, made these more conditional on work effort, and allowed wages at the lower end of the labour market to fall. All this was done by Conservative governments in the USA and UK, but by Labour administrations in Australia and New Zealand.

In the 1990s, the unintended consequences of the decade of individualism and markets – insecurity, poverty, rising crime, social divisions – have provoked reassessment in just those countries that pioneered the shift away from collectivist systems. The collapse of state socialism in the Soviet Union and East Central Europe, followed by the rapid decline in living standards that accompanied the beginning of the economic transformation, fuelled the debate about how to combine the benefits of free trade and the new international division of labour with an acceptable degree of social cohesion, solidarity and respect for law. The Third Way is the British response – very different from the even more successful Irish version, which has much less of a moral crusade about it, and more emphasis on social partnership and agreement in the reform process (Jordan et al., 2000, Chapter 1).

The main preoccupations of the Third Way's programme have been:

To make work pay. Tax-benefit reform has been a priority in all the Anglo-Saxon, liberal welfare states, and all have come up with similar technical solutions (Jordan, 2000). These involve running down social insurance systems, increasing the role of means-tested benefits for those outside the labour market, and giving support to low-wage workers through the tax system. The New Labour version is mainly modelled on the Australian, where these changes have been achieved without damaging the living standards of the poorest (Castles, 1996, pp. 103–4), but using US-style tax credits to improve work incentives. The Chancellor, Gordon Brown, has announced that these are soon to be extended to households without children (Treasury, 1999). Other EU countries would like to find ways to make work pay and to provide secure income (European Commission, 1999, p. 1) but they cannot adopt this approach because their social insurance systems are much more developed, and all economic actors have a greater stake in them (Streeck, 1999).

Our analysis shows that attempts to widen employment through tax credits are not sustainable. Although they mitigate the unemployment traps that have kept so many outside the labour market, they also extend poverty traps to a broader section of the working population, so more people have incentives to work less. Econometricians have calculated that the net effect of the Working Families Tax Credit scheme will be a reduction in overall labour supply (Blundell et al., 1999).

We show that these and other technical difficulties in tax-benefit reforms on this trajectory will take the New Labour government in unplanned and unexpected directions (Chapter 1, pp. 34–7 and Chapter 8, pp. 193–203).

Meanwhile, the welfare reform programme involves officials in a range of detailed transactions with claimants under the various New Deals, in which they are 'counselled' in the direction of employment, education or training, as a way of reinforcing the incentives provided and reducing benefit fraud. We argue that this signals two important messages. First, the New Labour programme has to be *negotiated* with citizens if its aims are to be implemented, which is why these quasi-social work methods are required. Second, it is time for a long overdue recognition that the social work profession should re-engage with economic issues, from which it has largely withdrawn since the advent of the welfare state. In Chapters 7 and 8 we show that many projects and units are already doing so, but that this should be an explicit reorientation of professional activity.

To strengthen responsibility and community. This part of the programme has mainly stemmed from alarm at the consequences of almost two decades of economic individualism, reflected in rates of crime, family break-up, drug addiction, alcoholism, truancy and so on. It consists mainly of ministerial rhetoric (with the moral exhortations of the Prime Minister especially prominent), combined with tough enforcement measures. Although the government is clearly serious about this aspect of its attempt to change cultures and attitudes, it seems to have very little idea about how to develop a policy programme to implement it.

We have borrowed the phrase 'tough love' from a newspaper article, written in the wake of the murder of Jamie Bulger (Phillips, 1993), as a shorthand way of encapsulating this aspect of the Third Way (see Box 3, p. 25). It conveys the key message that the reform of welfare systems is a moral enterprise that requires personal and emotional commitment by those engaged in its implementation. However, Third Way morality is itself empty and incoherent (Chapter 2), and its ideas on how to achieve change are almost completely undeveloped.

Behind these preoccupations lie crucial issues about the environment, human diversity and solidarity, faith and spirituality. Global markets promote social relations of instrumental exchange between individual bargain-hunters. Turning the world into One Big Market (Polanyi, 1944) necessarily provokes a counter-movement that tries to embed such individualism in a cultural context, and rein in the 'creative destruction' of capitalist development (Schumpeter, 1936), through institutions for restraining competition and promoting co-operation. But along with traditional structures like churches and the armed services, welfare states themselves have largely ceased to provide such orientations and restraints under global economic conditions. Increased mobility and better communication have created a more atomized society, where even politics is less organized. Roy Hattersley reports that, after he had written an article accusing Tony Blair of trying to 'take the politics out of politics', the latter remarked to him that the politics had gone out of politics several years ago (BBC Radio 4 *World at One*, 31 December 1999).

Our first criticism of the Third Way version of responsibility and community is that it extrapolates from the morality of small-scale groups and associations (families, clubs, voluntary organizations) and informal networks, and applies this inappropriately to large-scale societies and the formal rights and duties of citizenship (Jordan, 1998a, Chapters 2 and 3). Many of the principles that inform the New Deals are of this kind, prescribing obligations on the basis of work contributions which are the stuff of everyday co-operation in those informal systems, but cannot consistently be required by the state of citizens of a liberal democracy. This makes the task of implementing certain parts of the programme in a spirit of social justice more difficult, because 'counsellors' in those initiatives have the power to withhold benefits from those who do not meet tough conditions for eligibility. It would be possible to move towards a fairer version of responsibility if a wider definition of relevant contributions to co-operation and community were adopted (Chapters 2 and 8).

Second, the Third Way's attempt to counter the selfishness and greed it sees as characterizing economic individualism is applied only to those citizens who rely on welfare benefits and services, and not to the mainstream population. In order to replace the collectivism of the Old Labour welfare state, it draws on a largely traditional backward-looking, intolerant and prescriptive notion of community (Driver and Martell, 1997; Jordan, 1998b), with religion and the family as bulwarks of social discipline. This is closely allied with a very tough line on criminal justice, which has resulted in an even faster rise in the prison population than during Michael Howard's tenure at the Home Office (see Box, 5, p. 33).

Third, the changes in attitudes and cultural practices sought by the government require some kind of mediation between the formal rules and institutions of the economy and polity, and the informal, everyday order of households, neighbourhoods and associations. New Labour fails to recognize the need to channel and soften what we call the 'blood-and-guts codes' that rule the latter (Jordan, 1999a) through skilled, flexible and imaginative practice. Mechanistic or heavy-handed approaches tend to strengthen the resistance of subcultures. Coerced co-operation is based on feigned compliance, strategic shows of need and helplessness but covert deviance and non-disclosure. This is where the experience of social workers has much to offer to the implementation of the programme, since social work has always operated in the territory between the formal and informal systems, with a half-willing clientele.

Social Inclusion

As Ruth Lister has observed, social exclusion has replaced poverty and inequality as the focus of New Labour's programme (Lister, 1998). Indeed, in his book on the Third Way, Giddens suggests that

> 'the new politics defines equality as inclusion and inequality as exclusion ... inclusion refers in its broadest sense to citizenship, to the civil and political rights and obligations that all members of a society should have ... It also refers to opportunities and to involvement in the public space. (1998, pp. 102–3)

He goes on to argue that 'exclusion is not about gradations of inequality, but about mechanisms that act to detach groups from the social mainstream'

(p. 104). This implies that welfare systems should focus on making such groups more employable through education and training. 'The cultivation of human potential should as far as possible replace "after the event" redistribution' (p. 101). In what Giddens calls the Social Investment State, equality consists in equipping citizens better for participation in a competitive economic and political environment.

There are many difficulties about this view. If a person's life chances are determined by some combination of their external resources (wealth), internal resources (talent) and the effort they put into various activities, and if none of these is equally distributed in a population, then social justice (which both Tony Blair and Tony Giddens implicitly equate with social inclusion) requires an evaluation of the *outcomes* of competition; there must be a justification of the inequalities of these outcomes in terms of those original factors (Carling, 1999). As Giddens himself comments, 'nations are ethical communities, where those involved owe special obligations to other members not owed to others on the outside' (Giddens, 1998, p. 131). Old-style welfare states were just such communities, in that members paid taxes and social insurance contributions into collective funds, which were redistributed to those falling into appropriate categories of need. This was justified on the grounds that market competition rewarded wealth and talent too generously, and effort (including unpaid activity) insufficiently. If 'inclusion in the mainstream' means no more than competing in the market, then inclusion does not address the central issues of inequality relevant to social justice.

Furthermore, the 'mechanisms that act to detach groups from the social mainstream' are often the consequence as well as causes of poverty. Exclusion is not an incidental feature of human interactions; there is no inclusion without exclusion. Groups and collectivities form to share the costs and benefits of co-operation among members; but this is only possible if non-members are excluded (Buchanan, 1965). Members must be capable of making the necessary contributions, in terms of material resources or work efforts. Society can be conceived as an environment consisting of overlapping and competing groups, each supplying one or more collective goods for its members. Which particular combinations of members (in terms of their individual capabilities, resources and risks) these groups will contain is influenced by society's overall institutional framework (Starrett, 1988; Mueller, 1989). In the less constrained environment created by Margaret Thatcher's policies of deregulation and privatization, individuals have tended to form more homogeneous groups, based on narrower mutualities, individuals with similar incomes, and the pooling of similar risks, thus excluding poorer and more vulnerable people. Better-off households have pursued strategies for positional advantage, congregating in the best districts, around the best schools, clinics, hospitals, recreational facilities and so on (Jordan, 1996a; and see pp. 31–2). This has led to residential and social polarization, leaving poor people in the worst neighbourhoods and with the worst public services, as in the USA (Wilson, 1989, 1997). Hence social exclusion is as much a consequence of the choices of mainstream citizens who (like Tony Blair and Harriet Harman) seek the most advantageous education for their children, as of the deficits of the disadvantaged (Jordan et al., 1994, Chapter 7).

More generally, in a market economy collective actors like firms and trade unions organize to seek 'rents' (returns higher than they would receive under conditions of perfect competition), forcing unorganized individuals to accept market distributions. Thus the strongest are protected, while the weakest must compete, nowadays with enterprises and workers world-wide, because of globalization. In other words, the collective action of the organized excludes the unorganized, and the vulnerability of poor people consists in their exclusion from membership of rent-seeking 'distributive coalitions' within the economy (Olson, 1965, 1982). It is only by redistribution that vulnerable citizens can be compensated for the advantages enjoyed by members of these organizations; and it is only this redistribution that can justify those advantages.

The New Labour policy programme recognizes this in a number of ways. First, it transfers substantial new sums from tax revenue to low earners through tax credits and means-tested benefits (Chapters 1 and 8). Second, it has initiated a whole series of measures – through the New Deal for Communities, the Social Exclusion Unit, the Employment Zones, the Single Regeneration Budget, and so on – for the economic and social regeneration of the poorest districts. In Chapters 7 and 8 we reveal the tensions and contradictions between these initiatives, and show how their implementation is seriously hampered by these inconsistencies, and new exclusions are created.

Our analysis is intended to endorse the potential for community-based approaches which encourage democratic participation through local groups and associations. However, we argue for the addition of two important elements to this strategy, both largely absent from the present programme. First the public authority – in this case local government – has a key role to play in co-ordinating community responses, giving an overall direction to them, encouraging new needs to find organized expression, and avoiding duplication of provision. Because of New Labour's suspicion of local government, its agencies are unable to take this role, mainly because of lack of resources (Chapter 8).

Second, social work is in a good position to contribute to these initiatives, partly because of its engagement with the informal spheres of activity – households, support groups, self-help organizations, and so on. New Labour's programme is at present too focused on employment and the formal economy. It is as much through informal methods that inclusion will be achieved (Chapters 4 and 7). Citizens who are deemed incapable of formal employment may take part in work to improve the quality of life in their community, and thus become active and contributing citizens. But this alternative approach requires a culture shift towards a more plural, diverse conception of the contributions that citizens can make to society, and a valuation of difference rather than conformity.

Social Work

We argue for a broader conception of social work, that embraces community development (including economic and social regeneration of the kind just mentioned), and all the various projects and units that have sprung up in recent years, employing street-level, outreach or support workers. Many of these have not been trained as social workers, and do not even think of themselves as belonging to this occupational category. But they are doing just the kind of face-to-face work that we consider an essential part of the implementation of a revised New Labour programme.

One reason why these projects were proliferating – even before New Labour's measures began to come into effect – is that public sector social work had become locked into a style of practice that was legalistic, formal, procedural and arm's length. Both the local authority social services departments and the probation service were already increasingly concerned with assessing and managing risk and dangerousness (Kemshall and Pritchard, 1996). Social workers were thus primarily involved in allocating services and exercising surveillance through systems of rationing and control that made little use of interpersonal skills. The direct, face-to-face work that was required, both to implement government social policy, and to create a space in which needs, norms and rules were negotiated between the state and civil society, was increasingly done by voluntary organizations and community groups, through these projects, units and support schemes.

The New Labour reforms have consolidated rather than reversed these trends. The White Paper *Modernizing Social Services* (DoH, 1998a) is primarily concerned with regulating local authority departments, through a series of new supervisory and monitoring bodies; with setting new standards and targets against which to measure performance, and agencies to enforce these; and with establishing a new system of training for social care workers, under the guidance of a new Council for Social Care. All these developments are critically reviewed in Chapter 4.

At the same time, the government has also set up a number of new agencies with a strong deterrence and enforcement ethos – such as the Home Office service for asylum seekers – and put more funding into others with similar cultures and functions, such as the Benefits Agency Benefits Fraud Investigation Service (Home Office, 1998, Chapter 8; DSS, 1998, Chapter 9). This is part of the transformation of the welfare state into a tougher, more demanding and more punitive set of institutions, which New Labour attempts to justify in terms of 'fairness'. However, even these agencies must negotiate and use judgement and discretion in their dealings with citizens, and hence need skills that are related to those of social work. In Chapter 5 we analyse how these new agencies fit into the overall pattern of welfare state services, and point out that, far from contributing to 'joined-up policies' or 'holistic governance', they increase the incoherence of New Labour's programme.

Sooner rather than later, these tensions and contradictions will lead to a further reorganization of the social services. Already New Labour ministers are finding reasons to threaten suspension of local government departments and perhaps to hand them over to private firms or consultants. When change comes, there is a risk that it will either follow the route of privatization favoured by the Conservatives, or involve the fragmentation of the public services into a number of specialist functions, all with a narrow instrumental brief and dealing in a style of practice prescribed by detailed central government guidelines and manuals.

All these developments have been facilitated by a movement within research and training for social work that favours 'evidence-based' approaches to social care (Reid, 1994; Fischer, 1993). Its exponents claim that a more rigorous application of critical appraisal skills to existing research findings would yield clear guidelines about appropriate interventions for definable categories of cases. So it makes sense for practitioners to be guided by detailed and instrumental instructions on how to assess and deal with service users, in line with scientifically validated methodologies (Chapter 3).

In Chapter 9 we argue that these ideas are based on a flawed social science conception of what research can offer practitioners. The scientism and positivism of this approach has been discredited in sociology for many years, is methodologically unsound, and yields misleading conclusions. We suggest that the reasons for its current hegemony in social work have more to do with political agenda of New Labour than with the real needs of practitioners. While pursuing a rhetoric of improving educational and training standards (DoH, 1998a, Chapter 5), the government is in fact effectively deskilling the profession – social workers and probation officers alike. There is a real danger that social workers will become even easier scapegoats for policy failure than they were under the Conservatives.

Yet the work that practitioners do is vital for the success of the whole of New Labour's reform programme. It will influence how its increasing interventionism can be reconciled with democratic values; how the public authority relates to civil society in an increasingly heterogeneous, multi-racial society; and – above all – what success the programme has in motivating and engaging groups that had become disaffected and deviant under the Conservative regime.

All this poses a classic dilemma for social workers, one that has always haunted the profession. Should they seek to make Third Way policies more 'user-friendly' for citizens (reformism), or should they try to mobilize resistance to its oppressive features (opposition)? In practice, social work nearly always combines these two elements, and is therefore an ambiguous, ambivalent activity. We are arguing that social workers should make both aspects more explicit to themselves, and be more reflexive about them, recognizing common ground both with the 'enforcement counsellors' of the Third Way, and the community activists who resist them. At very least, they should mediate in conflicts over these crucial issues, and create a space for local criticism and debate, which can modify the impact of the programme on poor people and allow campaigns for more fundamental changes to develop.

Third Way rhetoric makes big claims about the need for cultural change, and New Labour policy documents proclaim ambitious plans to achieve such objectives. However, they offer no coherent account of how this is to happen. Social scientists have demonstrated that the diffusion process through which cultural change occurs relies on networks of contact, which expose individuals to the influence of new ideas and behaviours (Coleman et al., 1957; Valente, 1995, 1996; Diani, 1997). Individual and organizational factors interact in complex ways in such innovations and mobilizations (Krempel and Schnegg, 2000). Cultural shifts cannot simply be induced by ministerial fiat or official exhortation. To facilitate new patterns social work requires subtlety of methods and access to community networks, in order to facilitate the activities and interaction that give rise to change.

In the final chapter, we argue that there is an alternative set of resources available for a style of practice that could do justice to this task. Using research and practice experience from Australia, New Zealand and the USA (Fook, 1996), we show that a more imaginative, creative, democratic and challenging way of working can far better meet the needs of a cultural environment in which change, not stability, is the dominant mode. This 'constructive social work' (Parton and O'Byrne, 2000) is in fact better suited for the modified implementation of New Labour's programme, precisely because it embraces ambiguity and uncertainty, rather than trying to impose rigid order and discipline; and because it is open to new potentialities and interpretations, rather than trying to impose meanings and solutions. The success or failure of the New Labour project will depend on how practitioners and service users are able to accomplish a convincing version of its values and goals, to tell themselves and each other a credible story about their co-operative achievements, and to work together on future progress. This is the style of practice we commend.

In essence, social work is not a means of implementing policy formally and directly, but of mediating the local conflicts generated by new programmes, and engaging with service users over how to fit new measures to their needs. It bridges the formal rules of official systems and the informal order of everyday life – the 'blood-and-guts code' (see Box 9, p. 54–5) of families, groups and neighbourhoods. It is a waste of its potential for these tasks to treat it as a crude instrument for the imposition of government rules or the quasi-scientific application of research findings.

Box 1   After the focus groups

The Arbiter was full of earnest intent – energetic, youthful, with a charming smile and engaging manner.

'Our values do not change. Our commitment to a different vision of society stands intact. But the ways of achieving that vision must change', he explained, waving his hands in an inclusive, healing way.

The Median Voter shifted rather crossly in his seat, his face pink with indignation. 'Like I say, why should we pay for her and her like' (at this point he indicated the Claimant sitting on his left with an awkward twist of his head and neck, but made no eye contact with her); 'why should we pay for them to get council houses, and have social workers running around after them, when she's out every night, plenty of money to spend, cars outside the house ...?'

The Claimant stared defiantly at a point high in the far corner of the room, diagonally opposite her adversary. She flicked the ash from her cigarette. 'What are we supposed to do – hide away, be ashamed of ourselves, keep our children inside, just to please you? We've got a right to live as well, you know. We want to work, we do work, but what chance do you lot give us?'

The Arbiter interrupted enthusiastically. 'That's exactly the point', he said triumphantly, 'and that's why we want to rebuild the welfare state around work and opportunity – work for those who can; security for those who cannot. It will be our new contract for welfare, where we keep a system from which we all benefit, but on terms that are fair and transparent. No rights without responsibilities. So for every pound that *you* pay' – he beamed at the Median Voter, his eyes gleaming – 'we will expect *you*' – he turned towards the Claimant – 'to do something in return.'

PART I

1

The Dog that Didn't Bark

In the UK, we are living through a period of radical reform of the public sector, especially that part of it that is concerned with the welfare of citizens. The New Labour government of Tony Blair has declared its ambitions to 'break the mould of the old, passive benefits system' (DSS, 1998, p. 24), to establish a 'new social contract' between citizens and the state, based on 'a change of culture among . . . claimants, employers and public servants – with rights and responsibilities on all sides' (ibid.). Social care should be given in ways that 'promote independence' (DoH, 1998a, para. 1.8). By implication, the agenda is to pull away safety nets and replace them with trampolines, to bounce claimants and service users out of dependency, and to activate and motivate citizens for participation. If a public service occupation is not part of this solution to social issues, it is part of the problem.

The system of rights, services, institutions and practices that is being replaced was established by the postwar Labour government of Clement Attlee in 1948. Following the principles of the Beveridge Report (Beveridge, 1942), it set up a range of collective protections against problems such as poverty, unemployment, bad housing, physical and mental illness, family deprivation and breakdown, bereavement, disability and accident, all of which had been seen as individual, private or family issues in the previous century. The essence of this public sector system was that these problems were seen to be largely randomly distributed in an industrial society, that almost the whole population was at risk of suffering from them (especially at certain points in the life cycle, such as when children were young, or in old age), and that only state-funded and publicly provided benefits and services would adequately guard against them.

In 1948, local authority personal social services were among the new creations of that set of reforms, replacing the prewar Poor Law services for families, children, old people, and some people with disabilities and handicaps and mental illnesses. The profession of social work grew under the auspices of these services, as a predominantly public sector occupation in the UK – as in Scandinavia, but unlike in Germany, France, Italy and other West European countries, where social workers were mainly employed in voluntary organizations, even when they carried out work mandated by the state. Social work was therefore one of the chosen instruments of the 'Beveridge revolution' (Macadam, 1945) – particularly in the field of public child care, where the Curtis Committee launched something akin to a moral crusade against the appalling deprivations suffered by children in Poor Law institutions (Packman, 1975).

By the year 2000, local authority social work has become part of the problem addressed by Labour government reformers, and social work is clearly not part of the solution to the wider social issues the government identifies as needing to be tackled. The reformers have targeted a whole range of attitudes and cultures to be transformed, among service providers and service users. Many of the ways in which New Labour's programme is to be implemented are described in language that is very reminiscent of the concepts employed in social work services for children and adults. For instance, under the New Deals, unemployed claimants will receive 'an individualized, flexible service ... with personal advisers providing tailor-made packages of help' (DSS, 1998, p. 3). But the term 'social work' is never used to describe how these processes will be performed, the occupations of those performing them, the values they will subscribe to, or the training they will receive. (Those who perform them are given various new titles, such as 'New Deal advisers'; we shall use the generic term *enforcement counsellors* for them throughout the book.) The term 'social workers' is reserved by New Labour for the fairly narrow range of employees of the local authority social services departments, and their training now embraces none but themselves and a range of workers in the voluntary sector (but no longer probation officers, who from 1948 to 1997 trained with them).

All this is paradoxical, because it follows a period of Conservative government in which social work's position as an occupation, and local authority social services departments' role in social welfare provision, were consolidated. Although Conservative ministers in their party conference speeches regularly denounced social workers as 'looney lefties' or vegetarian wimps, and the popular press reserved its bitterest scorn for their profession, their budgets grew and their powers and duties enlarged during the long period of the Thatcher–Major administrations. Child protection systems were established; a new Children Act (1989) extended responsibilities for children in need, and included some who were previously in the ambit of education departments; hospital closures meant more work in supporting people with learning difficulties and mental illnesses. Above all, the NHS and Community Care Act 1990 gave social services departments the duty to assess all elderly people and adults with disabilities and handicaps for domiciliary, day and residential services, and passed financial responsibility for purchasing these from the Department of Social Security to the social services departments. All these changes were welcomed by the leaders of the social work profession, as recognizing its role in a new regime of personal social services, in which efficiency and cost-effectiveness, budgetary prudence and good management were enshrined alongside new techniques of care, support and risk management.

This book examines the complex relationship that has developed, in the wake of the Thatcher–Major reforms of social services, between social work and the Third Way. The Blair government's reform programme springs, in all its essentials, from the policy agendas of the previous administrations. One has only to glance across the Channel at the plight of the Schröder coalition to see how much harder it is to graft the 'Neue Mitte' on to Helmut Kohl's Christian Democratic stewardship of the German social state than it is for Tony Blair's Third Way to follow on from eighteen years of neo-liberalism – privatization, deregulation and a strong central state. For teachers, doctors and housing officers, like social workers, there is no respite from the relentless drive towards greater accountability. Equally, the thrust towards stamping out fraud and informal resistance practices, being tough on crime, and social inclusion through compulsory labour-market participation, are all strengthened rather than relaxed.

What is distinctive about the Blair agenda is its strongly moral rhetoric and its reliance on 'people changers' – agents to transform attitudes, cultures, practices and decisions both among service providers and service users. But not only are social workers not to be such agents themselves; they in turn are to be changed – controlled, regulated and quality-assessed in ways that will tie them more closely to their statutory tasks and to ministerial guidance, within a fairly circumscribed policy domain where they will be involved only marginally in new developments.

Unlike employment and social security, which are to be the expansionist flagships of the Third Way; unlike education, which is to be the main focus and measure of the programme's success; unlike the NHS, which is to be the long-term target of a major overhaul, local authority social services reforms are low-key and contained. These services will lose work when the new Immigration and Asylum Act spawns new agencies and partnerships to provide 'no choice' accommodation and supervision for asylum seekers (Home Office, 1998). As for the social work profession, in all the rhetoric about personalized packages of help and individual counselling under the Single Gateway and New Deals, it is not to be mentioned. Familiar, faded and slightly discredited, it remains unobtrusively in the background – the dog that didn't bark amid all the frenetic activity.

Why didn't it bark? And if the reason was that the new masters of the house had about them a well-known scent, and used well-recognized words in well-loved voices, why did not they in turn greet the faithful hound and reward it with a little praise, if only for past services? These are some of the issues for the early chapters of this book.

Social Work and Social Policy

The interaction of social work and the Third Way is, of course, a particular example of a general relationship between a reforming government and a relatively established profession – one thinks, for instance, of the interactions of the 1945 Labour government with the medical and legal professions, though they were immensely stronger, and in a far better bargaining position. It is also an example of the relationship between social policy and social work, with the latter as a means of implementing certain aspects of the former. What is interesting about this example for the history and development of social work – internationally, as well as in the UK – is that it shows that social work as a profession can take a backward step, even under conditions that seem especially propitious for its advance, if a government's programme for social reform cuts across its organizational position in the institutions for social provision. The Blair government is ambivalent about the public sector in general, and local government in particular. Social work in the UK is too strongly linked with certain public sector traditions and local authority interests to be a suitable instrument for its purposes.

To understand the evolution of the social work profession within social policy, one needs to analyse its emergence both historically and comparatively. This is not within the scope of this book. Here it suffices to say that social work requires certain conditions (a religious or humanitarian tradition of care and assistance, an ethic of individualism *and* altruism, the emergence of an educated bourgeoisie, and particularly of educated women) to come into existence at all; and other political and economic factors (a collective consciousness of personal and family problems as public issues, together with an element of paternalism, interventionism or authoritarianism) for it to emerge as a prominent feature of public sector services. Generally, the existence of the latter conditions without the former leads to official policies pursued through state agencies – such as the Poor Law in seventeenth- and eighteenth-century Europe and North America, and the state social services developed more recently by some Arab states – which are somewhat bleak, harsh and impersonal. The existence of the former conditions without the latter leads to a proliferation of charitable foundations and small local initiatives, focused mainly on individuals and families, and with a rather moralistic flavour. When both conditions hold, it is still more common to find social work located in voluntary sector organizations, but usually doing tasks paid for and promoted by the state's legislation and policy (Jones and May, 1992). The UK has been unusual in its adoption (in the immediate postwar period, and again in the period 1968–71) of a local government organization for its main employers of social workers (Jordan, 1997; Jordan and Jones, 1995).

The example of the former communist countries of Central Europe illustrates the situation in the absence of individualism, religious and humanitarian ethics and bourgeois culture. Although there was some voluntary sector social work (in Catholic agencies) in Poland, and some specialist counselling and group work in special education in all countries in that region, a distinctive profession of social work did not emerge until after 1989, except for one small precursor in Hungary some five years earlier (Gosztonyi, 1993). After 1989, when precisely these elements in political culture emerged strongly, social work training and employment sprang up everywhere (Jordan, 1997). The charitable ethos, the revival of Christianity and humanitarianism, and (above all) the notion of individuals as being morally responsible for their own life courses, all created – in the briefest of times – conditions in which social work was *possible*. The devastation of these economies, mass poverty and unemployment among whole populations, loss of security and the sense of collective solidarity, and the overall disruption and disorientation of the transitions to democracy and capitalism, made it a *necessary* part of these countries' social policy programmes.

In the UK it is hardly surprising that the role and significance of local authority social work grew in the 1980s and 1990s (Hill, 2000). During that period, poverty and inequality emerged as strong features of UK society, with the relative situation of the poorest declining more markedly than in any other country except New Zealand (Rowntree Trust, 1995). As policy moved towards restricting both the redistribution of income and the provision of public services to groups in 'genuine need' – through means-testing and other policies for 'targeting' those most at risk, or most threatening to public safety – so the residual elements in state systems, which had been adapted from the old Poor Law systems, became more important and prominent. Indeed, the meaning of the very terms 'social security' and 'welfare' changed from signifying National Insurance benefits to 'targeted' benefits like income support, housing benefits and family credit, as Conservative governments shifted expenditure away from universal provision and towards systems for the poor. Economic liberalization, labour-market deregulation and privatization dramatically increased differentials in earnings and life chances; the benefits system and the local authority social services had therefore to be adapted to pick up the pieces.

One strong feature of this shift was a greater emphasis on social control, discipline, surveillance and containment, an emphasis captured in the idea of a change from policies for *social justice* to ones for *criminal justice* (Hudson, 1993). The Thatcherite notion of a 'property-owning democracy', and its strong emphasis on individual economic choices, was always threatened by the persistence of an excluded minority, which tended to expand as Conservative policies unfolded. The urban riots of 1981 were followed by pragmatic programmes to reduce unemployment by various forms of temporary work, low-quality training (Youth Training Scheme) and mass occupational therapy (the Community Programme). Margaret Thatcher shared Friedrich von Hayek's view that social justice was a 'mirage' (Hayek, 1976) and went further by doubting the existence of 'society'; hence redistribution and the provision of services was to be undertaken only in cases of market failure (public goods might be necessary for the sake of economic efficiency, for instance in the case of law and order, basic education and health care, defence, etc.), or to ameliorate public harms.

It fitted well with this philosophy that social work should perform tasks that were directed at order and discipline, particularly in relation to an emerging 'class' of dependent and dangerous citizens. This was the period in which the notion of a morally degenerate 'underclass' was imported from the USA (Murray, 1983, 1989), and used to justify tougher attitudes towards the provision of benefits and services. It was reflected chiefly in two phenomena – the growth in the prison population after 1993 (Donnison, 1998), and the expansion of child protection systems from the early 1980s (Parton et al., 1997). What was interesting about the former was how late it came; under Margaret Thatcher's leadership, the prison population remained reasonably stable, although this was mainly a consequence of the transformation of the youth justice system – in the direction of *justice* rather than a welfare approach – and the conversion of the probation service from being primarily a court social work service to one that focused on criminal correction and providing alternatives to custody (Williams, 1996). Child protection systems developed – as in other countries, such as Australia (Thorpe, 1997) – mainly in response to the perception of risks to children arising from the lifestyles of poor people and members of minority communities. The dominant task of social workers with children and families became one of investigating allegations of abuse by parents, giving low-key support to a minority of these, and protecting a very small number of children by the use of court orders (Gibbons et al., 1995). Thus the disciplinary emphasis of child protection work reflected growing inequalities, and moral anxieties about the cultural practices of a burdensome and threatening 'underclass' (Jordan, 1996a).

However, not all social policy developments affecting local authority social services were unambiguously in this direction. Youth justice policies in fact kept numbers in custody very low in the second half of this period. Programmes for 'normalizing' the lives of people with learning disabilities, and providing better supports for their families, together with hospital closures, were predicated on progressive principles, even if the outcome was often 'micro institutionalization' in small homes and hostels, or the burdening of informal carers. Policies for reducing the population of mental illness hospitals had very mixed results, and led to serious boundary disputes between health authorities and social services departments, but were similarly inspired by notions of inclusion and empowerment, even if these turned out to be largely illusory and something of a backlash led to measures of increased control later. Above all, policies for community care of older people and people with disabilities and handicaps were inspired by social-work-orientated research (Challis and Davies, 1985), and aimed to improve quality of life by the provision of more flexible domiciliary and day services. Of course, the stated aims of empowerment and choice for service users and carers have been to a large extent sacrificed to the rationing of scarce resources, the assessment of means and risks, and the pervasive managerialism and budgetary obsession that accompanied the new administrative systems (Clarke et al., 1994; Hadley and Clough, 1995). But the original goals still stand as a challenge to the social work profession and local authority social services departments.

The New Labour government has picked up many of the positive elements in these policy and legislative developments, and in the Children Act 1989, and re-emphasized them in its official papers (DoH, 1998a). Using examples of best practice, and reasserting the values behind its whole reform programme – social inclusion, empowerment, autonomy, community and responsibility – it has set out guidelines, regulations and procedures for sustaining those goals. But it has not favoured the local authority social services with new resources, new principles or powers, or a new vision of their role in society. There is now growing evidence that this is affecting recruitment of social workers (see Box 12, p. 80).

Part II of this book will analyse the reasons for this relative silence, and the seemingly marginal role allotted to the social work profession and the local authority social services under the Third Way. We will argue that, like other local authority services, and like the public sector generally, this profession and these agencies are tainted, in New Labour's eyes, by involvement in the policies, practices and political cultures of the period 1948–79, when the public sector was the dominant one in policy and politics, when its expansionism threatened the market and civil society, and when the Thatcher reaction against all this began. Furthermore, they are tainted by association with the resistance of local authorities and the public sector generally during the Thatcher–Major period – with a culture of rule-bending and 'banditry' in favour of very disadvantaged service user groups, such as the poor, ethnic minorities, asylum seekers and homeless people. They are paying a high price for their ambiguous and ambivalent activities under Conservative governments.

This is because New Labour takes forward many of the themes of Thatcherism–Majorism, but under a new banner of moral revival and social inclusion. The instruments of Thatcherism – a strong central state, regulating the professions, trade unions and public sector interests for the sake of taxpayers and 'customers', favouring commercial and voluntary providers or public–private partnerships over local or central government agencies, and using new initiatives (zones, projects and new agencies and services) to subvert the established power of the large public sector organizations, through the creation of new sets of actors and professionals who owe no allegiances to those interests – are brought to bear on the new issues given priority within the Third Way. Furthermore, the Thatcher method – populist moral rhetoric, appealing to the electorate over the heads of local politicians and local political interest-group bargaining and compromise – is much favoured by Tony Blair. Finally, the Thatcher-style authoritarianism of appeals to the most negative aspects of a blood-and-guts code (Jordan, 1999a) to narrow-minded prejudice, judgmentalism, revenge, spite, prudery, retribution, shop-your-neighbour, patriarchy and religious bigotry, is far from abandoned. Instead, Tony Blair and Jack Straw invest this with an aura of sanctity, of *caring* bigotry, *responsible* retribution and *communal* revenge, giving a sort of proletarian respectability to lower middle-class values and bourgeois susceptibilities, in an era when 'competing for the middle ground' in UK politics translates as fighting for the most effective means to inflame the irritable sensibilities of the nearly-poor and the almost-rich (Dean and Melrose, 1998).

The Limitations of the Third Way

In the final part of the book we will argue that these aspects of New Labour's principles, methods and policy programme represent important weaknesses, and that they will need to be modified if the government is to succeed in its aims. At the level of political principles, the Third Way will have to find an accommodation with pluralism and a far wider variety of versions of the good life. Its small-minded communitarianism and narrow interpretation of social responsibility will have to be broadened, and its conceptions of relevant contributions to co-operation will have to embrace a wider range of activities. Above all, its conception of a civil society led by a moralizing central state and steered by enforcement counsellors will have to be abandoned, in favour of a new conception of public social services, more firmly rooted in neighbourhoods and linked with community groups, and less concerned with enforcement, surveillance and control.

The main features of the Third Way are summarized in Box 2.

Box 2   The Third Way

The Third Way is the name given by the New Labour leadership to its own political philosophy and strategy; it is also the title of texts by Tony Blair and his adviser, Professor Tony Giddens, both published in 1998. It purports to be an alternative to Margaret Thatcher's free-market model of the neo-liberal state, and to old-style socialism, both of the undemocratic Soviet, command-economy kind, and of the Old Labour variety (with a mixed economy and universalistic, collectivist welfare state).

What is distinctive about the Third Way in both accounts is the emphasis on the requirement to find new expressions for the *values* of socialism, feminism, anti-racism and justice. Tony Blair writes that Labour's values have not changed, but the means of achieving them must change: 'The Third Way is a serious reappraisal of social democracy, reaching deep into the values of the Left to develop radically new approaches' (Blair, 1998a, p. 1). Similarly, Tony Giddens writes of socialist values which 'remain intrinsic to the good life that it is the point of social and economic development to create' (Giddens, 1998, p. 2).

The following is a list of the Third Way's values, and how they are interpreted in these texts, following Carling (1999):

> *equality* – equal moral worth of all human beings; equality of opportunity, not outcome; protection of the vulnerable;
> *autonomy* – personal freedom; choice; political liberty;
> *community* – individual responsibility; reciprocity; obligations corresponding to social rights; social inclusion as the basis for social justice;
> *democracy* – empowerment; devolution of power.

The key question is whether these values have any substance when they are detached from the content of socialism, feminism, anti-racism and justice.

As Carling points out, the Third Way largely accepts capitalism as a suitable vehicle for delivering these values, and aims to modify it mainly in terms of the following policy goals:

> lifelong learning (the Social Investment State);
> a balance of rights and responsibilities;
> promoting independence through work;
> provision for genuine need.

New Labour's policies on employment and income maintenance – which form the central plank of its social programme – will have run their course within their next term of government. New issues about how welfare benefits can support active participation and prevent poverty will become recognizable (Jordan et al., 2000), and the technical problems of tax benefit reform will push the government towards the recognition of unpaid activities, informal support, community and neighbourhood groups and social regeneration (Ginsburg, 1999). The role of public social services will become crucial at this point.

The limitations of the Third Way are already visible in the government's failure to recognize a set of highly significant issues, and (despite its rhetoric of 'joined-up government') to see the connections between policy decisions on a range of current topics.

The implementation of programmes such as the New Deals, the Single Gateway, the various initiatives on crime, and the work of the Social Exclusion Unit all raise huge problems about how the public authority can deal with the most intimate, significant and distressing aspects of the personal lives of citizens, in ways consistent with democratic values of civil liberty, personal autonomy, collective responsibility and social justice (Jordan, 1998a). For all their weaknesses and failures, local authority social work and the probation service have been dealing with just these issues for fifty years. These traditions, and the cumulative experience embodied in these organizations, are not to be lightly dismissed or marginalized. At the very least, new agencies and new professions have something to learn from them.

New programmes, initiatives, projects, zones and schemes must all, at some point, interact with local authority social services, and with the public sector generally. In many cases they rely for partnership, co-ordination and coherence (and even for funding) on local authority or health service staff; in others they depend on them for referrals or delegated tasks. If these public services are themselves so under-resourced and overstretched that they are responding purely reactively to the most desperate of their service users, then the new projects, programmes, zones and initiatives will not be adequately co-ordinated with mainstream work in health and social care, or will not receive any referrals or delegated tasks from them. In the 1970s the voluntary and commercial sectors were too weak in relation to public services, and were dominated and marginalized by the expansionist public sector ethos. However, in the 1990s well-resourced voluntary and commercial providers, and these new agencies and programmes, are so much stronger and better able to plan and mount strategies that they dominate the underfunded and overburdened public services. In this situation, public agencies like local authority social services departments cannot conduct proper relations with formal voluntary organizations and private sector providers, still less with informal community associations, pressure and advocacy groups (see Chapter 8).

Even within the confines of the fairly narrow role now allotted to them, local authority social services are now charged with conducting the exchanges between the public authority and the commercial sector of social care provision. If the local authority social services departments are so weakened and under-resourced that they cannot do this efficiently, the consequences for service users will be very damaging. Purchasing of care involves the setting of appropriate terms for contracts – sufficiently detailed to ensure quality in very personal, individual issues – and monitoring compliance: checking that the contracts are fulfilled in all their specifics. The balance of power between public sector purchasers and commercial providers is already shifting. When the social services departments took over responsibility for funding care from the Department of Social Security, the bulk of commercial providers were small family businesses, often providing care in their own homes. But in a global economic environment, this situation is changing. Already firms based in the USA, owning funeral parlours and crematoria as well as elderly people's homes, are taking a significant share of the market in the UK. Protecting the interests of service users in this environment, where the headquarters of a provider enterprise is often in a completely different part of the country, and the firm has huge market power, is not a suitable role for a weak and overstretched local government agency.

The goal of empowerment of and choice for *both* service users *and* their family or neighbourly informal carers is a vital and noble one, but extremely difficult to achieve. It requires delicacy and a sure touch, and is not to be accomplished by pressured and harassed officials, working to tight agency deadlines and budgets, and focusing solely on a checklist of resources and risk factors. One significant factor that complicates this task is the potential conflict of interest between people with special needs and their carers, and between various members of the caring (family or neighbourly) network. For example, in the most difficult cases of a sudden need for extensive care provision (the impact of Alzheimer's disease causing a breakdown in caring relationships, or a stroke that deprives its victim of the power of speech), a social worker should try to negotiate new arrangements which take account of the needs, commitments and preferences of *all* the people affected. This is very delicate work, and it has to take account of the fact that both the carer and the person in need may be suffering from an enormous sense of loss and grief over the events precipitating the crisis, which pull them in different directions (Weinstein, 1997). Furthermore, different members of the care network may respond in opposite ways to the crisis; a partner in a relationship which has been drifting apart might want to pass responsibility for care completely to the public authority, while another relative (a brother or sister) might see the crisis as an opportunity to become more involved and take more responsibility (see case example, pp. 89–94). In the absence of skilled, sensitive work, these issues can be disastrously mishandled, particularly if the public authority uses its statutory power to overrule certain interests and preferences, as a shortcut to 'solutions'; there is evidence, which we present in Chapter 4, that this is happening at present.

These are specific examples of a general problem with public social services in the present environment, which is echoed in other European countries (Knijn, 1998). The fragmentation of the old, monolithic organizations of social care (local authority services in the UK, large voluntary organizations in countries like the Netherlands and Germany) has had the great advantage of allowing greater flexibility and a whole range of new domiciliary supports and services to be developed (Ostner, 1998). However, this can become a chaotic supermarket of commercial or small-scale non-profit organizations, which is difficult to use effectively in the interests of people in need and their carers. A pressurized public authority comes to rely on pre-selected 'packages of care', which are not really tailored to individual needs, so the experience becomes more like that of a 'consumer' under a communist regime – queuing up for commodities which are strictly rationed by the authorities according to their own criteria of risk and need, and then being given something that does not fit or suit, and certainly is not chosen (Knijn, 1998). This again illustrates the difficult and demanding nature of local authority social services' task – the management of risk (Kemshall and Pritchard, 1996), and the rationing of resources in a political culture of cost efficiency and value for money, over intensely personal issues, open to a range of subjective interpretations, and requiring detailed individual attention.

CASE EXAMPLE: JOHN AND MARY RYAN

The points above are illustrated by this example of the recent experiences of a vulnerable woman and her carers.

John and Mary Ryan were both in their mid-eighties when the events leading up to her death occurred. She had for some years been suffering from Alzheimer's disease, and he was rather physically frail, but able to care for her at home without assistance from social services. A devoted couple, who had always lived in the same district of the city, they had one daughter, who had a responsible job in a large organization but gave them much emotional and practical support. Two years ago, John became ill and had a short admission to hospital. On discharge, practical assistance in looking after the home and caring for Mary was requested, and a care manager from the local authority social services department called to make an assessment. A care package was agreed, but nothing followed from this. It was only when they received a bill for support services they had not been given that they realized that there had been some contracting or compliance failure with the provider agency, and telephoned to point this out. Eventually a community care assistant from this (private) agency did start to call, and this was the beginning of the family's tragedy.

The care assistant did not keep the hours stipulated in the written contract, and when she did come she did not do the tasks required; instead she talked mainly about her own domestic problems. On a couple of occasions, she very disruptively arrived just as John was feeding Mary her meal, according to their established regime, and then tried to intervene. John became flustered and angry with the care assistant, remonstrated with her for interfering and coming at the wrong moment, and in the process Mary became distressed and spilt her food on herself. On the second occasion, the care assistant arrived late as John was undressing Mary for bed. Again she intervened with criticism and attempts to take over the handling of Mary, John was distracted in what he was doing, there was a semi-scuffle between the two of them, and Mary fell on to the bed.

Soon after this, the care manager contacted the family and strongly suggested that Mary should be admitted to hospital for a full assessment of her needs. John and their daughter were surprised by this suggestion, and resisted it for some time, but were eventually persuaded that it was in Mary's interests to have this assessment, as her quality of life might be improved by additional care services. In the event, the admission to hospital was an unmitigated disaster. Mary had never slept alone in a room in her life, and was used to having John at her side by night, to comfort and reassure her. Disorientated by the new environment, and terrified by being put on her own in a single room, she tried to get out of bed, fell and broke her hip. A far longer stay in hospital was therefore necessary. She reacted very badly to these events; her mental health deteriorated, she cried out in anguish, and drew the wrath of other patients, one of whom even hit her.

Very distressed by these events, John and their daughter met the care manager to arrange for Mary to be discharged as soon as possible. However, they were informed that she had been assessed as needing full-time psychiatric nursing because of her mental condition – which would cost £3,000 a week. The local authority could not afford this out of its budget, so she would have to remain in hospital until a suitable residential placement was found.

John and their daughter said that in this case they would like simply to arrange for Mary's discharge, and that they would take full responsibility for her care, if necessary employing a qualified nurse from their own funds. At this they were told that the care assistant had alleged that John had been violent towards Mary – they assumed to cover up for the incidents where she, in their view, had been at fault for her lack of punctuality and clumsy handling of a delicate interpersonal situation. If John attempted to discharge Mary, the local authority would apply for guardianship over her, taking away his rights as nearest relative.

John and their daughter were completely shocked by this allegation, and the whole turn of events. They consulted a solicitor, who advised them that on balance it was better not to contest the decision, but to wait until the placement in residential care was made, and then try to win the trust of the owner or manager of the home. They accepted this advice, and told Mary that she would soon be moved into residential care.

On receiving the news, Mary (who had become slightly calmer with medication and reassurance) simply said 'No', dropped her chin on to her chest, and refused to raise her head or eyes again. It was as if, on hearing she would not be going home, she simply gave up on her life, and chose to die. Her neck became locked in this position, and it proved impossible to feed her adequately. Nursing staff made half-hearted efforts to overcome her resistance, but she quickly got weaker.

John and their daughter made frantic attempts to save her life, including trying to get treatment or assistance to change her posture and enable her to be fed – but in vain. She died of exhaustion and near-starvation a couple of weeks later. After her funeral, neither the hospital nor the social services department sent letters of condolence (or any other sentiments) to the family.

Discussion

This is not a case where divided responsibilities of health and social services caused poor communication between practitioners. Mary Ryan's condition was undisputed, and the two agencies worked closely together. What went wrong was that social services were acting on an undisclosed agenda about the possibility of abuse by John, following the report from the community care assistant. It seems that the whole admission to hospital was a pretext for assessing the allegation that John was becoming violent towards Mary. In the event, she suffered serious injury as a result of the hospital's neglect of her emotional needs, followed by physical and emotional abuse at the hands of other patients because of her resultant distress and mental disorientation. Her death was the final chapter in a story of the tragic mishandling of a frail old lady's vulnerability (see also pp. 89–94).

In this case, the care manager took an authoritative approach towards the issues that emerged, without consulting with, or listening to, carers. Of course, there is such a thing as abuse of vulnerable older people by their carers, just as there is such a thing as child abuse – but such interventions without discussion or the chance to rebut allegations by a third party (a virtual stranger) are not justifiable in either type of case. Here again there is an overwhelming argument for professional training and supervision that takes account of the emotional dynamics and moral perplexities of such situations, and respects the individuality and value of all the parties. But since 1990 such skills are at a discount, while competence in budgeting, contracting and managing is highly valued. Even work with grief, loss and bereavement, fundamental to all the tasks concerning disability and dying, are no longer widely valued (Weinstein, 1997).

Finally – and crucially – there is the emergence of a range of linked issues relating to the position in society of an impoverished and excluded group of people seen as troublesome, burdensome or threatening. It is over these people that the Third Way makes its most distinctive – and most dubious – contribution to social policy. In its emphasis on social responsibility and social discipline, and the need for public agencies to make more *demands* of such citizens (Mead, 1986), to require them to prove the *genuineness* of their need, to change their behaviours and attitudes (Waddan, 1997), New Labour principles attempt to shift the moral basis of official relations between the state and citizens – the 'new social contract' (DSS, 1998). The central idea behind this new approach is '*tough love*' (Phillips, 1993), a concept borrowed from the USA, which entered British public consciousness during the moral panic over the killing of Jamie Bulger by two children (Jordan, 1999a). 'Tough love' means that service providers must expect more from service users, must test their eligibility for services more strictly, must activate them more vigorously, and support them more strongly in any efforts they make to be independent. The hallmark of the new basis for social provision is *achievement* and *participation* rather than passivity and need. The provenance of this phrase is given in Box 3.

Box 3   'Tough love'

The phrase 'tough love' was the title of an article by journalist Melanie Phillips, published in the *Observer* on 13 June 1993, and calling for a return to family values in the face of the 'collapse of moral certainty'. Like John Major's 'Back to Basics' campaign, this plea was made during the media-generated frenzy of soul-searching that followed the revelation that the toddler James Bulger had been killed by two 10-year-old boys. This in turn provoked a national debate about society, morality and the socialization of children (Franklin and Petley, 1996; Davis and Bourhill,

1997). Although the Labour Party under John Smith did not clarify its stance on these issues at the time, when Tony Blair was elected leader his consultations with focus groups revealed the popularity of traditional values and retributionist invective on crime and disorder. This ensured that the form of communitarianism adopted by New Labour was conformist, conservative, prescriptive, moral and concerned with individual responsibility (Driver and Martell, 1997).

We have chosen the phrase to encapsulate characteristics of the Third Way:

- its emphasis on the family and education as sources of norms and discipline;
- more demands for a reciprocal effort from those who receive support from welfare services;
- a tough response to crime, truancy, drug use, begging and other forms of 'disorder';
- the prescription of moral standards and obligations;
- support for those in 'genuine need'.

The phrase has continued to circulate as a description of New Labour's policies on social issues. On 8 December 1999 the *Guardian* ran a news story about a leaked letter from the Home Secretary to his cabinet colleagues suggesting that the new title of the probation service (the Community Punishment and Rehabilitation Service, incorrectly abbreviated by offenders to CRAPO) 'nicely balances "tough" with the constructive tone of rehabilitation'. In a letter to the paper the following day, Paul Boateng, the Home Office minister, wrote: 'I can accept your characterisation of the change of name of the probation service ...'. The *Guardian* leader was called 'Jack's Tough Love'.

The moral intuitions on which the Third Way bases its approach are perfectly plausible. Society is a system of co-operation, founded *on rules that restrain competition* between members (citizens) and outlaw violent conflict, without which neither prosperity nor peaceful co-existence is possible (Hobbes, 1651). Criminals, vandals, beggars, drug dealers and pushers, unruly ruffians and all who use intimidation and violence to achieve their ends threaten the order, stability and progress of society – so it is necessary to be tough on them and the conditions that cause them. Under Margaret Thatcher, UK society fragmented and divided, with a large group excluded from the formal economy, who adopted a counter-strategy to compensate for their disadvantages (Jordan, 1995, 1996a). This involved cash-in-hand work combined with claiming social assistance benefits, hustling, dealing and petty theft – all of which were largely overlooked, because the 'property-owning democracy' could not afford to confront and challenge those it had marginalized and demeaned.

New Labour's policy programme seeks to *include* these elements (Lister, 1998), while simultaneously containing, disciplining and controlling them. If they are to be returned to full membership, then they must be reminded of the second principle of social co-operation – that in every association the benefits of membership are derived from the *contributions* of members. Poor and marginal people cannot contribute money through taxes, but they can contribute *work*. Hence they must be restored to a place in the formal economy, if necessary under the threat that their benefits will be taken away (the New Deals: see Box 4, below). The Third Way's clear moral stance (inclusion conditional on orderly contributions under fair rules) replaces the mixed message of Thatcherism–Majorism, which told poor people to fend for themselves, and largely turned a blind eye to how they did so.

Box 4   The New Deals

The New Deals for increasing labour-market participation are the centrepiece of New Labour social policy. At a cost of £3.2 billion (raised from taxes on windfall profits by the privatized utilities) they offer subsidies to employers, education and training to participants, but all on condition of co-operation; non-compliance means loss of benefits. The six New Deals are:

- Young unemployed people (18–24), on Job Seeker's Allowance for 6 months (cost £2.2 billion);
- Long-term unemployed people, out of work for over 2 years (£350 million);
- Lone parents – compulsory interviews and work and training advice;
- People with a disability or long-term illness (£195 million) (see pp. 119–23);
- Partners of the unemployed (£60 million);
- Communities – to 'combat social exclusion' in deprived areas (£15 million).

In addition the Employment Zones, targeting districts with high unemployment (see pp. 185–90).

The flagship of the New Deals is the one for young people. Although its achievements are disputed, because it is impossible to tell how many would have found jobs without it, the shift out of unemployment in this age group is impressive.

- 155,500 New Dealers had left unemployment by November 1999.
- 59 per cent of the first cohort of New Dealers were placed in unsubsidized, open-market jobs.
- When the New Deal began, 62,000 young people had been unemployed for more than one year; two years later (November 1999) this had fallen to 9,200 – an 85 per cent drop.

The New Deal has revealed the extent of deprivation and damage among young people. Only 19 per cent had five or more GCSEs, and there were high rates of illiteracy and personal problems. Polly Toynbee writes that the emphasis of the programme has shifted towards education and training, and that the advisers have good street credibility in the Lambeth New Deal Centre among young black people ('A Very Good Deal', *Guardian*, 26 November 1999).

Between May 1997 and September 1999, the government claims that jobs growth (many part time) was a total of 648,000, with a fall in unemployment in the same time (Gordon Brown, speech to Labour Party Conference, *Guardian*, 28 September). During the implementation of the New Deals, conditions – such as compulsory interviews – have been intensified; most recently (*Guardian*, 30 December 1999) to include a call centre to ring long-term claimants about vacancies.

The most glaring *limitation* in the Third Way's programme lies in its *implementation* (Pressman and Wildavsky, 1973; Lindblom and Woodhouse, 1993). In principle, the demands on citizens are unambiguous and reasonable at first sight – though as we shall show in Part III this clarity dissolves into cloudiness when we come down to specific instances. But even if it is possible to demonstrate the fairness of the requirements on claimants and service users to be as active and independent as possible, to provide for themselves as much as they can, and to be responsible members of their communities, it is quite another thing to show how a state official can translate such requirements into a negotiated 'deal' relating to social inclusion.

The Third Way cuts a swathe through a century of knowledge and experience of how such officials actually handle their relationships with marginal, disadvantaged, unorthodox or deviant members of society. It goes back to the crude psychological certainties of the eighteenth century – the authoritarian utilitarianism of Jeremy Bentham (see Box 10, p. 62–3 and pp. 62–5), with its mechanistic reliance on reward and punishment, and the more abstract legal and administrative formulations of the Scottish Enlightenment philosophers (Spragens, 1981). It bypasses the expertise and traditions embodied in the old social services, in favour of the relatively naïve energy and enthusiasm of new and untried groups of 'counsellors', 'advisers' or officers. At best, this approach is risky; at worst, it is crude and hazardous, with the danger of all kinds of unintended consequences (see Chapter 3).

This is particularly the case because of the *authority* vested in the new enforcement counsellors by the Third Way. Since they have the power to demand attitudinal and behavioural change from claimants and service users, and to enforce this by withholding benefits and services for non-compliance, these forms of casework combine state paternalism (all this is for the sake of inclusion and the long-term good of the client) with social control (the client has a duty not to burden or disrupt the taxpaying community more than is absolutely necessary). Although these services are highly fragmented, provided by various programmes, units, schemes, zones and budgets, they have in common a strong emphasis on enforcement (as in the Benefits Agency Fraud Investigation Service, the Child

Support Agency, the Home Office Immigration Service Enforcement Directorate, the Home Office Partnerships for Asylum-Seeker Accommodation, and the Social Exclusion Unit Initiatives, as well as the New Deals and Employment Zones). So these new or reformed agencies share a common theme with the directions of policy in adult and youth criminal justice, child protection and mental health. The importation of crude enforcement slogans from various American sports – such as 'Three Strikes and You're Out' – or American police cultures ('zero tolerance') reinforces this obvious reliance on *toughness*, on pressure, persuasion and confrontation as central elements of implementation and practice.

What remains largely unaddressed in the Third Way's philosophy and policy programme is how the 'love' bit in 'tough love' is supposed to be grafted on to this enforcement ethos. There is a tradition, an approach and a method that has flourished in the USA – in 'drugs courts', for example, where vigorous, energetic judges (often black women) confront, challenge and harry somewhat crestfallen junkies into reforming their ways, using peer pressure as well as exhortation, shaming and comforting. Similarly, there is a culture of street-level work – with homeless people, alcoholics and addicts – that relies on tough-and-tender methods, by getting alongside lost souls and helping them back into the mainstream. But these traditions are strongly based on *personal charisma* of a kind that is rooted in certain aspects of US culture, notably evangelical Protestant churches, cults and prayer meetings, especially in black communities. It is far from clear how easily these practices can be transplanted into the more reserved and ironic British culture, where religious enthusiasm has always been regarded as more embarrassing and potentially dangerous than either alcoholic intoxication or drug abuse, and where this kind of personal charisma is prized only in live stage performances and sports personalities (and then only very provisionally).

Furthermore, the attempt to combine programmes for personal development and change with functions of income-testing, rationing, risk management, control, surveillance, and enforcement defies at least three centuries of historical experience (Jordan, 1974; Moroney, 1976). Poor Law institutions, houses of correction, prisons, reform schools and mental hospitals have all at one time or another in their evolution made serious attempts to combine caring and disciplinary functions. Some have had a degree of temporary success – for instance the UK prison service in the Alexander Paterson era, the early part of this century, until the Second World War (Behan, 1956) – but all have reverted to type in the end, as highly stigmatized and damaging experiences for their inmates. The local authority personal social services which were set up in 1948, and developed in the next four decades, were an attempt to combat this stigmatization and identity spoiling by making services more widely accessible, more firmly based in local communities, and more focused on supporting people in their 'natural' environments. Although not entirely successful, these approaches certainly represented advances on previous methods, especially for children and families (Packman, 1975).

Tough love relies on making benefits and services that were formerly entitlements into conditional privileges; on making services that were standardized and generalized across wide swathes of population 'tailored' to individual needs through close assessment processes; and on rationing and 'targeting' them on people seen as most at risk or dangerous to others. History suggests that these processes – making benefits and services more conditional on 'deserving' or 'co-operative' behaviour, conducting detailed assessments of eligibility, especially enquiries into means and resources, and focusing on the most risky and dangerous elements in the population – are precisely what make these benefits and services least acceptable to claimants and service users, their receipt most shameful, and their provision most resented and begrudged by taxpayers (Titmuss, 1968; Jordan, 1974). In order to succeed in its implementation, the Third Way on social welfare will have to overturn this enormous weight of adverse historical evidence.

The Way Ahead

All this so far sounds very critical of New Labour's programme, and gloomy about its future prospects. In assessing the likely outcomes and options for the development of social policy, and of social work within it, we now introduce a more positive and constructive note. The Third Way has notched up some notable achievements, and its programme has dealt with many of the most pressing issues inherited from the Conservative years. In the concluding chapters, we will take a more upbeat view of the way ahead, and argue that, although the road chosen by Tony Blair is a cul-de-sac, his government may ironically, in trying to find its way out from this, stumble upon a quite different path, that takes it by another route to its goals. This accidental change of direction is likely to come about for reasons of technical rationality rather than ideological conversion. Social work could have an important role to play in these more viable long-term policy directions, but only if it rediscovers some almost lost aspects of its historical legacy, and adapts radically to its new circumstances.

The crucial point to make about the Third Way's success is that it has been required to address one central and completely unresolved problem of Thatcherism–Majorism (see pp. 26–7 and Box 1, p. 11). What the Third Way calls 'social exclusion' was in fact a set of issues relating to divisions and conflicts in UK society, through which poor and marginal people came to rely on strategies and practices which pitted them against the majority and drove them into further isolation and disadvantage (Jordan, 1996a; Jordan and Travers, 1998). The starting point for New Labour's social policy programme was – especially in this respect – particularly undesirable. UK society was divided, lacked cohesion, purpose and common bonds of community. To this extent, the Third Way's diagnosis was quite correct. Even though we disagree with the *means adopted*, there can be no doubt that radical policies were required, to tackle these structural problems.

The neo-liberal measures undertaken by Margaret Thatcher's ministers were aimed at encouraging UK citizens to become *competent market actors* in a competitive economic environment, as part of a programme to make the UK economy more successful in competition with other states in a global system. The assumption was that market opportunities, created by breaking down a set of interest-group coalitions (established through trade unions, local government and other public sector empires, business cartels and bureaucratic controls) would benefit the poor at least as much as the better-off (Olson, 1982). Since free voluntary exchange (individual transactions of all kinds, but especially through markets) was a better engine for growth than protectionism (including the *social* protectionism of welfare states), the Conservative administrations of the 1980s were confident that less skilled workers could 'price themselves into jobs', and improve their situation. In practice, the greater freedom created by the deregulation of labour markets, the privatization of services and the weakening of trade unions, all created opportunities for better-off people (who either still enjoyed the protection of good jobs, or formed new protective organizations) to gain at the expense of the worst-off. It also provoked resistance by poor people, most of which involved compensating themselves for their increasing disadvantage by means which are unorthodox or plain illegal (Jordan et al., 1992; Evason and Woods, 1995).

What the Thatcher programme failed to take into account was the development of new *strategies* by both mainstream and minority citizens, through which they took individual and collective action within the reformed institutions of the UK state. For the mainstream section of the population, these involved strategic mobility, both geographically (to more favoured districts in terms of the physical and social environment) and towards the best schools, health clinics, care facilities, etc. For the wealthier few, it meant joining private pension schemes, taking out private health insurance or sending children to private schools; for most, it involved doing whatever was necessary to get the best from state services (Jordan et al., 1994). As better-off households moved out of city centres to more congenial districts, better-paid working-class families left poorer council estates, and those with greater income security or fewer ties to neighbourhoods gained access to, and concentrated in, the better schools, clinics and care services, so less-favoured districts came to be reserved for people with low incomes and other social needs (sink estates), less-favoured schools reserved for their children (sink schools), and the clinics, hospitals and care services allotted to those districts began to decline in quality. Local economic boom or depression mirrored this social polarization (Jordan and Redley, 1994; Marske, 1991; Power, 1997).

As we have seen earlier, poor people's reaction to the decline in their relative position brought about by better-off households' strategies for positional advantage (Hirsch, 1977) was to develop strategies of their own, which used benefits and services to compensate for these losses in welfare. Research studies show that they justified actions like earning undeclared cash while claiming benefits by insisting that this was the only responsible way to protect their families from the adverse consequences of loss of the right to payments for exceptional needs under reformed Income Support regulations; or the only way they could adapt their working patterns to highly fragmented labour markets without risking destitution or debt (Jordan, 1995; Dean and Taylor-Gooby, 1992; Rowlingson et al., 1997). Similarly, young people leaving home and getting into trouble with the law, or getting pregnant, can be seen as using the care system strategically to counteract their adverse situation in the labour market and the housing system.

However, although these strategies were rational for individuals and households, collectively they frustrated each other and caused the situation of the worst-off to deteriorate (Jordan and Travers, 1998). If every person with low earning power works 'off the books' for marginal employers or for themselves, this tends to drive down wages at the bottom of the labour market, and to further fragment employment patterns by undercutting those in regular jobs with decent wages and conditions. The result is *unrestrained competition*, leading to 'hypercasualization' (Jordan, 1996a, Chapter 4): the downward spiral eventually damages the welfare of the poorest. It was necessary for the new government to do something to arrest this. The combination of the New Deals (to drive claimants off benefits and back into the formal labour market of regular employment and self-employment), the national minimum wage and the new Working Families Tax Credit are designed to re-regulate the chaotic world of low-paid work, improve incentives for the 20 per cent of working-age households with no one in formal paid work when Labour came to power, and clamp down on benefit 'fraud' and the whole informal economy.

There is, therefore, an important sense in which New Labour has tackled a problem, inherited from eighteen years of neo-liberal policies, that had to be addressed before any other approach to reform could succeed. There was simply no way to get poor people off benefits and back into the mainstream economy, or to live with the rules of mainstream society, so long as the cash-in-hand and petty criminal sectors prospered. However much this shadow world might have been romanticized in TV series like *Boys from the Blackstuff, Aufwiedersehen Pet, Common as Muck,* or *Making Out,* or in films like *The Full Monty, Trainspotting* and *Brassed Off,* the fact that undeclared cash work and dealing gave payoffs (in the short run) so superior to formal employment meant that the vicious circle of hypercasualization could not be broken. In effect, poor people had reformed the benefits rules in their favour, to allow them to do occasional work, or gain occasional income, without losing a secure, regular weekly payment. Official surveys of earnings showed they had much less than in 1979, but expenditure statistics suggested that their unofficial work compensated for this (Goodman and Webb, 1995). This gave able and enterprising claimants an unfair advantage, *both* over those who chose to do low-paid jobs in the formal economy, *and* over those (mainly women) whose caring responsibilities made it hard for them to undertake these activities, or who lacked the networks to find them (e.g. minorities and loners). Where the young, able and advantaged were organized to rob and terrorize the weak and minorities, this added an oppressive dimension to the injustices built into such social relations of unrestrained competition – the law of the jungle.

The approach that New Labour has taken to these problems is different from the one taken by governments in Denmark (Jordan and Loftager, 1999), the Netherlands (Cox, 1998) and Ireland (Jordan et al., 2000), all of which faced variations on the same problems. It is characterized first by the Prime Minister's moral crusade against irresponsibility and wrongdoing (Blair, 1999a), with its highly selective version of the ills that afflict UK society; second by a very strong form of conditionality, compulsion and activation, embodied in the New Deals; and third, by a US-style approach to enforcement that moblilizes popular prejudice and lust for revenge against lawbreakers of all kinds. Those other countries relied on higher minimum wages (the equivalent of £8.50 an hour in Denmark; £4.50 in Ireland) and generous rules on permitted earnings and benefits tapers. Their activation programmes are much more low-key, and they still rely on a moral consensus that has prevailed since the end of the 1970s. In Ireland this is particularly striking, because it had a similar institutional system to the UK's before 1979, and was experiencing similar problems of unemployment, inflation and low growth. The Irish way out of these problems was through European-style social partnerships, wage restraint, tax reform and national solidarity, not the neo-liberal dogmatism of the UK's Thatcher period or the communitarian moralism of the Blair one (Jordan et al., 2000, Chapter 1). The Irish way has recently been delivering an even faster reduction in unemployment and growth in income than the Third Way, as the compact Celtic Tiger has outstripped the more ponderous British Lion.

If, however, we accept (provisionally) the heavy-handed conditionality and compulsion of the UK programme, as the means that was the logical political follow-up to the Thatcher–Major period, then the achievements of New Labour in its first three years in office are impressive, in relation to expanded labour-market participation and reductions in claimant numbers. This must of course be qualified by the other side of strong enforcement – an ever steeper rise in the prison population in the period 1993–99 (Home Office, 1999). While a higher proportion of claimants have moved into employment than during the Major administration's 1992–97 economic expansion, there are still large numbers who simply 'disappear', either into invisible informal activities, or into crime and (eventually) into prison (see Box 5). There may be fewer suffering 'social exclusion' through unemployment, but there are more suffering the ultimate exclusion of imprisonment.

Box 5   Tough on crime

Criminal justice is an example of New Labour's tendency to adopt populist rhetoric, while quietly pursuing some rational (and even occasionally some liberal) policies which it seldom discusses.

In 1999, recorded crime in the UK fell for the sixth successive year. This was a record for the twentieth century, bucking the trend of an average 5 per cent rise in recorded crime every year since 1918. But rises and falls in the crime rate tend to follow a long-term pattern, closely linked to economic factors. The upheavals of the Industrial Revolution brought rising crime throughout the early nineteenth century, followed by greater stability and prosperity with falling crime from 1860 to 1918 (Nuttall, 1999). Since the recession of the early 1990s, crime figures have fallen with economic growth and rising employment, but it is too soon to tell whether these falls will be sustained over a longer period – indeed, figures for most forms of crime had risen again in statistics published in January 2000.

New Labour came to office in the aftermath of a rapid rise in the prison population since 1993, and a £2 billion prison building programme, under Michael Howard's regime at the Home Office. With Jack Straw as Home

Secretary, the prison population has grown faster. By the end of 1999 there were 66,000 inmates, compared with about 40,000 in 1993.

Thus New Labour's punitive regime has continued, despite falls in the crime rate – but the former cannot be the cause of the latter. It requires a 25 per cent increase in prison sentences to produce a 1 per cent reduction in crime rates (*Guardian*, 13 October 1999). Meanwhile, the government is also pursuing a long-term low-key crime-reduction strategy that could well contribute to reducing crimes, and especially burglaries, in areas (mostly deprived) of high offending.

More generally, it seems that high crime rates and imprisonment are part of the 'trade-off' between employment and equality. More poverty means more crime, even when employment rates are high, and more inequality means more fear of crime, and more popular pressure for punitive measures. In the USA, crime is falling too, but by the year 2000 there will be over 2 million prison inmates (*Guardian*, 29 December 1999), double the number at the beginning of the decade (Donnison, 1998). Although a quarter of California's prison population of 165,000 are detained under the deterrent 'three strikes and you're out' laws, there has been only a 1 per cent fall in violent crime in that state since this law was introduced. And 'tough love' boot camps for young offenders are now being closed in several states, after scandals over bullying by staff, including the death of a 16-year-old boy in Arizona and a 14-year-old girl in South Dakota (*Guardian*, 20 December 1999).

With this caveat, it is still possible to look with some optimism at the prospects for the labour market. What follows will be set out in more detail in Chapter 8. We attempt to look beyond the New Deals and Employment Zones, to anticipate the *long-term* trajectory of tax-benefit reform and its effects on the other reforms of the public sector. In our sketch of these developments, we assume that the Chancellor of the Exchequer will have substantial sums – around £2 billion a year for the next ten years – to redistribute, because of the buoyancy of the economy. This, of course, could be threatened by a whole range of world events, especially by the collapse of the US stock market or a European economic crisis, but it is the best available forecast at present.

We also assume that he will not want to redistribute these sums through the benefits system, because the New Labour government has already declared that it sees benefits as trapping people in poverty and social exclusion (Brown, 1997, 1999). As 'work is the only reliable way out of poverty', reform of the tax-benefit system will be required to improve the situation of the *working poor* without making anyone else worse off, except the very rich. But because of sustained economic growth, it is possible to launch a number of reforms that would redistribute towards low earners, and correct anomalies in the present distribution of incentives and advantages. Furthermore, this strategy would be a politically strong one, in competition with any tax-cutting regime proposed by the opposition Conservatives under William Hague.

The first target of such a programme would be *low-earning households without children*. This sounds improbable, but the Chancellor has already said that it is the way he is thinking (Treasury, 1999). The fact is that working-age households without children form the largest group of individuals of working age in the UK population. They are at present strongly disadvantaged, compared with households with children, because they cannot claim Working Families Tax Credit. But the clear problem about such measures is that, in improving incentives for people to *enter* the labour market (either from income support, or from unpaid household roles), these measures fail to provide incentives for people to *increase* their earnings, either by working longer hours; or by seeking higher wages (Jordan et al., 2000). So although they alleviate the *unemployment trap*, by making those who came off benefits a lot better off on starting work, they also intensify and widen the *poverty trap* by extending the range of incomes across which in-work benefits are withdrawn as earnings rise (Redmond and Sutherland, 1995).

Worse than this, employment credits tend to redistribute most to people who work shorter hours. Under Working Families Tax Credit, by far the greatest gains are made by those working sixteen hours a week or just over (Jordan et al., 2000). This makes sense in the case of a benefit targeted at people with child-care responsibilities, many of whom are lone parents. However, it gives perverse incentives to work part-time for people without such responsibilities. Given New Labour's concern to get citizens to maximize their contribution to the economy through paid work, it makes little sense to encourage them to work so few hours (or to do formal work for so few hours, and informal, off-the-books work for the rest of the week).

To mitigate these problems, it would be most logical and effective to raise the tax *allowance*, benefiting every earner, but especially those with lowest incomes. In addition, the best way to give comparable advantages to the workers with fewest hours or most irregular employment would be to introduce a tapered withdrawal of income support say of 50 per cent, so that these claimants were able to use income support as an in-work benefit, as a step back into the labour market. By this route, a point would be fairly quickly reached at which it would be technically simple to integrate the tax-benefit systems, so as to create a *negative income tax scheme*. This is because, after reforms lasting the period of the next parliament, the value of increases in tax allowances (rising with earnings) would have come to equal the value of far slower rises in the value of benefits (since these would continue to be pegged to prices, in line with the Chancellor's determination not to let benefits trap people in 'dependency' and 'exclusion'). Hence people in the labour market would get the same amount through 'fiscal welfare' in the form of a tax allowance as those outside the labour market through the 'social welfare' of the benefits system (Jordan et al., 2000).

However, this would also signal the end of the 'New Contract for Welfare' (DSS, 1998), which has been the cornerstone of New Labour's programme, for two reasons:

1   At present, New Labour is able to argue that the current claimant population is a product of eighteen years of Conservative government, and the exclusions

and perverse incentives of its policies. People now claiming not only want to work, but are able to do so if opportunities and incentives are given, and if they can be suitably trained and motivated. Hence it is fair to reserve benefits for those who are in 'genuine need', i.e. quite incapable of work, who form a very small proportion of the present claimant population. But after five to ten years of New Deals, All-Work Tests and strict conditionality, the claimant population will presumably *mainly* consist of people in 'genuine need', or New Labour policies will have failed. Any programme which continued to disadvantage this residue of 'deserving' claimants would appear to violate principles of social justice. An integrated negative income tax system would also make it technically difficult to do this, even if benefits and credits continued to be delivered by different administrative processes.

2 A great deal of socially valuable activity does not take the form of paid work – in particular caring and supportive work by family members, neighbours and volunteers, community, cultural and political work. Full-time carers, volunteers and activists deserve recognition and reward. Under a negative income tax such citizens would get neither benefits nor credits, and there would be strong incentives to commercialize all forms of care and support. This would favour paid work unduly, and penalize informal household work, neighbourliness, volunteering and other communal activities unfairly.

These factors would give rise to campaigns, social movements, lobbies and pressure groups, all protesting about the distortions caused by the excessive priority given to paid employment in the Third Way's system. These interest groups would argue that this was neither fair nor efficient. Above all, many would insist that households, kinship groups, friendship networks, neighbourhoods and communities are more sensitive and appropriate ways of caring for, nurturing, socializing and supporting children and adults with special needs than the various kinds of paid and for-profit services that prevailed. They would argue that society itself was weakened by such developments, because they destroyed the bonds of trust, co-operation, mutuality and community on which it relies for its prosperity *and* quality of life (Putnam, 1993; Fukuyama, 1994).

Those mounting such campaigns would not necessarily be poor and disadvantaged people, or members of opposition political parties. There would be supporters of the main charities, of smaller groups for people with disabilities and handicaps, women's groups, associations upholding family and community values, religious faiths, early-retired people, members of rural communities and many others, all pressurizing the government to recognize informal carers, volunteers, political activists and social entrepreneurs. Research suggests that they would be strong in the Labour Party as well as in opposition parties (Jordan, 1999b).

The political difficulties that would face New Labour at this stage point towards more promising directions for tax-benefit reform, and for the programme itself. They also indicate that social work – in a broader, more generous and transformed version – would come to play a very positive role in the implementation of a new approach. But the important point is that the present reforms are only a temporary stage, and are themselves unstable. The Third Way is in this sense a cul-de-sac.

Conclusions: The Future of Social Work

In this chapter, we have explored the origins and implications of New Labour's doctrine of 'tough love'. The ideas behind the Third Way's policy programme prescribe a new kind of relationship between those who give social services and those who receive them, one that embodies a more effective communication of key values, especially those of 'reciprocity' (something for something) and 'responsible community' (respect for order and the needs of others).

These changes raise questions about how local authority social services in particular, and social work as a profession, make themselves relevant and significant for the government's new programme. As more commercial organizations, employing fewer trained social workers, move into service provision, both local authorities and the profession have become more specialized around assessment of resources and risks, the investigation of abuse and rule-breaking, and the setting up and enforcement of contracts.

Conversely, the growing role of the voluntary sector in service provision, and the mushroom-like spawning of new projects and initiatives under new partnerships, challenge social workers' conception of their roles. Another theme of this book is whether professional social work any longer seeks to be credible at street level, with service users and carers, or whether it is developing into an arm's length, office bound, report-writing, official kind of practice, which leaves face-to-face work to others.

In so far as voluntary agencies do employ professionally qualified social workers, and often use them far more flexibly than local authorities or other public sector agencies do, the answer to this question is clearly in the affirmative; social workers still need the interpersonal skills, moral maturity and broader vision to be able to improvise on their feet in face-to-face encounters with people in need. There is much more of a continuum between local authority and voluntary sector practice than our categorization so far allows. Many who work in the former services still practise in ways that have much in common with workers in the latter, who in turn overlap considerably with project and community workers, often in the same organization. But the uncomfortable fact remains that many new workers, with just these skills, are now practising *without* social work training, and with no intention of seeking such training. People doing the same sort of work ten years ago would certainly have considered this form of training; many today do not, and do not regard themselves as social workers (see Chapter 5).

In one sense, these workers have come into existence as a new tier of practitioners – street workers, support workers and project workers – acting as intermediaries between service users and officials, negotiating solutions to intractable conflicts and misunderstandings as well as helping their clientele in the daily struggle to get by. In part, this is a response to the managerialist, rationing and controlling turn in local authority social services, and the authoritarian tendencies in broader government policy. It is as if these more 'hands on' workers, who get alongside service users, understand their subjective experiences, advocate for them, and help them organize to represent and meet their needs, are filling a vacuum left by the profession's bureaucratization. It is also as if they are supplying the missing element of 'love' in the Third Way's unbalanced version of its policy formulation.

Another paradox of social work's role in social policy under New Labour is that the personal social services have never been more closely identified with the quest for a rational, instrumental and bureaucratic approach to social engineering and the top-down management of social problems. But present organization and methods reflect the Conservative agenda of the 1980s – concerns with cost-effectiveness and budgetary control. The new forms of accountability introduced in the reforms of that era make economic criteria and business methods at least as important duties to the state. 'Tough love', as a philosophy and a policy programme, has developed from a number of factors – the 'normative turn' in political thought, a revival of interest in the notion of community as a basis for moral rules and political membership, moral panic about the excesses of individualism and materialism (Jordan, 1999a, 1999b), and a perceived growth in lawlessness and disorder. The intellectual and social background to all these developments will be analysed in the next chapter.

These policy and professional tensions are reflected in theoretical developments in social work. Mainstream theory and research seek reliable knowledge for practice that give both legitimacy to professional interventions and techniques, and direction to the detailed implementation of more general policies. 'Evidence-based' approaches in social services (as in health) seek to interpret research findings, and translate them into prescriptions for practice (MacDonald and Sheldon, 1992). In this, they employ the institutional frameworks of managerial and bureaucratic control, and the guiding hand of central government, to steer what happens between providers and service users, using rational scientific analysis and measurable outcomes, so that resources can be deployed in the most efficient way.

But there is a strong undercurrent of critical scepticism about this project which casts doubt on both the managerialist and scientific credentials of the evidence-based approach. Among a minority of academic researchers and theorists, as well as some practitioners, attention is being redirected towards the detailed face-to-face transactions between social workers and service users, either as narratives (Hall, 1997), or as social constructions (Parton and O'Byrne, 2000), or as emancipatory efforts (Shaw, 1997). In such encounters, these authors suggest, what has been transacted is not a one-way implementation of policy or method (Jordan, 1970), but a negotiation of meaning and identity. Those who give and receive social services obstinately refuse to interpret their work or describe their tasks in the way that law, policy and guidance require. Instead, they continue to insist on giving versions of practice in which values, cultures and interpretations at adds with those of managerialism and the Third Way are the main elements.

The New Labour project challenges social work practice, but also creates opportunities for it. On the face of it, a programme for cultural and individual change, which emphasizes sharing and mutuality and takes its exemplars and principles from the family, the neighbourhood and the community, should provide fertile ground for a healthy, expanding social work profession. If it does not, then this says something about the adaptability of a still-young occupation, as well as the prejudices of its political masters.

2

Values, Morals and Emotions: The Shifting Ethical Foundations of Social Work

The Third Way has been described as an attempt to change the moral and political culture of the United Kingdom (Marquand, 1998; 6, 1999a). The Prime Minister regularly takes the moral high ground in his political speeches, and does not shrink from demanding fundamental moral shifts in social relations among citizens – for instance, in his speech to the 1999 Labour Party Conference (Blair, 1999b). These cultural developments, partly attempts to lead society from above, partly efforts to surf the wave of changes already occurring spontaneously in society, have important implications for social work and its place in social policy.

At the same time, the New Labour government employs a different language to describe its reform programme and its agenda for change – the language of contracts, risks and penalties. While giving moral reasons why citizens should be more responsible, should participate more fully, and should show concern for each other, it also talks frequently of the need for 'prudence', the duty to 'invest in the future', to be 'flexible, 'adaptable', and 'competitive' (Brown, 1997, 1999 *passim*). Often these words are employed in the Chancellor of Exchequer's descant on the Prime Minister's themes. This language spills over the sphere of economic policy into the social programme, for instance in ideas about a New Contract for Welfare (DSS, 1998), the need to control and punish fraud, and the overall emphasis on compliance and enforcement (Home Office, 1998).

In this chapter, we will analyse the implications of the first of these elements in the Third Way. Here we will look at how the new ethics both develops the moral themes of Thatcherism, and introduces significant new elements. New Labour morality and its social implications combine two versions of ethical reasoning in new ways which attempt to capture the emerging consensus on welfare and communal responsibility in the USA (Waddan, 1997) and the UK (Jordan, 1998a). The first part of the chapter examines how these developments can be squared with social work ethics, as they have been adapted to fit the changes of the 1980s and early 1990s.

These questions of moral and political culture are connected to ones of rationality and the implementation of policy. The distinctive feature of the 1990s has been the emergence of new thinking about 'risk' (Beck, 1992) and 'risk societies', all of which has clear significance for social work (Parton, 1998; Parton et al., 1997). Many of these ideas have been imported into the Third Way and to New Labour political strategy from the work of Anthony Giddens (1998). Giddens' thought has influenced New Labour thinking about social justice and social inclusion, and hence about the reform programme of the government (see Box 2, p. 20). The concept of risk provides one of the links between the moral and the economic elements in the Third Way.

Our goal is to look at how a version of political rationality and planning founded on these new ethical principles makes sense to workers at street level, carrying through some of the measures outlined in the first chapter. At this stage, the purpose is to look behind the details of the New Labour programme, at its philosophical basis and its concept of governance, and the relation of the state to civil society. Later we will move on to a more detailed consideration of the programme's impact on social work practice.

This does not imply that we will not be concerned with implementation here. On the contrary, it will be with implementation of values, reasons and knowledge that we shall be centrally concerned, because (in one sense) social work *is* the implementation of these things. Indeed, we will argue that implementation (like practice) needs to be understood in its own right (Hill, 1993; Pressman and Wildavsky, 1973; Lindblom and Woodhouse, 1993). New Labour's thinking about this key part of cultural change and institutional reform is still under-developed and shallow, and this is reflected in its approach to local authority social services, and to social work more generally.

The Third Ethical Way

In his essay on the Third Way in politics, Tony Blair claimed that the central values of his new direction were 'equal value, opportunity for all, responsibility and community' (Blair, 1998a, p. 3). In many of his speeches and writings, these themes are echoed and elaborated. For instance, at the party conference of 1999, he talked of:

> Solidarity, social justice, the belief not that society comes before individual fulfilment but that it is only a strong society of others that the individual will be fulfilled. That it is these bonds of connection that makes us not citizens of one nation but members of one human race .... We are putting our values into practice; we are the only political force capable of liberating the potential of our people. Knowing what we have to do and knowing how to do it. (*Guardian*, 29 September 1999, p. 6)

What stands out about these sentences (apart from their conspicuous lack of verbs) is the strong linking of a political programme with a moral purpose, first for the nation, and then for humanity. This is picked up in policy documents, where the Prime Minister writes of 'national renewal' as the ambition of welfare reform: 'Reform is a vital part of rediscovering our true national purpose' (Blair, 1998b, p. iii). What is therefore required is 'a new contract between the citizen and the state, where we keep a welfare state from which we all benefit, but on terms that are fair and clear' (ibid., p. v).

The distinctive feature of this new political morality is the attempt to combine elements of individualism with aspects of collectivism. By philosophical tradition, these are two different modes of ethical reasoning. The postwar welfare state was grounded primarily in collective morality, though severely limited by the constraints of a long-term path of liberal individualism in British political culture. Margaret Thatcher elevated individualism and the values of liberty (personal and property rights) to primacy, in combination with hierarchy and the values of order and control, in a successful shift which reinstated many of the ethical priorities of the nineteenth century ('Victorian values'). Tony Blair's project is to find a combination of the three elements (individualism, hierarchy and egalitarianism – see Box 6) which is adapted to today's economic and cultural environment (6, 1999a). This is a deliberate attempt to *redefine* the centre ground of UK politics, to establish a new consensus around work, welfare, citizenship and community (6, 1999b).

Box 6   Institutions, moral character and political settlements

Politics is always concerned with the 'moral character' of citizens (6, 2000), in that political mobilizations make implicit or explicit assumptions about the relationship between institutions and the nature of citizens' commitments to each other.

Moral character is 'largely an interconnected set of traits, such as honesty, fairness and fidelity, which, in turn, are largely deep-seated dispositions to do certain things for an appropriate range of reasons' (Audi, 1997, p. 160). It reflects the pattern of a person's thoughts and actions concerning the relationships between themselves and others (Kupperman, 1991, p. 17).

Political thought since Aristotle has been divided over whether the *institutions* of a good society (norms, rules, educational systems, civil society organizations and the structures of governance) can be designed to create citizens with good moral characters; whether individuals are in fact more deeply influenced by other factors, such as biological evolution or original sin; or whether institutions should allow individuals to develop spontaneously, but be robust against strategies they might invent to exploit or cheat each other (see pp. 179–82). Constitutions might be seen as attempts to balance these three views (6 and Randon, 1995, Part II).

Political mobilizations, such as Margaret Thatcher's 'property-owning democracy', and Tony Blair's 'Third Way', rely on reaching new *political 'settlements'* that combine two or more of four apparently conflicting *cultural projects* in new ways. The stability of the settlement depends on its capacity to create cohesion out of conflict (Douglas, 1996, p. 42).

The four cultural projects can be represented as follows (6, 2000):

A. Fatalism: Individuals make themselves. No form of morality is reliable. Luck or fate determine outcomes. Institutions are incidental.	*C. Hierarchy*: Individuals should keep rules. Institutions should reinforce rules; they should punish wrongdoing and reward virtue.
B. Individualism: Individuals should pursue their own projects. Institutions should prevent them from violating each other's rights to do so.	*D. Egalitarianism*: Individuals are made by communities. Moral character is the product of membership and belonging. Institutions should protect communities.

Thatcherism was a mobilization that combined B. *Individualism* and C. *Hierarchy*, against the collectivism of the 1970s under Old Labour. The Third Way introduces D. *Egalitarianism*, but in combination with B. (the individual as the moral unit in society) and C. (the need for law enforcement and strong central government leadership).

In this section, we will try to show why the liberal individualist and egalitarian collectivist traditions do not mix very easily, but go on to show that social work, as a practice and as an element in social policy, does not make much sense without both of them. The Third Way's attempt to find a new synthesis between them *should* therefore provide friendly conditions for social work to expand and thrive. As a general rule, individualist ethics plus collectivist ethics equals a good time for social work to prosper. This still holds – but only if we widen our view of what constitutes 'social work' to include things called something else by New Labour and (often) by its own practitioners (see pp. 37–9).

Values are moral principles that guide policy and practice. They can and do conflict, because all political cultures and programmes represent some kind of balance between principles – such as liberty and equality – that often pull in opposite directions. In social policy, one fundamental moral issue is whether to provide services on the basis of the value of human life (i.e. as basic rights for all citizens, as human beings, whatever their social virtues or vices, their contributions or costs to society); or whether to provide them on the basis of membership (i.e. as entitlements deriving from what they do, or have done, for the public good, or what they merit or deserve).

This division between two ethics of social provision is not a left–right split; it reflects a deeper tension between two whole approaches to ethical reasoning. The former is characteristic of the Kantian tradition, of progressive liberal and Christian Democratic thought. The latter is the hallmark of utilitarian thinking, and of authoritarians in both conservative and socialist traditions. In the first approach to ethical reasoning, individual moral autonomy is the basis of a free society and a healthy community. The fundamental moral principle is individual choice and self-determination in all social questions – decisions about relationships and organizations as well as personal issues. In the second approach, membership of groups and the interdependence of members is the basis for all human well-being, and the fundamental moral principle is responsibility towards the community, and fairness between members who co-operate.

Box 7   Individualist and collectivist moral reasoning

There are important differences between the two main cultural projects or moral traditions that the Third Way attempts to combine with order and hierarchy – liberal individualism and egalitarian collectivism.

Individualism is biased towards institutions that enable individuals to be responsible for themselves, to be morally autonomous, and to be committed to personal projects and relationships. It sees group ethics and collectivist institutions as intrusive and distorting of individuals' potential. It holds individuals to account for the outcomes of their decisions and choices. It sees *justice* primarily in terms of the procedures and rules that govern interactions, and therefore favours institutions such as markets and adversarial court hearings.

Collectivism is biased towards institutions that promote care, mutuality, solidarity and interdependence. It emphasizes *equality of membership*, dignity and decency in all interactions, as factors enabling trust and co-operation. It sees individualist ethics as promoting selfishness and social irresponsibility. It holds individuals responsible for contributing to the common good, and restraining their competitive impulses. It sees justice in terms of the distributive process, as concerned with fair shares of the benefits of co-operation.

There are significant common elements in the two systems of ethical reasoning, such as moral autonomy, responsibility and trust (6, 1998; Margalit, 1996); but the Third Way's attempt to reconcile them relies heavily on creating a set of double standards. Mainstream citizens inhabit markets and are held accountable in terms of individualist ethics. Public sector employees (such as teachers and social workers) and welfare claimants and service users are subject to collectivist rules over obligations and contributions, and held accountable in terms of membership of a *responsible community*. Tony Blair says: 'This generation wants a society free from prejudice, but not from rules' (Blair, 1999a). But there are different rules for different parts of society.

The creation of the postwar welfare state in the UK was clearly a strong move in the direction of the second approach to ethical reasoning, signalled in the Beveridge Report (1942). Starting from the experience of the Second World War, and the common struggle against totalitarianism, the programme of the 1945 Labour government accepted Beveridge's vision of new institutions to protect *all* citizens from the shared risks of an industrial society – the five giants of Poverty, Idleness, Disease, Ignorance and Squalor. The major social services would use resources gathered from everyone, through taxes and National Insurance contributions, to give all citizens basic protection against the costs associated with dependence in childhood, sickness, disability and old age, and to bring all up to a decent standard in education, health, housing and welfare. As well as being collectivist in its programme, Labour did not hesitate to use the power of the state to require such contributions. But – in the spirit of the liberal tradition of UK politics – the new services were presented as basic rights, to give each individual citizen a platform on which to build through individual choices and projects, rather than a system of interdependence of strata in the social order (as in many European countries).

It was these elements of *individualism* in the UK political tradition that were strongly revived and re-emphasized by Margaret Thatcher after 1979. The central thrust of her thinking was that collectivism had gone too far by the 1970s, and had fallen prey to the collective selfishness of groups like trade unions, local authorities and bureaucrats, who exploited its moral principles for their own benefit, using their power to pursue their own interests at the expense of less organized citizens (Olson, 1982; Peacock, 1979). Social policy reforms should aim to restrain the power of these interests, and restore autonomy and choice to individuals.

Individualism as an ethical tradition is quite distinct from the narrow economic views of those who advised the Conservative governments of the 1980s. It does not imply that everyone is required to be, or assumed to be, a rational egoist, seeking the best available bargains in the global marketplace. It means that every individual matters, and is in some sense *sacred* (Durkheim, 1933) – that human life and human rights have special value, that each person is unique and, in a fundamental sense, all are of equal worth. But this in turn implies that in this version of ethical reasoning each person is morally responsible for his or her own life, and for the consequences of their decisions. It means, in fact, that they *hold themselves responsible* for their choices and the results of them. It respects the subjective view of the good life (Weale, 1983), of the individual's own versions of what makes his or her life worth living, and how to live it, and insists that it is this, and not politicians' or bureaucrats' view of the public good, that must count for most in a properly organized society.

These ethical ideas are not confined to Thatcherite Conservatism, but were central to the Reformation of the sixteenth and seventeenth centuries, to the Enlightenment of the eighteenth century, to the reform movements of the nineteenth century (including that for the emancipation of slaves), and to the resistance against both fascism and communism. But also, they are central to social work's professional ethics – to the principles of confidentiality, self-determination, non-judgmentalism, and even to the more recent anti-oppressive values that entered the social work lexicon in the 1980s (CCETSW, 1990).

The key moral intuition behind ethical individualism is that (in West European countries since the Reformation) we *want* to be responsible for ourselves, and we are only truly human when we do so. We want to be the *sovereign authority* over our own lives, the captains (as it were) of our own ships; this implies a degree of autonomy and independence, and a capacity to make informed decisions.

It means that we choose our relationships, and reach agreements about the extent of our interdependence with others, relying on a kind of 'contract' that is negotiated and may be quite flexible, but does not simply reflect tradition or convention. This in turn implies that we hold ourselves accountable for the failures as well as the successes of our relations with others (Jordan et al., 1994, Chapter 2). It means that we try to anticipate, calculate and manage the risks associated with the lives we choose, including their economic hazards.

According to this ethical standpoint, the Old Labour version of the welfare state, like Soviet-style state socialism, was not only morally wrong because it denied citizens the right to choose the kinds of social services they wanted, and largely denied them the opportunity to criticize those they got, but wrong because it put the collective good before the freedom of each individual to be critically responsible for his or her own life. It therefore violated the fundamental human right to be individual and different, by subjecting everyone to the same regime, standardizing provision for their needs, telling them what they required, and giving it to them without asking them what they wanted. In this way, Thatcherism was able to conflate all forms of collectivism and socialism as sharing the same weakness – putting equality before freedom, and *compelling* people to be equal.

These individualist values are still strongly present in the Third Way, in Tony Blair's insistence on individual fulfilment (Blair, 1998a), and Gordon Brown's on equality of opportunity to achieve, not equality of outcome after redistributive social welfare provision, which he described as 'not a socialist dream, but other people's nightmare of socialism' (Brown, 1997, p. 16). But they have been offset by collectivist values and principles of a kind, that attempt to balance individual responsibility by the sense of community membership and bonds of mutuality.

What is new about the Third Way is the perception of a different set of risks against which the state should help individuals protect themselves. In the 1945 version of the welfare state, the hazards of industrial society were seen as the result of class conflict and the power of capital; new collectivist institutions were designed to mitigate the wasteful and damaging effects of such conflicts, and of the industrial process itself (Marshall, 1950). They were also to insure and protect citizens against the hazards of 'nature', 'misfortune', and the life cycle, unavoidable shared hazards of the human condition.

The Third Way sees the risks that threaten citizens as stemming from quite different sources. Since the task of the state is to close the gap between individuals' human potentialities and human achievements – 'between what they are, and what they have the capacities to be' (Brown, 1997, p. 16) – it is essential to identify the factors which prevent people from exercising their autonomy in the most effective way, and hence achieving their potential. One of these is lack of information and (in a deeper sense) *knowledge*. People are vulnerable in so far as they make choices that are actually damaging their own prospects, and distance them further from their goals. This can also result from weakness of will or motivation, from inexperience, or from harmful cultural pressures. Hence state services should inform *and* guide individuals to make wise decisions, taking account of their personal projects and commitments.

The most obvious choices that affect health and welfare concern use of drugs, alcohol and tobacco; activities that increase the risk of skin cancer, HIV/AIDS, heart disease, burnout and being overweight (leading to hypertension and other vulnerabilities) are others. The aim is to assist citizens to make better choices, and to manage their own risks more effectively. The idea that such risks stem from our own actions, and not from impersonal economic forces, class competition, state oppression or natural hazards, transforms the role of the state into an educative and guiding one, and justifies a degree of paternalistic intervention (6, 1999b) in the lives of citizens, especially those vulnerable as a result of poor education, weakness of will or damaging early experiences. It justifies a greater focus on individual casework which combines 'care and control' elements across a far broader spectrum of health and welfare issues than traditional liberal political culture or the individualist ethic of strong personal rights and liberties would allow. All this points towards an expansion of something like social work; in New Labour's programme it involves new policy initiatives and new occupations for its implementation.

The second new kind of risks identified by the Third Way are those that stem from the actions of *individual others*, and especially irresponsible or antisocial others. Whereas Old Labour values saw citizens' vulnerabilities mainly in terms of the impersonal effects of 'society' on individuals, New Labour emphasizes the damaging consequences of the behaviour of various groups – delinquents, criminals and truants (Straw, 1999a), 'travellers' (Straw, 1999b), bogus asylum seekers (Straw, 1999c), beggars (Blair, 1997) and so on – and different kinds of irresponsible or feckless action, such as under-age sex and drug abuse (Blair, 1999a). All this justifies tough policies, not only in the field of crime, but also towards children and young people generally (such as curfews and fines on parents), and again a degree of paternalism (classes on parenting). It heightens awareness of individual vulnerabilities of citizens in the private sphere of their lives (domestic violence, child abuse, the damaging consequences of separation, divorce, neglectful or inconsistent parenting) and in situations not previously perceived as risk-laden (bullying at school, harassment in the workplace, racism and sexism in the police, stalking, passive smoking in public places). Dangerousness of, or oppression by, individual others therefore becomes a major factor in the protection against risk offered by state services, and this again influences the shape and implementation of government programmes, towards a more educative approach for mainstream citizens (greater awareness, assertiveness and more demands on other citizens or on officials) and new interventions to raise behavioural standards or punish infractions.

Finally, there is an increased awareness of the risks associated with scientific 'progress' or 'expert systems' (Giddens, 1998). The Third Way recognizes this, though it is ambivalent about the government's role in, and responsibility for, managing these risks, as can be seen from the controversy over genetically modified (GM) crops. The implication of recognizing that many risks previously seen as 'natural' are in fact caused by human agency, that they are the unintended, long-term consequences of scientific experiments (nuclear testing) or the result of individual irresponsibility (asbestos pollution), medical incompetence

(Bristol Hospital heart surgeons), unforeseen disaster (Chenobyl), or the cumulative effects of individual actions (hole in the ozone layer, global warming) is that it increases the government's role in regulation and self-regulation. But it also involves it in very difficult issues, both because the agencies to be regulated are often very large and powerful (e.g. multinational drug companies, GM crop developers), or because other policies are at stake (e.g. employment in the arms industry), or because large claims for compensation by injured parties are involved. The obvious policy implications – fuller and more accessible information, by means of which the public can protect itself against these risks – are less readily accepted by New Labour in relation to these risks than those identified above. This is partly because freedom of information goes against the grain of the paternalism and interventionism allowed by the other new kinds of risks recognized.

All this amounts to a new element of collectivism in the Third Way's ethical reasoning, but of a very different kind from the one that informed the postwar welfare state. Whereas the individualist elements in the Third Way point towards personal responsibility, small-group mutuality and voluntarism, as well as commercial and private self-provision in health and welfare, these collectivist elements indicate a need for more state intervention, regulation and steering. Most of them also justify selective interventions, focusing on protecting and controlling targeted individuals, either because of their dangerousness or their vulnerability, or both. It is this individual focus for collectivist measures that is distinctive about the Third Way and gives a special flavour to its social policy programme. The implications of this will be analysed in the next chapter.

'Community' as a Moral Basis for Social Work

So far, we have argued that the Third Way attempts to combine the individualist tradition of ethical reasoning in social policy issues with a collectivist ethic, in new and distinctive combinations. In this section, we will look at the part played by the notion of 'community' in synthesizing these two traditionally antagonistic elements in ethics and politics. But first we will consider how social work stands in relation to these two modes of moral reasoning, and whether its professional ethics can be squared with the kind of synthesis that is emerging within the Third Way.

The first idea to be developed is the one that was briefly made on pp. 16–17 – that professional social work as an aspect of public policy is only possible in political cultures containing both elements of individualism and of collectivism. Without individualism, there can be no good reasons for focusing on the subjective, the personal and the interactive elements in social phenomena, because the behaviour of human beings makes sense only as a reflection of some higher or deeper powers at work in the world – God's purposes, evolution and genetics, the iron laws of economic determinism, original sin, alien invaders, or something else. But without collectivism, social work will remain the province of charities, churches or other civil-society organizations, and will never enter the sphere of governance as an aspect of social policy. Although there are fewer state-employed social workers in the Netherlands and Germany, for example, than in the UK or the Scandinavian countries, those employed by voluntary organizations are *trained* under licence to the state, and do statutory tasks – so they too are involved in public policy.

Thus any coherent ethic for social work practice in public service work must contain a balance between individualist and collectivist moral reasoning, and must link morality with politics. In the postwar welfare state, the dominant solution to this problem was to subscribe to the ethical goals of the 'Beveridge revolution' (Macadam, 1945; Cormack, 1945), and hence to identify with the goals and purposes of the major social services – health, social security, education and social housing. The rationale for public social work thus became the existence of *special needs*, not catered for within the standardized and generalized provision of those (universal) services. People in unusual situations, or in personal crises, or in conflict with each other in the family or neighbourhood, or simply failing to adjust or adapt to 'realities', provided the mainstream justifications for social work interventions (Timms, 1964). Alternatively, the need for more generous provision of individual attention, to respect the personal, the subjective and the interactive, and to create a space for critical reflection on society and social relations, was a later (and more radical) gloss on this function (Statham, 1978; Simpkin, 1979; Jordan, 1974, 1976, 1983, 1990).

Such justifications became increasingly problematic in the period between the late 1970s and the mid-1990s. This was the result of two factors. The first was the erosion and fragmentation of the major social services, which has exposed a large section of the population (far larger than the one that required personal social services during the 'golden age' of the welfare state) to the adverse consequences of global economic change. This intensified social divisions and conflicts, and resulted in the development of resistance strategies – many illegal, or damaging for others – among poor and marginal citizens (Jordan and Redley, 1994; Jordan, 1995, 1996a). Social workers and local authority social services have been required to work with these people, and to deal with the damaging results (for themselves, their children, their neighbours, etc.) of their resistance strategies. This has led to the second problem – the increasing role of public social work in assessing, rationing, investigating, controlling and enforcement among disadvantaged people.

To counter these tendencies, and deal with obvious contradictions between ethical aspirations and everyday practices, social work theorists have put forward a series of new principles and new dimensions of moral awareness, aimed at addressing hitherto unrecognized aspects of oppression and exclusion. These have included racism and sexism (Dominelli, 1988; Thompson, 1997), ageism, ableism and discrimination based on sexual orientation. All these new ethical principles have now been gathered up under the portfolio term 'anti-oppression' (Thompson, 1998), and provide the basis for a more balanced set of professional ethical principles. However, these fail to capture the essential element in most service users' oppression – exclusion and marginalization stemming from poverty, from lack of access to mainstream economic, social and cultural facilities, and from divisions and conflicts in society caused by injustice and inequality (Jordan, 1990). By focusing on 'oppression' in relations between men and women, white and black, able and disabled, young and old, they have largely failed to address the fact that most social work is implicated in oppression based on those fundamental sources of social injustice shared by the largest number of service users.

The great strength of the Third Way is that it does directly address exactly this source of oppression and injustice, via its philosophy of social justice through social inclusion, and through its policy programme. But it does so in a way that has a limited shelf-life (see pp. 35–7). Furthermore, its ethical basis rests on a concept – 'community' – which is highly contested. In the rest of this section, we will focus on New Labour's version of community, and its relevance for social work.

The idea of 'community' notoriously has many meanings – fifty-seven, according to Leaper (1968) – but its key role in ethical reasoning is to bridge the gap between individualist and collectivist ideas. What all the different meanings imply is *membership* involving a degree of reciprocity and co-operation, and hence mutual obligations and responsibilities. In liberal political thought, the high priority placed on individual freedom, and hence on personal and property rights, and on protection against interference or coercion by others or the state, implies a *thin* (abstract, impersonal, insubstantial) version of the duties of citizenship, and of commitments to the common good (Taylor, 1989; Sandel, 1983; Walzer, 1983). Conversely, socialist ethics implies a form of collectivism that often invests the state with formidable coercive powers, involving strong restraint of individual liberties and interests, and an authoritative role in the pursuit of common purposes – an 'objective' version of the good society, which turns out on closer inspection to reflect the interests of political, bureaucratic or military élites, and to institutionalize their power. The communitarian turn in ethical and political thought (MacIntyre, 1981; Kymlicka, 1989; Kymlicka and Norman, 1994; Etzioni, 1988, 1993) attempts to provide a 'thicker' (more concrete, morally binding and substantial) version of the obligations that individuals owe each other in a good society, and of the duties of citizens towards the state. But it tries to do so in a way that locates these duties in relationships between members of a moral association, co-operating for the mutual benefits of their membership, rather than in the overpowering legitimacy of the authoritative collective, or a grand political vision of social improvement.

Box 8   Community

Community is both a system of order and membership, and a way of getting things done; it is both a *form of social organization* and a *kind of economy*. In the latter sense, as a way of producing and distributing goods and services, it is an alternative to markets *and* state services.

The Third Way focuses on community almost entirely as a system of social control, with members holding each other responsible for orderly conduct and work contributions, and thus providing the 'glue' to bind the inclusive society together (Williams, F., 1998, p. 12). As has been clear in Tony Blair's speeches, this is closely tied to 'family values':

'I have no doubt that the breakdown of law and order is intimately linked to the breakup of a strong sense of community. And the breakup of community is in turn, to a crucial degree, consequent on the breakdown in family life.' (speech in 1993, quoted in Hughes and Mooney, 1998, p. 68)

'... strong families are the foundation of strong communities'. (Blair, 1996)

However, in this book we emphasize community as a source of economic and social regeneration, as one means by which marginal individuals can take collective action to pursue their interests. Community differs from formal production in several ways:

	Community	*Market/state*
Mode of exchange relationships	reciprocity, social obligation	exchange under contract
Type of property	inclusive, shared, collective	exclusive, private- *or* state-owned
Medium of exchange	labour contribution	Price *or* financial contribution
Distribution	sharing in (collective consumption) *or* sharing out (voluntary redistribution)	Contractual *or* compulsory redistribution

Markets and states marginalize community as a way of doing things. Marginal groups (such as immigrants from rural settings) retain community as a way of surviving in markets and states.

This approach is particularly attractive at the end of a century in which the weaknesses of socialism (both in its democratic and its authoritarian versions) have been cruelly exposed, in economic competition with varieties of capitalism (both liberal and authoritarian); but when economic individualism, as preached by such leaders as Margaret Thatcher and Ronald Reagan, turned out to have many unintended and costly social consequences also. The hope is that the notion of community can provide a 'cement' for society (Elster, 1989), repairing some of the fractures and fragmentations brought about by the neo-liberal hegemony of the 1980s, and the impact of global market forces. Indeed, it sometimes seems as if Thatcherism saw only the individual bricks in the wall of societal relationships ('there's no such thing as society') whereas Blairism sees only the mortar ('we must rebuild the bonds between people').

However, the version of community implicitly or explicitly embraced by the Third Way (in the USA under Bill Clinton, as well as in the UK under Tony Blair) is quite specifically conservative, compulsory and prescriptive (Driver and Martell, 1997; Hughes and Little, 1999; Jordan, 1998b). In Blair's vision

no country can ever prosper economically or socially unless all its people prosper, unless we use the talent and energies of all the people rather than just the few, unless we live up to the ambition to create a society where the community works for the good of the individual, and every individual works for the good of the community. (Blair, 1996, p. 5)

At this level of generality, no one could take exception to such sentiments, or even to the more specific version of the good society put forward by Amitai Etzioni, an important influence on the Third Way.

First, people have a moral responsibility to take care of themselves ... the second line of responsibility lies with those closest to the person, including kin, friends, neighbours and other community members ... As a rule any community ought to be expected to do the best it can to take care of its own. (Etzioni, 1993, pp. 145–6)

It is the last line of this quotation that is most telling in relation to the Third Way on welfare provision, citizenship and law and order. The New Labour government seeks to transform UK political culture from above, but by 'restoring' the sense of family, kinship, neighbourly and local 'ownership' of social issues, as diverse as child care, care of older people, drug use, truancy and crime. For instance, a Department of Health consultation paper says, 'We believe that the community as a whole has a responsibility for promoting the welfare of children and preventing child abuse' (Department of Health, 1998b, preface). But this moral responsibility is located in social relationships which are an idealized reconstruction of past working-class 'communities', and bear little relation to actual relations in a mobile, cosmopolitan, ethnically plural, market-orientated society.

Furthermore, the Third Way is very questionable at the level of ethical and political philosophy. New Labour's version of communitarianism is (like Etzioni's and Bill Clinton's) aimed at instilling the sense of responsibility for providing reciprocal care between members of all levels of associations, both informal and formal, in society. It is also aimed at supplying mechanisms of social discipline and control, to restrain unruly, damaging and deviant behaviour among such members – through parenting, neighbourly surveillance (e.g. Neighbourhood Watch) and a degree of challenging and remonstration. State systems are supposed to come into play partly to reinforce the values of these family, kinship and neighbourly systems, and partly to back them up by enforcement (e.g. reports of 'benefit fraud', or allegations of child abuse). This suggests a new accommodation between informal, communal systems of social order, and the state's official systems of regulating relationships between citizens (Jordan, 1998c, 1999a, 1999b).

First, the Third Way takes moral intuitions from the sphere of the small-scale, informal association, and applies them to membership of large-scale, plural society. As we have seen (pp. 18–20), these ideas about responsibility and obligation are problematic in two main ways. Since the birth of liberalism – ethical reasoning about economic relations put forward by John Locke at the end of the seventeenth century (Locke, 1698) – the strong tendency has been to disconnect citizenship from obligation, except the duties to pay taxes in return for such collective goods as law and order, and to give military service. Liberal rights *plus* market economics provided a trade-off: freedom from the traditional duty-based relationships of feudalism and patriarchal, paternalistic monarchism – what Marx and Engels called 'the idiocy of rural life' (1848, p. 11) – in exchange for the loss of the 'protections' of a hierarchical social order, based on the 'reciprocities' between landowners and their dutiful serfs. Commerce under liberalism runs on self-interest, preferences and incentives, not obligations, as Adam Smith so clearly demonstrated in his famous account of the 'invisible hand' that redistributes through voluntary exchange, not duty (Smith, 1767, Part IV, Chapter 1).

Second, even if it is accepted that a nation state is a moral community, it is unclear in what sense a national economy is a system of co-operation between members. If capitalists are free to produce anywhere in the world, and investors can move their money where they choose, why should poor and immobile citizens be obliged to work for the good of the community? We are now all part of a *world* system of production and exchange under globalization; our welfare depends as much on the efforts of Chinese workers as on those of fellow citizens (because of overseas investment and transnational companies), and it is not obvious either why my neighbour should have to be responsible for my welfare by making a productive contribution in the labour market, or even that such a contribution will improve my welfare – it may cost me more in taxes to retrain him than if he stayed on benefits for several years (Jordan, 1998a, Chapter 2).

But also – and more seriously from an ethical perspective – the Third Way introduces a new approach to how the informal order of family, voluntary and local associations can be combined with the formal order of state regulation, law and policy. It is new because it embraces and promotes informal systems, and adopts many of their values and principles into the rational-legal systems of the public authority, while using the power of the state to reinforce the moral messages and the methods of the local community.

In liberal ethical and political thought, this approach has never been favoured, because of the high priority given to individual liberty and choice, and to personal rights to freedom of conscience, morality and practice. After all, in his famous essay *On Liberty* (1889), John Stuart Mill was concerned to define 'a circle around the individual' that protected him or her against interference or pressure as much from 'public opinion' (i.e. the community) as from the arbitrary or coercive state. Mill, as a true representative of liberalism, wanted to uphold the individual's uniqueness, originality, creativity and free-thinking dissidence from the conformities and compliances of the moral majority, because he believed this was the only reliable source of the energies that drove forward artistic, scientific, cultural and economic progress. 'Public opinion', in the form of the tyranny of convention and tradition, was a threat to all these, and to democracy itself, in mainstream progressive thought (Tocqueville, 1836).

To this end, all state regulation (law, policy and their implementation by public officials) in liberal polities is framed in terms of basic civil, political and economic rights, giving citizens the opportunity to test the powers of the state in the courts. Rights are abstractions from the above aspects of human personality and activity, seen as crucial for the free flourishing of human capacities (Freeden, 1989). They are established and sustained through the political pressure of free associations within civil society, by processes which abstract, formal universal principles consistent with such flourishing from the messy world of everyday social relations, and encode them in rules that can be interpreted by judges, bureaucrats and professionals.

Social Work and the 'Blood-and-Guts Code'

All this is in marked contrast with the ways in which social interactions in the everyday world are regulated through informal rules of conduct which we have elsewhere called the 'blood-and-guts code' (Jordan, 1999a, 1999c). By this we mean the processes of mutual recognition, exchanges of meaning and communication among members through which the sense of order, predictability and reliability are maintained in purely informal interactions, which lack of sanction of law or policy (Hilbert, 1992; Jordan, Redley and James, 1994, Chapter 2). This everyday order has a distinctive reality and binding power of its own, through interactions themselves (Rawls, 1989), and makes everyday life liveable.

Social work is performed partly through the formal regulatory systems of public authority (courts, offices, records, interagency meetings), and partly within this informal everyday order, in service users' homes, neighbourhoods or groups. Much social work is simply done through communications between professionals and service users, using an informal code (sometimes one *created* within their interactions) and relying on its meanings, its values and its regulatory powers. This includes much work in day centres, residential homes and other official facilities. However, informal, discursive methods of regulation of this kind are always ultimately accountable to formal systems (e.g. of child protection, or community care, or risk management). Part of what professionals do is to identify serious issues from informal practice that require adjudication within the formal system (e.g. in court), and refer them on – for instance, deciding which allegations of child abuse should result in Emergency Protection Orders or court hearings.

Box 9   The 'blood-and-guts code'

The term 'blood-and-guts code' is a shorthand denoting the way in which members of social units order their everyday life. It is the largely unnoticed, taken-for-granted system of cognitions and concepts according to which they hold themselves and each other accountable for their decisions and actions, giving these moral and social significance, and creating the sense of *order*, *stability* and *external reality*. All social units (e.g. occupational groups, friendship networks) develop their own codes, and these adopt various ethical ideas from the wider cultural environment.

As an example of one blood-and-guts code, from a deprived neighbourhood in Exeter (Jordan et al., 1992), we give the following interview extracts. On the role of men and women in the labour market:

Mr Ribble: 'If ... I was on the dole and Sheila [pregnant wife] had the chance of getting a job, I wouldn't let her do it ... . I couldn't be kept like [laughs] ... . No way. ... I would have felt inadequate by not bringing in the money ... a man should be the money bringer, you know.' (pp. 88–9)

Another interviewee indicated awareness that others, inside and outside the community, did not necessarily share this code:

> Mr Tamar: 'The man should never live off a woman. I don't think so anyway. Probably that's a different attitude than most, than most blokes got, but that is my attitude: a man should never live off the woman.' (Mr Tamar, interview, p. 42)

In this rather tight-knit community, members saw themselves as accountable to each other. But they also constructed their versions of their actions in terms of the *official code* of rules and structures. For instance, Mr Bow's whole account of hunting at night with his four dogs was given in such a way as to be in line with the Social Security regulations:

> Mr Bow: 'If I go out rabbiting ... it's me dogs do the work, see .... And that money don't go into me wife's ... or me, it actually goes back into food for the animals.' (p. 316)

Similarly Mrs Bow explains throwing his dinner at her husband and running away from home in terms of the categories and concepts she has derived from a mental health clinic:

> Mrs Bow: 'I can't enjoy me life 'cause I got this nerve trouble, you know, panic attacks, can't breathe, and funny heads and ... I had an illness I couldn't go out for 12 months, that sort of thing ... it makes your relationship very hard, 'cause I'm always leaving, see, running away from it. My husband accepts it but ...' (p. 314)

In every political system, and under every moral consensus or sustainable ethico-political culture, there is a kind of accommodation between the formal order of rights, rules and procedures, and the informal everyday order of the 'community' (i.e. relatively unstructured interactions in civil society). But it is important to recognize that these two operate in very different ways, and are always in some tension with each other. The formal code of law and policy is a modern construction; it is a rational-legal-bureaucratic system (Weber, 1922). Under a liberal political regime like the UK or USA, it deals in citizens' liberties and state powers, and regulates market and civil-society exchanges between them.

The blood-and-guts code is far older (as old as human society itself). It knows little or nothing of rights, legal powers, or the protections of professional ethics. It deals in love, loyalty, commitment, faith, patriotism, sacrifice and all the emotional ties between members of families, clans, tribes, nations and 'races'. It also deals in blame, fear, rejection, hatred, revenge, domination, xenophobia, bigotry and scapegoating, using methods of bullying, shunning, shaming, rape, punishment, injury, excommunication, violence and war. It knows only the passions, the bonds of affection, belonging, kinship and territory, and the sometimes brutal ways in which these are sustained. It has survived the imposition of every official system of regulation (slavery, feudalism, absolute monarchy, democracy, state socialism); every political regime must come to terms with it, and each must be cautious in dealing with its unpredictable forces.

Liberalism (as a moral philosophy and a political practice) is traditionally *very* cautious about the blood-and-guts code, and strongly liberal polities like the UK have resisted populist politics that mobilizes this code to achieve its purposes (the USA has always been more ambivalent, with strong but transitory traditions of populism, especially in the South). This is because liberalism's system of rights is abstract, artificial and *thin*. The formal order of individualism (a protective circle of rights around each citizen) and markets (the exchange of labour-power and goods for money) makes few emotional claims upon us – it is structured by efficiency, convenience and rules of fairness that are accepted intellectually, but make few connections with our deepest feelings. Hence this whole order (the laws of non-interference, non-violence, property, free mobility, trade and commerce) is highly vulnerable to the more earthy and substantial pull of our everyday commitments – the pressing claims of sex, power and religious belief. After all, international law is a flimsy construction when faced with the passionate and primeval drums of race, blood and soil, as the break-up of the political order in the Balkans and Caucasus has recently shown; and religious hatred is a far older and more enduring force than religious tolerance, as we have been almost daily reminded by news from Northern Ireland for thirty years.

Liberalism deals with all this by a firm separation between the public worlds of political authority and economic organization, and the private worlds of blood and guts, with an elaborate bridging system between the two. The professions, including social work, are part of that bridging system; they operate in both worlds, and use both codes – or at least they should, if they are to be effective. They contribute the system of social regulation through which the two codes are both linked and separated – essential for the whole social order, yet traditionally not allowed to be mixed.

This separation was strongly reinforced in the first half of the twentieth century by the experiences of fascism and communism, which equally horrified ethical liberals. Fascism mobilized blood-and-guts enthusiasm – racism, patriarchy, patriotism and folk-dancing – to destroy all the fragile structures of liberal democracy and release the demons of naked violence, domination and conquest lurking beneath the surface of the everyday world. Communism coercively imposed the formal rationality and bureaucratic order of its political and economic philosophy on the whole of civil society, engineering and controlling the family, the neighbourhood, the village and the community, as well as the factory, the office and the farm. It attempted to suppress all the sentiments and emotions that fuelled relationships and actions other than those of solidarity and obedience to the will of the party and the state.

The ethical innovation of New Labour is its embrace of the popular moral order. It appeals directly to blood-and-guts values on traditionally judicial, technical, administrative or professional issues like crime, child care and education. It goes over the heads of the policy community, academics and experts, and relies on focus groups and public opinion canvassing for its policies on social security and employment. It goes well beyond Margaret Thatcher's populism; she tried to reconstruct citizens as *market* actors, and to privatize aspects of the public infrastructure, including parts of the welfare state. But her goal was to make both public sector staff and service users more cost-conscious, competent and effective in a competitive economic environment, where there was no such thing as a free lunch. Tony Blair's citizens of the Third Way are held accountable to a morality of mutual concern and responsibility, discipline and sacrifice, as well as the rules of independence and choice within markets. They – and the providers of services – are required to uphold an ethic of giving, a rule of restraint, *and* a gospel of prudence. Blair and Jack Straw invoke the norms of the blood-and-guts code to mobilize the public against wrongdoers and deviants, and encourage 'the community' to adopt informal means of policing its own systems of regulation.

Towards a Responsible Community

We have just taken a highly critical line in relation to the Third Way's version of community as the ethical basis for its social reform programme. The bonds of solidarity and co-operation forged by everyday interactions, and sustained by the blood-and-guts code, cannot provide moral and political principles on which liberal democratic institutions can safely rely. However, New Labour ministers could argue that they are not depending on unmodified versions of these everyday, homespun notions, nor are they leaving communities to interpret, practise and enforce them without guidance from officials and professionals.

Indeed there is some justification in this defence, since government ministers are quick to take every opportunity to speak and write (often in newspapers like the *Daily Mail*) about their principles, and to explain how the programme seeks to implement them. They are also relatively generous with funds for the appointment of new echelons of advisers and counsellors, to help citizens and communities to understand and then put them into practice. But Driver and Martell (1997), in their careful analysis of 'New Labour's Communitarianisms', conclude that on six dimensions of analysis the Third Way's philosophy and programme come out as conformist rather than pluralist, more rather than less conditional, conservative rather than progressive, moral rather than socio-economic, prescriptive rather than voluntary, and individual rather than corporate (see Box 3, p. 25). Although this is not necessarily always in line with populist sentiments on crime control, the work ethic, immigration and asylum, benefit fraud or redistribution, it rides and steers public opinion in directions that are perilously close to these.

This is because the Third Way uncritically adopts principles from the family, the small group and the informal club which are entirely appropriate to these spheres, and applies them inappropriately to larger-scale interactions (Jordan, 1998a, Chapter 2). For example, Tony Blair's claim, 'For every right we enjoy we owe responsibilities. That is the most basic family value of all' (Blair, 1996, p. 2) is generally true of partnerships and other long-term, face-to-face relationships between adults, but not always directly applicable to large, impersonal associations. In liberal democracies, wealthy people have a right to hold property in land, but there is no corresponding duty to them to maintain it, to provide employment, or to work on it themselves. They also have the right to transfer financial assets abroad, with no penalties, simply because tax rates elsewhere are lower there. Conversely, people born with severe disabilities or handicaps have the right to care, but no corresponding duties towards others.

Furthermore, the moral idea behind all small-group units – reciprocity, give-and-take – makes sense in such informal situations mainly because they involve individuals who are *equal* in some fundamental sense, and because their co-operation concerns tasks which they *share*, to produce goods which cannot be bought and sold in markets. Reciprocity (White, 1996) means exchanging services, either on a very long-term basis, without any attempts to calculate equivalencies (the *generalized* reciprocity of most nuclear families) or over a shorter period, according to rough-and-ready versions of like-for-like or taking one's turn (*balanced* reciprocity, as in doing one's fair share in preparing the pitch and serving behind the bar at the local hockey club). Such rules apply because members regard the sharing of their lives, or part of their lives, as a benefit rather than a cost of belonging to the group, because the nature of the group's task of co-operation is complex and changeable and demands frequent changes in role allocation, or because they lack the resources to buy these services on a paid basis. But labour markets begin where such reciprocity ends (and vice versa); it is simply more efficient, in a large-scale economy, to exchange specialized, skilled and repetitive work for money than to provide it for each other on a reciprocal basis – that's why we have labour markets, formal employment and paid work. As Adam Smith pointed out, it is convenient and economically advantageous to pay for goods and services on the basis of price, rather than to shop and work according to a system of reciprocal obligations (as under feudalism), and it is this gain in welfare for all that morally justifies the commercialization of productive relationships (Smith, 1776, Part IV, Chapter 2). In other words, the reciprocity principle does not apply to the economic sphere of paid work; preferences, choices, and incentives do.

Finally, the moral force of reciprocal bonds is greatly weakened by the use of *power*. Reciprocity is a morally powerful principle because individuals feel obliged to do their fair share of work for the group, and to do it voluntarily or under the persuasive influence of peer-group pressure, rather than because they are forced to do so (see Chapter 8, pp. 198–201, for examples). As soon as power enters the equation, the moral force behind the principle of reciprocity dissolves. In partnerships of men and women, under the old 'breadwinner–housewife' role division (Lewis, 1992), this was supposed to reflect a reciprocal exchange between equal but different individuals, who shared a life together. The moral intuition behind feminism is that such patriarchy is not based on equality, but on the domination of women by men. True reciprocity can only be achieved under a much more flexible division of roles, in which unpaid household tasks are more fairly shared, and women have equal access to the public worlds of the economy and polity (Greer, 1970). Similarly, politico-economic systems that claimed to be based on reciprocity between powerful landowners and warlords and humble peasants and serfs, such as feudalism, were in retrospect not morally justified, since the former could and did kill the latter if they did not fulfil their obligations, whereas the latter could do nothing about it if the local nobility rode their horses through their crops, or raped their daughters. And Marxist-Leninist state socialism, which posed as a system of 'scientific co-operation' for the benefit of the working class, was in fact a vehicle for the unrestrained power and privilege of a Communist Party élite, that gave citizens very low wages and low-quality services in exchange for their forced labour (Fehér et al., 1983).

However, something can be rescued from this Third Way muddle about community responsibility and reciprocity. There is, as Anthony Giddens claims, a sense in which community is fundamental to an ethical approach to politics (Giddens, 1998, p. 79), and 'nations are ethical communities, where those involved owe special obligations to other members not always owed to others on the outside' (p. 107). The main way in which large-scale communities reveal their ethical principles is in how they share the advantages of common membership among the whole of their citizen populations (Carling, 1999). Without the idea of a society as a community in this sense, there can be no morally coherent version of social justice, since justice consists in giving each member his or her due as one of the collective. The 'special obligations' owed by citizens to each other are revealed mainly in systems that gather contributions according to ability to contribute, and redistribute them as benefits to those who qualify for them, mainly by need – in other words, welfare states. While it is true that such systems, as they were established after the Second World War all over the developed capitalist world, are now revealed to have flaws that distort their intentions – perverse incentives, moral hazards or other in-built unfairness with their rules and structures – this does not undermine the fundamental moral principle behind them, which is the same moral principle that underlies all the great world religions' commandments: that the rich and able should help the poor and vulnerable, by giving money for their assistance.

Furthermore, despite the Third Way's insistence that economic globalization has changed the terms on which citizens co-operate within a national economy, and sharpened the requirement on all to make themselves employable, efficient and competitive, liberal democratic principles still apply to the *means* by which social justice should be achieved. It is still unjust to compel individuals for the sake of the public good, or to use the power of the state against those who are not able to move abroad to escape such power (i.e. benefits claimants) for the sake of reducing the tax burden of those who *are* able to escape abroad in search of higher earnings (skilled workers) or lower taxes (capitalists). Finally, it is inappropriate and unjust to demand that some citizens do demeaning or dangerous work for others simply because they depend on the state's redistributory systems for their livelihood, when others are in a position to choose what work to do, and how many hours to do it (Jordan, 1998a, Chapters 2 and 3).

All these qualifications to the moral notion of community should provide openings for social work. A truly responsible community, organized according to the principles of social justice, equality of membership, respect for difference and individual liberty, should contain considerable public space for negotiating the terms on which members co-operate for the sake of a good life together. It should be committed to democratic and voluntaristic ways of allocating roles between paid and unpaid work roles, and to the fairest way of improving the quality of life of all members of the community.

It is an odd fact that the conventional analyses of social work values and professional ethics seldom mention democracy and social justice as basic principles of social work (Jordan, 1990, Chapter 6). Yet there must be a sense in which they are fundamental to ethical practice, and this seems to remain implicit rather than explicit in books on the subject. Above all, the ethical rules which prohibit social workers from abusing their power over service users (rules against judgmentalism, oppression and discrimination, and against imposing their own standards on them) stem from the equal value of all members of an interdependent community, with responsibilities to listen to each others' points of view, share resources, give support, and provide a fair deal for all, because they belong together in some deep sense (Jordan, 1990, prologue and Chapter 6).

None of this allows social workers, and especially public sector workers, to escape from hard questions about how such work is best organized and delivered. These are not simply questions for politicians and managers; they apply to each distinct team, day centre and residential unit. They are questions about relationships with policy makers, between members of these working units, and with service users, their carers, support groups and community organizations (Jordan, 1990, Chapters 1, 5, 6 and 7).

During the 1980s, public sector social workers devoted a good deal of their energy (through trade unions and working groups) to 'defending jobs and services' in local authority social services departments. Such actions were partly motivated by concern for the welfare of service users, but they did not always take full account of the possibility that these departments fell short of the old ideals of social justice they claimed to uphold (Jordan and Parton, 1983). In the 1990s these organized coalitions were broken up, as more social workers left the local authorities and moved into voluntary sector organizations or community projects. Within these structures, the danger is more of the loss of a coherent view of social work's role in the wider scheme of things. In striving to implement good practice at the level of a team or unit – to open up possibilities for all team members to participate in decisions, or for service users and carers to be involved in policy, strategy and planning meetings – they do not always make time to recognize common cause with other teams or projects, or with those in other organizational systems. Above all, local authority social workers may find it difficult to raise their heads above the daily grind of assessments, child abuse investigations, reviews or care plans to get a wider picture of the needs of their communities, or to work more closely with groups and associations active within their districts.

The Third Way's version of community as the moral basis for social justice is a partial and misleading one: there are much more promising approaches to the ethics of membership and belonging. Radical versions of communitarianism have not flourished in the UK (Hughes and Little, 1998, 1999), but there is scope for them to emerge. Social work, as an ethically informed profession and as a practice, needs to develop its understanding of these if it is to break out of some of the limits that constrain it under New Labour, and be available to take the opportunities that are likely to appear in the next decade.

Conclusions

The ethical foundations of the Third Way are shaky. Its attempt to combine individualist and collectivist elements in moral and political culture is a necessary corrective to the unintended consequences of Thatcherism, but its version of community as a system of membership and mutuality is flawed. This is partly because it relies on the values and emotions of the 'blood-and-guts' code, and fails to recognize how the rational-legal regulation of liberal democracy protects freedom and difference. It is also because it transposes principles of reciprocity and fairness in co-operation from the sphere of small groups and associations (where they belong) to that of large, complex market societies (where they do not). As a result, the Third Way is much more authoritarian, monolithic and narrow than is needed to restore the sense of belonging and sharing in our culture.

The paradox at the heart of Third Way ethics is that New Labour's programme requires citizens to be more self-responsible and more aware of their interdependence, yet its style of governance gets in the way of this cultural shift. If what are needed are more morally autonomous, active citizens, then the enforcement of obligations to the state is unlikely to produce them. If change is what is to be promoted, enforcement counsellors are not the best agents to achieve this.

In the next chapter we will turn to the economic and social theory on which the Third Way is based, and to how this can be squared with the theoretical foundations of social work practice.

3

Reasons, Motives and Evidence: The Theoretical Basis of the Third Way and Social Work

Although the Third Way introduces new collectivist ideas, and especially the idea of community, into UK political culture, it does not radically shift from the theoretical basis of the reforms of the Thatcher–Major period. This was – and still is – an *economic* analysis of the main forces driving individual actions and strategies, and the best means of modelling the interactions that make up a political society. In other words, the communitarian ethics analysed in the previous chapter are grafted on to a neo-liberal model of what motivates citizens and how to influence their decisions towards more socially desirable outcomes; and the join between the ethical and the economic shows.

In this chapter, we will argue that the version of human rationality and motivation that lies behind the Third Way's social policy programme is a somewhat crude eighteenth-century utilitarianism in which the influence of Jeremy Bentham is clearly recognizable. This is distinguishable from the rather more sophisticated, subtle and sympathetic moral and psychological theories of Adam Smith (1767, 1776) mainly in Bentham's optimism about the possibilities of, and insistence on the necessity for, steering, guiding, nudging and shoving citizens towards the kinds of behaviour favoured by the government. In this, Bentham relied heavily on surveillance, reward and punishment, as he devised the first systematic model of a bureaucratically and professionally ordered society, in which officials and experts shaped every sphere of interaction, from environmental safety and sustainability to arrangements for the custody of children in parental separation and divorce.

Box 10   Jeremy Bentham (1748–1832)

A trained lawyer as well as a philosopher and political economist, Jeremy Bentham devoted his long life to the development of the instruments of governance, through reform of the law and design of new institutions. He advised the Russian Court and published several of his works in French. His influence greatly increased after his death, when a series of British governments adopted administrative structures and principles that owed much to his grandiose schemes, and his disciples became influential in the later reform process.

A founder of utilitarianism, he did more than any of its exponents to translate this new approach to social relations into policy and practice. One of the many ways in which he might be seen as the ancestor of the Third Way is in his insistence on free markets in goods and services, but a highly intrusive, organizing and supervisory state to regulate the social sphere. His ideas found their clearest expression in the period after his death in the New Poor Law of 1834 (and especially in its new model workhouses), and in the prison building programme of the mid-nineteenth century. Our present prison buildings are indeed monuments to Bentham as much as to John Howard.

Bentham's work culminated in a codification and classification of all of the executive, administrative and judicial functions of the modern state, which foresaw many of its extensive powers. This whole grand design was based on the idea of educating, training, supervising and punishing subjects conceived as self-interested seekers of pleasures and avoiders of pain. He particularly influenced the founders of the welfare state a hundred years later, the institutions of twentieth-century social democracy, and more generally the conception of the state as an 'ideal collective capitalist', using rational-legal authority to harmonize class interests. Although illiberal in many ways (criminals were to be treated as state property for life, and released only on the most restrictive conditions), he anticipated such recent social work innovations as a family conciliation agency, under a Preventive Service Minister for the 'prevention of calamity; or of delinquency' (*Constitutional Code*, Book II, Chapter 11, sect. 5, p. 439).

It was Bentham whose ideas inspired many of the great pioneering social reformers of the nineteenth century, such as Sir Edwin Chadwick (Finer, 1952), who in turn strongly influenced the Fabian thinkers at the end of that century and the beginning of the twentieth – Sidney and Beatrice Webb, George Bernard Shaw, H.G. Wells. New Labour's programme is firmly in that tradition, in its search for administrative structures of hierarchical supervision and accountability to ensure that the philosophical and social purposes of the Third Way are implemented. In particular, in its programme for regional government, the general principles of which are set out in the White Paper *Modernising Britain* (DETR, 1998), the government puts forward its plans for introducing a whole new tier, to exercise more control and steering over local authorities, using various mechanisms for allocating new resources in a 'stick and carrot' approach that is typically Benthamite.

The aim is to induce local authorities to restructure along Third Way lines, so as to be better adapted to the purposes of social and economic regeneration envisaged in New Labour's programme. Regionalization and 'modernization' are the two arms of an ambitious plan to recast the whole administrative system of the UK, both institutionally and culturally, not along the lines of a minimalist purchasing and contracting agency (as under Nicholas Ridley and Margaret Thatcher), but as a partnership-building and commissioning authority, with a strong brief to organize and shape civil society in an interventionist and super-vising way. These plans, and the model of social intervention and surveillance that underpins them, will be analysed and criticized in the first part of this chapter.

For all the rhetoric of community and empowerment in many of the documents emanating from Whitehall under New Labour, this is a strictly top-down approach to institution-building and cultural change, based on the idea of a Bentham-style enlightened legislator who leads citizens towards socially desir-able goals. Bentham was far less convinced by the 'invisible hand' argument about the beneficial effects of markets and voluntary exchanges of Adam Smith, that so strongly influenced Margaret Thatcher and her philosophical gurus (Hayek, 1976, 1980). However, like Thatcher, he was no believer in concepts like 'society' and 'community', holding that any such collectivity is a 'fictitious body', created by law and administration (Bentham, 1780, p. 2); and that citizens' actions must be moulded by the lawgiver and the magistrate into whatever patterns give rise to the greatest 'happiness' (i.e. utility, welfare) of the greatest number.

In many ways, all these developments in Third Way thinking about social policy are strongly reflected in theoretical and methodological developments in social care, and in the professional literature of social work. On the one hand, there is the proliferation of guidance from the Department of Health on every aspect of social care, steering practice towards specific interventions and out-comes. Much of this concerns the assessment process – the requirement to iden-tify risk factors (and particularly dangerousness), and indicators of priority need. This in turn gives rise to systems of resource allocation, review and monitoring in which service users are kept under constant surveillance, and interventions can be adapted and recast to keep control of risky or fragile situations.

Within the academic study and professional literature of social work, this in turn reflects the increasing influence of *research* on practice methods, and the movement for *evidence-based practice* in social care, as well as in health care (MacDonald and Sheldon, 1992). This approach insists that social services staff must understand research methodology and be up to date with research findings, so that they can intervene in human situations in ways that implement the best available knowledge about effectiveness. Clearly such ideas see practice as a means to the ends of policy, a rational form of social engineering which aims to accomplish the purposes of government in the most cost-effective way. In this sense, it closely resembles the Third Way, in that it emanates from the Benthamite and Fabian traditions of governance, with their combination of economic-utilitarian philosophy and behaviourist psychology.

Yet there is a counter-movement in social work thinking and research methods that criticizes or rejects these approaches and re-emphasizes the qualitative, interactive and process-orientated aspects of interventions. In particular, authors who reject the positivist version of instrumental, means–ends rationality and top-down policy implementation try to reclaim notions of meaning and subjectivity, reflection and judgement (Gould and Taylor, 1996), emancipation (Shaw, 1997) and social justice (Jordan, 1990). In terms of research method, others see social work practice as narrative (Hall, 1997), as social construction (Parton and O'Byrne, 2000) or as user participation and empowerment (Beresford, 1997). All these alternative views see service users as active subjects making their social worlds and co-operating with professionals in constructing the meanings and outcomes of their encounters, rather than merely implementing the purposes of central government and local policy makers.

In all this, the role of 'social work theory' is at issue. In the second part of the chapter, we will analyse the relationship between theory, policy and practice in social work, and the impact of the Third Way on professional thinking. We will also examine the debate among social work academics about the profession's position within the polity, in relation to government programmes and civil-society associations. The Third Way raises acute issues about the role of social work in civic governance and a democratic civil society, because its social engineering approach to moulding and steering all forms of interaction among citizens can be seen as what Habermas (1987) calls the invasion of the sphere of civil society (the 'lifeworld') by that of the 'system' of technical management by instrumental methods. We will discuss whether social work rightly belongs within the former sphere or the latter, and how it can act to define its proper role within a more interventionist and control-orientated policy programme.

Remodelling Society: The Basis for the New Labour Programme

There are certain themes running through the Third Way's whole project for social reform, which are well reflected in New Labour's plans for *Modernising Social Services* (DoH, 1998a). One of these is to promote the *independence* of citizens – their competence to choose, to achieve, and above all to work and contribute to society as participative economic actors. One of the declared aims of the reforms of local authority social services is to

promote and enhance people's independence, with better prevention and rehabilitation services established with the help of additional funding the Government is providing; and many more people will use direct payments schemes to have real control over how their care needs are provided for. (DoH, 1998a, p. 5)

The same goals can be seen as informing the changes in services for children, to enable those in need to get a better start in life, and become fully competent, contributing citizens:

children looked after by local authorities will benefit from the radical improvements to be made in the care system, backed up by substantial extra funding. Our specific targets to improve education for children in care will be met, and care leavers will get a better start to their adult life. (ibid.)

Better education and training will also make staff more competent and skilled, able to give an improved quality of care:

> social care staff will have clearer standards and better training arrangements, overseen by the General Social Care Council. Our targets for improving training levels will mean that people will benefit from safe, skilled and competent care staff. (ibid.)

In all this, there are hints of the model and the method by which the Third Way seeks to transform society and improve outcomes. It will target resources on the promotion of independence, activity and achievement, offering incentives and inducements for even the most disabled and handicapped, disturbed or deviant citizens to be self-responsible and to participate. It will focus on education and training as a means of making disadvantaged people more adaptable, mobile and effective. And it will introduce new supervisory bodies and scrutiny committees, new layers and tiers of government, and new agencies and experts, to ensure that its goals and standards are accomplished and implemented.

It is difficult, in contemplating these ambitious goals and putting them along-side those of all the other reforms of the social services, not to be reminded of the eighteenth-century British Enlightenment project, summed up by Sir James Steuart in 1767 as

> to adapt the different operations of [political economy] to the spirit, manners, habits and customs of the people; and afterwards to model these circumstances so as to be able to introduce a set of new and more useful institutions. (1767, p. 17)

Jeremy Bentham's version of this new science of government was based on the idea of an authority that works principally through the medium of education, 'operating in the character of a tutor upon all of the members of a state' (Bentham, 1780, p. 30). Legislation should 'promote the happiness of society, by punishing and rewarding' (ibid., p. 35). His approach aimed at 'abundance' (prosperity through economic growth) by increasing the workforce, the amount of work done, its effectiveness, the volume of capital, and its most advantageous use. The method used was mainly based on rewards, and operated through markets (Hume, 1981, p. 129); he thought that legislation should aim at improving incentives to maximize outputs and minimize costs.

But Bentham saw a need to reinforce these measures by a broad and detailed range of state regulatory and supervisory bodies, for the sake of internal security and order. He thought that government consisted in securing *obedience* to the legislators' rules (or 'commands'), which defined citizens' duties, along with their corresponding rights (Bentham, 1780, pp. 30–5). He outlined systems of surveillance, for guiding individuals into harmless amusements, for licensing activities and trades, for regulating firearms and other dangerous implements, providing public information about crime, and so on (Hume, 1981, p. 95). His systems for dealing with poverty and idleness involved 200 to 250 'Houses of Industry' where paupers would be accommodated, and all but the frailest and most ill would be employed, with maximum efficiency, until they earned enough for an independent life outside the institution (Bentham, 1798). His proposed range of services was intended to manage subjects' behaviour through a network of institutions which prevented or treated 'moral pathologies' by guiding or manipulating individuals' behaviour, and by disincentives for any action that caused public harm. Lacking a theory of natural or human rights ('nonsense on stilts', Bentham claimed), or of citizens' consequent entitlements to liberty and self-direction, he regarded anyone who was not economically independent as a legitimate target for therapeutic intervention, including all women and children who were not fully supported or self-supporting. In the Panopticon, Bentham designed 'a new principle of construction applicable to any sort of establishment, in which persons of any description are to be kept under inspection; and in particular to penitentiary-houses, prisons, houses of industry, work-houses, poor-houses, manufactures, madhouses, lazarettos, hospitals and schools' (Bentham, 1791, p. 40). Panopticons could equally serve the purposes of 'punishing the incorrigible, guarding the insane, reforming the vicious, confining the suspected, employing the idle, maintaining the helpless, curing the sick, instructing the willing in any branch of industry, or training the rising race in the path of education' (ibid.).

In his *Constitutional Code* (1843), Bentham extended his notion of government activities to include a vast number of preventive and supervisory agencies for environmental and social control, including public health and sanitation, crime and delinquency, bereavement and widowhood. This whole system was deduced from abstract principles of utility, yet to a remarkable extent it anticipated the modern state, and especially the 'modernization' programme of New Labour. He addressed current social issues and problems through social engineering of a largely piecemeal kind (Popper, 1950), using bureaucratic-authoritarian methods. His insistence on property as the source of abundance made him give high priority to law and order, for the sake of unlimited accumulation; and his concerns about security led to a high degree of regulation, enforcement and punishment to achieve this goal.

The Third Way adopts a similarly regulatory approach, based on a similarly crude psychology of rewards and penalties, applied as much to the old regime of local government departments as to the citizens it seeks to remould for its purposes. This is particularly evident in its plans for *Modernising Britain* (DETR, 1998) which introduced an intermediate tier between central and local government. The modernizing agenda is concerned with evaluating and grading the performance of local government, and differentially distributing large sums of money, the most generous amounts going to those with 'beacon' status. In return for this, they are required to restructure their committees, and move in the direction of mayoral and cabinet-style government. Typically such authorities will have an executive board and a scrutiny board to replace the former departmental structures. Local authorities which fail to push through these reforms, or to achieve targets in key policy areas, will be penalized by losing grants, especially for health and social regeneration initiatives.

All this has important implications for social services departments, which are among the main targets of the government's reforming zeal. If they do not come up to the standard required, or if there are further high-profile scandals and tragedies, there is a real threat that their duties will be farmed out to new agencies (public–private partnerships) on the model of the new services for asylum seekers (Home Office, 1998). This would put them under the direct control of central or regional government, and allow them to be firmly steered and controlled (Milburn, 1999). This 'devolution of power' to Scotland, Wales and the regions turns out – on close inspection – to be more about ensuring that local authorities perform up to the centre's standards.

In the same way, the New Labour government's relationship with civil society and with individual citizens is tutelary and supervisory as well as regulatory. For all the rhetoric about independence, self-responsibility and community, the Third Way is low on trust, and puts little value on freedom from intervention or compulsion by the public authority. The 'contract' between the state and citizens is carefully policed and enforced by officials who constantly monitor performance wherever public money or central government purposes are involved. In true Benthamite fashion, it builds layer upon layer of officials, experts and advisers to make sure that every organization and individual is reminded of the government's goals and their duties towards these, and to use the sticks and carrots available to them to drive forward the reform programme.

However, the crude Benthamite psychology and sociology on which such methods are based makes little allowance either for the subjective identities, meanings, projects and commitments of individuals, or the common goals, purposes and programmes of groups and associations. Implementation of New Labour goals therefore comes to depend on direct persuasion, inducement or penalty, administered through transparent manipulation and pressure, rather than a subtler process of encouraging individual and collective actions that lead to socially desirable outcomes. It also focuses on direct contributions to outputs, or improvements in productivity, or the accumulation of physical capital, rather than on less visible or measurable targets, such as a better quality of life or an increase in social capital (trust, co-operation, participation in voluntary organizations, etc.).

The Third Way collects together a number of overall objectives which are common to all the domains of social policy, and pursues them using administrative methods and processes applied to all these domains (Jordan et al., 2000, Chapter 3). In addition to the themes of rights and responsibilities and lifelong learning already identified and discussed as ethical goals (promoting autonomy and independence and contributing to community) these are:

1 *breaking down barriers* to participation, inclusion and opportunity. Reforms of rules and institutions, and new agencies and systems, are intended to provide better access to work resources and civic roles, by building citizens' capacities (education, health and disability policy), by empowerment (social care policy) and by regeneration of disadvantaged communities (Social Exclusion Unit, Single Regeneration Budgets, New Deal for Communities);

2 *harmonizing policies* across domains ('joined-up government'), by ensuring that there is consistency in the goals of, and co-ordination between, the means of implementing, the various aspects of the whole economic and social programme;

3 *indicators and targets* to allow central and regional government to monitor and publicize the successes and failures of the programme, to publish league

tables (health and education), to 'name and shame' failing units and authorities (health, education, social care), and to hold staff to account for their work, through new regulatory bodies (Milburn, 1999);

4   *tendering for and contracting out* services, as a way of making public services more cost-conscious and to keep them focused on their targets. Where they are identified as failing, new competitive tendering for services is introduced (accommodation and services for asylum seekers; failing education authorities, social services departments);

5   *public–private partnerships* as a way of encouraging innovation and matching localized supply and demand, as well as creating able new services (asylum seekers' services, regeneration, social care).

In Chapter 8 we will review these objectives and implementation strategies, and argue that they are often clumsy and ill-conceived. We will suggest that there are other, more promising ways of pursuing the Third Way's goals, which would allow social work to play a more constructive role.

Box 11   Setting objectives – delivering change

The flavour of the government's method of implementing its programme for modernization and raising standards can be gleaned from this small sample, from *Children's Services Planning: Planning to Deliver Change* (Social Services Inspectorate, Department of Health, September 1999).

> The Government believes that setting national objectives is the essential first step to improving the effectiveness of children's social services. They are supported by more detailed sub-objectives and performance indicators through which local authority performance will be measured. (para. 1)

'1.0   *Objective*: to ensure that children are securely attached to carers capable of providing safe and effective care for the duration of childhood.

1)   *Sub-objectives*:
1.1   to support children in need and their families in order wherever possible to prevent family breakdown and promote better life chances for the most vulnerable children.
PAF Performance Indicator E44 Relative spend on family support:
Expenditure on children in need (and not looked after) as a proportion of expenditure on all children's services ...'
[There follow 11 objectives, each with up to 6 sub-objectives.]
'2:   *Definitions of Indicators*
The following 19 indicators are included under both Quality Protects and Performance Assessment Framework.
A1   The percentage of children looked after at 31 March with three or more placements during the year.

The denominator: The total number of children who were looked after at 31 March. Exclude from the count any children who were looked after on that date under an agreed service or short-term placements (under the provisions of Reg. 13 of *Arrangement for Placement of Children (General) Regulations, 1991*) ....

The numerator: Of the children defined above, the number who had three or more separate placements (as defined by the SSDA903 collection) during the year ending 3 March. ... Indicator A1 differs from the Audit Commission indicator L9c. A1 is the count of placements rather than moves and covers all placements in year rather than the latest period of care ...'

[Then follow the other 18 indicators, with their numerators and denominators, and a further 15 Quality Protects indicators that are not included in the performance Assessment Framework, with their numerators and denominators.]

These developments quite strongly reinforce the tendency for local authority social services to become more engaged in tasks of assessing risks and resources, reviewing, managing and enforcing its care plans and interventions, contracting for services, and enforcing compliance. They are in line with the Thatcher reform agendas that shifted the emphasis of the public sector personal social services away from provision of care, towards an investigative, purchasing, planning, prioritizing and rationing function, and from the political negotiation of social needs towards the cost-conscious management of how its revenues are spent. Although this is less the emphasis of the Children Act 1989 than of the NHS and Community Care Act 1990, it is clear that the ethos and the organizational imperatives of the latter have strongly influenced thinking and practice in the former.

In the Conservative years, however, the interventionist and power-laden elements in these developments were limited by the requirement to minimize public spending and the scope of bureaucratic authority. Managerialism (Clarke, et al., 1994) was established as the means of governance in the local authority social services for the purposes of introducing the contract culture and devolved budgets and thus restricting the power of both professionals and bureaucrats (Niskanen, 1975). In the Third Way no such restrictions operate, because of its strong commitment to rational-legal authority in the Bentham mould (Weber, 1922; Hume, 1981, p. 4) and the social engineering approach to implementation.

This tradition of politics and administration sees little reason to limit the concentration of political power, since it provides the means of solving social and economic problems, overcoming the failures of market institutions and the frailties of human nature, and steering economy and society towards optimal outcomes. It adopts an instrumental approach to social well-being, and its main instruments are tutelary bureaucracy, economic incentives, material penalties, and physical punishments of a liberty-restricting kind. Bentham's Panopticon regimes were designed to give inmates inducements to work, and no opportunities to do anything else; while his punishment for criminals (monotonous confinement) was indistinguishable from his provision for elderly, widowed and disabled dependants, or his training and treatment for young people and those with mental illnesses (Bentham, 1798, pp. 4–5; 40). Like Bentham, New Labour finds it difficult to conceive of a right *not* to be guided, *not* to be conditioned, *not* to be moulded or trained for the public good.

All this stems from an approach to human subjects which sees them first as rational agents, who will maximize their utility (i.e. choose according to their schedule of preferences for all kinds of goods) in transactions with any formal systems. A well-devised economic and political system will be self-enforcing (Elster, 1986), in that it reminds citizens of the reasons they have for acting in socially responsible ways. This form of top-down social engineering varies in its models and methods to the extent that it sees human subjects as able to discern their own long-term good, to conceive and carry through projects to those ends, and to recognize risks, hazards and potential harm on the way. It also tends to categorize both subjects and risks (a favourite activity of Bentham's), and to devise complex systems for classifying individuals and designing particular forms of tailor-made guidance to help them choose wisely.

Finally, the Third Way has a very limited view of the role of democracy in society, and a specific conception of how government should relate to the electorate. This is revealed in its blueprint for the modernization of democratic governance (DETR, 1998). Because the 'community' in New Labour's version is very much led and steered towards 'responsibility' from above, local councillors who cannot find a seat on the executive board of their authorities, or a place in its scrutiny committee, are – since other committees would be abolished – cast in the role of 'community champion'. They are to be expected to spend time in their neighbourhoods, often as chairs of local associations and groups. Apart from the obvious problems of connecting civil society organizations with particular party colours, this seriously undermines the independence of community organizations, and the scope for self-generating criticism and democratic pressure. It is more like Bentham's post of 'local headman' in every district – a sort of conduit for the will of government, and a link with all the labyrinthine quangos and services of the state (Bentham, 1843). This approach discounts the autonomy of civil society, its potential for creativity and new social movements in the development and adoption of democratic politics (Jordan, 1996b). While democratic community is consistent with elements of social engineering in governance (see Chapter 8), it can only be accomplished if these are balanced by informal, discursive and participatory interactions between members.

Social Work: Theory, Research and Evidence

In view of the fact that New Labour thinking and policies on social services in many ways develop and extend aspects of Conservative reforms, it's not surprising to find that the theoretical, research and policy orthodoxies already current in professional social work are not strongly opposed to these principles. Indeed, the current domi-nant theme of official publications – evidence-based approaches to social care – is also the emerging hegemonic discourse of research and professional literature, and it closely reflects the versions of governance, accountability, rationality and human psychology that we identified as underpinning the Third Way. However, there is an undercurrent of very different perspectives and approaches to the theory–practice relationship, and to practice itself, that has developed in reaction to, and in resistance against, these orthodoxies. This new tradition (which builds on many of the theoretical development of the 1970s) can provide foundations for the alternative model of practice that we will elaborate in Chapter 9.

First we must interpose some comments on this history of the search for theoretical foundations for social work practice, since this provides the context for the current struggle for the soul of social work, and for influence over practice methods. Because it has only fairly recently been accepted as a profession – or semi-profession (Etzioni, 1969) – and as part of the official range of state service provision, social work's claims to exclusive knowledge, and to scientific credentials for its theoretical basis, are extremely shaky. The defining features of its practice historically (Jordan, 1983) have been:

- its reliance on *informal, interactive, and discursive* methods, rather than formal prescriptive or 'expert' prescriptions and treatments;
- its preference for *negotiated* agreements and *co-operative* approaches rather than imposed 'solutions' to problems, and to the resolution of conflicts;
- its recognition of *social* factors (such as structural disadvantage, poverty, exclusion, discrimination and domination) as factors in behaviour and problems, rather than individual personalities and pathologies;
- its concern with the provision of the *means of survival in adversity*, and with essential services for people with special needs, rather than with remedial, corrective or therapeutic measures (i.e. 'care' rather than 'cure');
- its inevitable involvement in the morally and politically contentious issues of society, because of its focus on interdependence and conflict within families and communities; and hence its unavoidable concern with moral and political issues (Jordan, 1978, 1983, 1990; Parton and O'Byrne, 2000);
- its practice in '*natural*' settings (such as family homes, community centres or residential units), rather than clinical, forensic or education facilities, or other controlled environments structured by the needs of experts;
- its operations on the *boundaries and borderlines* of institutions, or between the major social institutions (courts, hospitals, schools, factories, etc.) rather than within any one of these;
- the *lack of any stable political or public consensus* about the nature or causes of the distress and damage suffered or inflicted by service users, and hence about the political and moral basis for social work practice, or its proper legal and organizational context.

Because of all these factors, and especially the last one, it has been extremely difficult for social work to muster a body of 'theory' or 'knowledge' that it can put forward as a reliable basis for its professionalism and expertise, or even as a sound foundation for education and training for practice. Such claims have, of course, always been made on its behalf, by academic social work educators, and even by government officials from time to time, but the frequency with which particular versions of this 'knowledge' and 'theory' are abandoned and replaced with quite different elements is a telltale sign of the weakness of the claims.

It is a familiar old chestnut in the accounts given of the evolution of social work theory that the period between the foundation of local authority social services after the Second World War and the fairly recent past was one of the dominance of *psychodynamic* approaches (Stevenson, 1998a, 1998b). In fact, such theories were far less influential on practice than this suggests, and even in education and training they were always balanced by 'agency-function' approaches (Timms, 1964), which emphasized the legal, policy and service provision elements in practice. Psychodynamic ideas and methods were derived from the USA (Hollis, 1960), and originally imported into the UK for the training of psychiatric and child-guidance social workers (Jordan, 1983, Chapter 3). By the time they came to be extensively taught in university courses, they were already coming under challenge from other ideas, which drew attention to quite different aspects of the exchanges between social workers and service users.

These included the sociological work on deviance and its amplification that emerged in the USA in the mid-1960s (Becker, 1963); the deeper understanding of stigma and normality and the effects of institutionalization that was developed from Goffman's (1968) research; the radical social movements for gender and racial equality, participative democracy, peace and the overthrow of political oppression that spread from the USA to Europe in the late 1960s (Bailey and Brake, 1975); and the various revisions to psychodynamic theory itself that were undertaken in the early 1970s, in the direction of a more interactive, interpersonal or transactional analysis of relationships between social workers and service users (Jordan, 1970, 1972; Mattinson, 1975). All these contributed to the more subtle and extensive range of ideas that was influencing practice by the early 1970s, when the psychodynamic 'dominance' that had existed only on a very few university courses was already broken, and both students and practitioners had many other sources of inspiration for their dealings with clients. They enriched social work theory with new insights from sociological and interactionist theory, from social movements and other civil-society groups, and improved the analysis of face-to-face exchanges at the level of practice, by providing far more realistic versions of what was at stake, and what occurred, in such encounters.

This process continued in the mid- to late 1970s, but by then the new sources of ideas were more clearly political, and authors began to present them more systematically (as *theory*), but less *practically* (as applied to the detail of face-to-face work). Examples of this were Marxist approaches (Corrigan and Leonard, 1978), 'systems theory' (Specht and Vickery, 1977), community development approaches (Butterworth et al., 1981), and other radical ideas. These prepared the way for the developments of the 1980s, when new forms of political oppression were identified and used as a theoretical springboard for ideas about the purposes of social work interventions (Statham, 1978), especially racism (Dominelli, 1988) and sexism (Dominelli, 1989). So books about 'social work theory' tend to classify and categorize this according to its provenance in other disciplines and social movements (Howe, 1987; Payne, 1991), when in fact 'Marxist social work', 'anti-racist social work' and 'feminist social work', for example, consist of ideas borrowed from these fields, with general prescriptions about how they might be applied in practice. In the 1990s, the latter increasingly consisted of checklists and schedules, rather than attempts to make sense of the detail of face-to-face encounters with service users, or to develop practice-based methodologies of analysis and intervention (Stevenson, 1998a, 1998b; Parton and O'Byrne, 2000, Chapter 1).

Meanwhile, however, the Thatcher years had witnessed a more influential – indeed over-determining – change in the thinking, the rules and the institutional structures underlying social work practice. The central thrust of developments at the policy level in that period was to shift local authority social services from a mind-set of responsiveness to political factors (the current opinions and interests of local politicians and activists, community groups, lobbies and service user organizations) to one of responsiveness to economic and technical factors (the costs and effectiveness of their interactions, and how to maximize value for money). Hence whatever their 'theoretical' (in the sense understood on training courses and in books on social work 'theory') commitments, social workers were expected to, and increasingly *required* to, subscribe to ideas and methods that subordinated such commitments to the roles, functions, tasks and disciplines of matching their practice to certain predetermined policy outcomes, by following the guiding principles of central government procedural handbooks and manuals, in the most cost-effective ways.

The legislative and managerial changes of the late 1980s gave shape to new structures, links and administrative practices in local authority social services departments, and new relations with expanding voluntary and commercial agencies, reinforcing the rhetoric of central government and the shifting spirit of a new age. Social work has always been strongly led by policy, politics and moral culture, from the individualistic religious and charitable era of its beginnings in Victorian Britain, to the pioneering crusade of the early welfare state and the politicized expansionism of the 1970s. It was therefore not surprising that Thatcherite ideas and institutions strongly influenced professional thinking about practice. But since local authorities were among the main centres of resistance to those ideas and policies (especially in urban areas, and in Scotland), many of the moral and political commitments of the 1970s lived on in social services departments, vilified by the Tory press, attacked by ministers and blamed for the scandals and shortcomings revealed by various inquiries during that decade (Parton, 1991).

Parallel to the diversity of moral and political 'theories of social work' that proliferated in this period was an increasingly binding orthodoxy that drew social workers towards instrumental and technical rationality in their assessment of, and planning for, service users' needs. This was the whole tenor of government regulation and guidance, first for the Children Act 1989, and then in the field of adult services under the NHS and Community Care Act 1990 (F. Williams, 1994). In the latter case, it was strongly reinforced by administrative structures and management methods that linked these processes with budgetary control, financial accountability, the assessment of service users' resources, and the prioritization of serious risks. Finally, the circle was closed by a growing volume of research literature, especially in the field of child care (Packman et al., 1986; Millham et al., 1986; Fisher et al., 1986; Gibbons et al., 1995), financed by central government, which addressed the often hidden or unintended *policy* elements and implications of practice, and the collective consequences of individual decisions and methods. These studies were collected up, co-ordinated, combined and delivered by central government in the form of *Child Protection: Messages from Research* (SSI, 1995), which was intended to have a direct influence on practice; they also informed new policy, guidance and regulation, which in turn steered both managers and practitioners.

These background conditions have strongly favoured the emergence of a movement for strengthening the scientific credentials of social work, its claims to exclusive professional knowledge, and the links between research evidence and practice. This movement for 'evidence-based' approaches (Sheldon et al., 1999) goes much further than central government's continuing attempts to orientate practice towards the findings and policy messages that its funded studies have revealed, and argues that practice should be rooted in an *experimental* method for choosing appropriate interventions, and *evaluative* skills in assessing the implications of others' research findings. As one exponent argues:

> Our clients deserve the best services our profession can provide, and for the determina-tion of social work effectiveness there is no substitute for controlled experimental research, guided by the philosophy of science known as logical positivism and the tenets of the hypothetico-deductive process. (Thyer, 1989, p. 320)

The central message of the 'empirical practice movement' (Reid, 1994) is that social workers should 'move away from the vague, unvalidated and haphazardly-derived knowledge traditionally used in social work toward a more systematic, rational and empirically-oriented development and use of knowledge for practice' (Fischer, 1993, p. 19), and that research and practice can become 'essentially the same form of activity, since practice should consist of clear and consistent assess-ment, formulating hypotheses, collecting information and resolving problems' (ibid., p. 21). The evangelical nature of the movement is betrayed by Fischer's prediction that 'by the year 2000, empirically-based practice – the new social work – may be the norm, or well on the way to becoming so' (p. 55).

This movement is paralleled in health care practice, where professionals are similarly being urged – by government and by academics – to ground their interventions more firmly in research, to become competent, critical evaluators of journal articles, and to pursue 'evidence-based' methods. In medicine and nursing, such ideas merely reassert the claims of an already-strong faction within the professions – academics, experimental scientists and researchers – to posi-tions of power and influence. They aim to equal the existing authority of man-agers and accountants in determining outcomes and decisions. In social work the movement is far newer, and reflects an *ad hoc* alliance between one part (hitherto a very small one) of the academic community and the policy makers and research funders of central government. It also reflects an opportunistic (but understand-able) bid for professional power from a party that has hitherto had little support, enjoying its moment in the sun that has stemmed from a change in the moral and political climate.

It should now be obvious how well 'evidence-based' social work appears to fit with New Labour's model of human rationality, behaviour, policy, governance and implementation. The psychological theory underpinning evidence-based approaches is strictly behaviourist; social problems are traced to patterns of behaviour which are learned, and which can be changed by programmes that exert systematic influence on the cognitive, emotional and functional elements in such patterns. By tradition, behaviourist methods deal in reward and punishment, and operate under a fairly simple and mechanistic notion of the motives for action, often derived from experiments with animals as well as human subjects (Skinner, 1973). Deviant behaviour can be corrected by the application of the right balance of reinforcing or aversive stimuli, and human subjects can be induced or trained to change their behaviour by well-chosen programmes. The best results are obtained by breaking down complex problems into smaller constituent elements, and focusing such programmes on changing the actions revealed as dysfunctional for the persons themselves, or for others (Reid and Epstein, 1977). Like the Third Way itself, the movement for 'empirical practice' is brisk and businesslike about changing people; it recommends pragmatic approaches on the grounds that 'it is better to build on what might conceivably be so ... than not to build at all' (Scriven, 1997, p. 479), adding that it is 'a waste of time to try to solve the problems of epistemology without getting on with the job' (ibid.).

Like the Third Way, the evidence-based approach relies on top-down social engineering, on the power of the expert over the lay person, and on the prestige of official science and programmes for social improvement in order to overcome the resistances of identity, locality, particularism, idiosyncrasy or creativity. It insists that its methods are objective and scientific and that they work for progress and human welfare. It sets little store on democracy or service user involvement: 'so-called participatory design ... is about as sloppy as one can get, short of participatory authoring of the final report' (Scriven, 1997, p. 486). It justifies social distance between researcher and research subject, for the sake of rationality and reliability. In the name of establishing a sound knowledge base for social work, 'science provides us with the key to the development of a cumulative evaluation of its different theoretical components' (Sheldon, 1978, p. 17).

The new orthodoxy in social work is, like the Third Way itself, a rational technical approach to social issues (Parton and O'Byrne, 2000), which fits well with its goal to make social work more accountable and transparent. It allows the prescriptive style of central government regulations and guidelines, and its messages from research, to serve as a model for how learning is transmitted, and presents practice as a vehicle for implementing well-evaluated knowledge and well-considered policy. In all these ways, the profession of social work and the local authority social services departments are seen as instruments of a Benthamite steering of society towards more desirable outcomes, and are required to perform this function under the supervision of managers and administrators who are the guardians of progress and order (see Chapter 9).

Subjectivity, Meaning and Culture

Although these principles have come to the fore in the 1990s, aided by the models of economic rationality that prevailed during the Thatcher–Major and the

Blair administrations, they could scarcely conquer the territory of local authority social services and professional social work without resistance and struggle. This is because of the far longer tradition of practice as concerned with subjectivity and meaning in personal experience, and culture as a variable mediating between the formal systems of the legal-bureaucratic authority of the state, and the informal everyday world of lived experience. Social work practice has always worked in the space between law and policy on the one hand, and family, neighbourhood, and community on the other (see pp. 54–7) – the space created in democratic and pluralistic societies for critical reflection on social interactions, social groupings and social systems. Hence it has never been closely associated with the top-down implementation of central policies in UK political cultures, or indeed in any democratic society – the Nazi period in Germany being an instance of just such direct implementation, as Lorenz (1995) shows. Instead, its established role is that of mediating between dissident, disaffected or 'maladjusted' individuals and the mainstream, between people with special needs and those agencies that provide for more generalized or universal needs, and between minorities, the disadvantaged and the unorganized, and the majority's organizations (Jordan, 1983, 1990, 1997). Hence 'the early moral and social orientations of the profession run deep in memory, but they have become part of our increasingly silent language as the weight of the scientific world view suppressed these appreciations' (Weick and Saleeby, 1998, p. 22).

So during the 1980s and 1990s there was a quiet counter-movement towards the analysis of just those factors that escape a positivist approach to social interactions, an instrumental perspective on policy, and a Benthamite version of governance. This is not a movement, still less an orthodoxy, in the sense of the movement for empirical or evidence-based practice. Rather it is a diverse collection of research methods, perspectives on evaluation and ideas about practice that are semi-organized in loose groupings and networks, and constitute an undercurrent of resistance to, and criticism of, the hegemonic discourses of management science and policy implementation.

There are plenty of sources on which this counter-movement can draw. The value of the subjective and idiosyncratic, of fantasy and creativity, was part of the psychodynamic heritage that reached social work not so much through the bowdlerized Freudianism of mainstream American theorists of the 1940s and 1950s, as via the work of British writers like Bowlby (1951) and Winnicott (1958), and the more popularised versions of child psychotherapy such as *Dibs: In Search of Self* (Axline, 1964), and educationalists like Barbara Docker-Drysdale and Richard Balbernie. These more imaginative, less mechanistic versions of the psychodynamic approach have continued to survive in the profession, for instance in the concept of social work as art (England, 1986) rather than science.

There is also the interactionist tradition in sociology, with its understanding of how meaning and order are constructed through face-to-face communication, and hence *accomplished* co-operatively in exchanges between selves, rather than being part of a structure within which individuals follow rules and procedures (Goffman, 1972; Hilbert, 1992). The notion that social work consists of a process of constructing mutually meaningful frames for interpreting and managing the world was implicit in much influential research and writing of the 1970s and 1980s, such as Mattinson and Sinclair's *Mate and Stalemate* (1979); conversely, the notion that social work practice could be demeaning and disempowering if what was constructed was stigma, blame and the humiliation of self was explored by Simpkin (1979) and Satyamurti (1980). Interactionism has left a legacy for new ideas such as social constructionism (Parton and O'Byrne, 2000; Karvinen et al., 1999) which emphasizes the role of language and interpretation in the analysis of practice.

Another source was the attempt to derive theory and deeper understanding from the details of practice, from the subjective impact of service users' emotional responses and behavioural manoeuvres on the worker (Mattinson, 1975; Jordan, 1970, 1972). The notions of intersubjectivity, reflection and transmission of feelings have all become deeply unfashionable in mainstream present-day practice, but they survive in much of the best practice teaching in UK agencies, and in some research literature also.

In addition there is the newer notion of the *reflective practitioner* (Schön, 1983), which was developed for a far wider range of human-service professions than social services – including architecture and planning – but which revalues judgement, experience and learning from doing as aspects of professional skill. Schön criticizes the view of practice that conceives it as a 'rigorous application' of research-based knowledge; he insists that the kinds of problems human-service professionals address are 'complex ongoing messes', the elements of which cannot be easily separated and subjected to scientific assessment and testing. Understanding in such situations develops out of a dialogue between the professional and the service user, which results in 'a new theory of the unique case'. Practice knowledge is therefore derived from 'reflection-in-action', from an interactive process in which the professional brings to bear experience, judgement and intuition in a creative response to the specifics of the situation and the person (Gould and Taylor, 1996).

Then there is the *emancipatory* agenda in social work and research (Shaw, 1997). The main common themes of this diverse set of ideas are that behaviourism and positivism overlook issues of *power* in social policy and practice, that researchers must *take sides* when such issues are at stake in social relations (because to ignore them is covertly to side against the dominated and oppressed), and that service users should *participate* in policy-making practice and research (Beresford and Croft, 1993, 1995). This points towards *qualitative* methods of research, which reveal the strategic, cultural and institutional aspects of power relations, and how these are practised by social workers. These methods uncover the cultural diversity and pluralism of service users' social worlds, and the artfulness of their resistance practices, which are obscured by quantitative methods that treat them as objects of policy programmes.

Another source consists of the emerging critiques of *post-modernism* (Parton, 1994, 1998) and *social constructionism* (Parton and O'Byrne, 2000). These reject the notion of a grand progressive purpose for social intervention (such as the ambitions for reform and cultural change presented as the Third Way) in favour of more modest goals in often fragmented and incoherent policy domains. They seek to revalue the personal and discursive elements in practice, and to recognize the extent to which social work is a *narrative* activity (Hall, 1997) in which dialogue is the vehicle for support and change. This in turn acknowledges subjective elements in individual experience as valid and empowering, and the goal of strengthening individual identity through group and collective processes. It also sees social reality as essentially provisional and advocates an approach to social work which is 'open to real moral, social and political dilemmas, and ... learns to live with inevitable uncertainty, confusion and doubt' (Jordan, 1978, p. 25).

Finally, there is the tradition of *community work* and *community development*, which was part of mainstream social work briefly in the 1970s and has now fallen right out of the education and training curriculum and come to be practised mainly in voluntary organizations and projects, often by practitioners who do not think of themselves as social workers. This tradition in professional literature has been kept alive largely by the work of Bob Holman (1981, 1988, 1998), who almost alone in social work combines commitment to the needs of disadvantaged people, accountability of academic and professional interests to local and democratic ones, and empowerment through collective action. Holman is widely idealized and marginalized by being regarded as a saint, but his influence and inspiration live on in scores of underfunded and unsung initiatives. The now tenuous links between official, professional social work and the whole community sector of projects and units will be a major theme of the third part of this book.

Far from constituting a movement, all these are separate elements in a still-surviving alternative version of social work's role in society, its practice methodology and its relationship to expertise and knowledge. They help to explain New Labour's ambivalence about social work as a profession, and local authority social services departments as social welfare organizations. In so far as these are deeply engrained in the fabric of social work and public social services, they represent forces of resistance to the views of rationality, policy and governance advanced through the Third Way.

These factors also help explain New Labour's keenness to regulate and supervise local authority social services departments, through new inspectorates and regional targets and standards, and to monitor and evaluate social work through a new General Social Care Council (DoH, 1999a, p. 5). Given the Third Way's claim to a progressive programme of reform, based on a sound and scientific analysis of the UK's problems and prospects, they represent obstacles to its purposes that need to be cleared away or minimized. But we will argue in Chapter 9 that these alternative approaches have great potential for implementing its values and goals, if it is willing to rethink its means.

Conclusions

In this chapter we have reviewed the basis of the Third Way's programme, and shown how it reflects a top-down, social-engineering approach to social intervention, based on an instrumental conception of technical rationality, and an understanding of human motivation derived from economic and utilitarian analyses.

New Labour is an interventionist, regulatory government, which is optimistic and ambitious about the possibilities of changing individuals and cultures, but relies on crude notions of reward and punishment to implement its plans.

Local authority social services departments had already been reformed under the Conservatives in the late 1980s and early 1990s, to make them more suitable instruments for its regimes of efficiency, cost control, targeting and risk management. In this way, public sector social workers were already operating at some distance from the 'front line' of human problems, engaged in assessment, investigation, care planning, report writing and evidence collecting. They were already deployed in processing 'needs' in a largely bureaucratic way, slotting human misery into dry categories of risk, vulnerability and dangerousness. In the probation service there is already a precedent for the view that such work can be more efficiently done by people with minimal instrumental training in procedures, in prioritization and in enforcement, whose vision has become so blinkered that they are focused on a limited number of predetermined 'factors', which they match to individuals using checklists. Thus the whole occupation of social work is at risk of having the exercise of professional judgement squeezed out of its practice in favour of mechanistic obedience to government guidance, research indicators and managerial commands.

Box 12   Disappearing social workers

Falling recruitment to and mass resignations from local authority social work began to attract attention in early 2000. The *Guardian* (26 January) reported that Essex County Council was bringing in qualified South African staff to fill vacancies; Canadians had previously been recruited, but soon left. At the time, overall vacancies for qualified social workers in England and Wales stood at 7.1 per cent, in Greater London at 10.4 per cent, and in the south and south-east of England at 11.2 per cent.

The social work admissions service reported a 45 per cent decline in applications for places to train as social workers between 1995 and 1998, from 11,526 to 6,521, with a further predicted 25 per cent drop in 1999. In a letter to the *Guardian*, Professor Laura Middleton commented that trained practice teachers in child care specialisms were being transferred to management posts because of pressure of child protection work, so that facilities for practice education were also being lost (Letters, 25 January 2000).

Although Health Minister Alan Milburn acknowledged that 'social services help more vulnerable people than any other part of the public sector', average pay for care staff working for private homes or agencies was revealed in a survey by Pay and Workforce Research in 1999 to be £3.80 per hour. In spite of this, two important groups of commercial providers, Grampian Care and Advantage Care, went into receivership that year, blaming inadequate local authority fees for residents (D. Brindle, 'Care Less', *Guardian*, 27 January 2000).

But this is not the whole story. In order to implement the positive side of its programme – social inclusion, empowerment, equality of opportunity, lifelong learning for all, social justice – New Labour will eventually have to recognize the need for subtler, more sensitive methods. Responsibilities cannot simply be enforced, they must be negotiated. The relationship between family obligations and civic duties is a complex one, and will require skilled and thoughtful interventions. Above all, the idea of community as the basis for membership and participation implies a dialogue with groups, associations and organizations in civil society, rather than the tutelary steering and surveillance that is the Third Way's main instrument. Although much of this can be done through voluntary and community sector agencies and projects, it will require a public sector agency if it is to be co-ordinated and coherent. Social work still has something to offer in all this.

The biggest challenge facing New Labour is learning how to reconcile its aims for the economy (especially for regulating the labour market and increasing participation in the formal economy) with its plans for social regeneration and the restoration of order and respect for law. These issues will emerge through increased pressure from civil-society organizations for the recognition of unpaid work, volunteering and community activism, to balance the emphasis on employment as a contribution to a responsible society. This in turn will redirect attention towards community development, and the possibility of channelling the 'informal' (often illegal) local economy in disadvantaged areas towards improving the quality of life for residents.

We have raised the big question for the Third Way of how its philosophy of 'tough love' will be implemented in practice, and by whom. There is something unconvincing about the images of New Deal counsellors and their packages of help; and something deterrent and aversive about many of the new officials in 'no choice' services for asylum seekers, or law-and-order projects for rough sleepers or truants. Tough love implies exceptional skills in communication, and a charisma sadly lacking in the Benthamite images of the government White Papers. The question is whether social work contains within it traditions, cultures and practices that can supply some of these missing elements.

Above all, neither New Labour's policy programme, nor the prevailing orthodoxies of social work research and theory, allow for the uncomfortable fact that most of the behaviour seen as increasingly problematic in the past two decades (crime, drug taking, benefits fraud, single parenthood, and serial relationships) was a rational adaptation by disadvantaged and marginal people to their deteriorating circumstances (Jordan, 1990, 1996a). This now confronts politicians as a perceived 'moral breakdown' in family values, moral bonds, community solidarity and law and order (Jordan, 1999c). It justifies the conservative communitarianism and social engineering approaches of the Third Way. But 'tough love' requires a challenge to the cultural adaptations of millions of people under Thatcher and Major, and one which requires them to break the patterns of behaviour through which they have pursued their interests (MacNichol and Smith, 1999). It is a far more ambitious and demanding programme than any hitherto conceived (let alone achieved) by 'people changers' in the UK; some might argue that it is bound to fail, and that social work is better off out of it. But we will argue that it is an opportunity for social work to prove itself, and to evolve into something new, energized by the spirit of those marginal people, cultures and practices.

PART II

4

The Third Way in Local Authority Social Services: Modernization and Management

The second part of this book advocates a broader understanding of social work, both as a professional activity, and as a means of implementing social policy. There is a wide range of practice concerned with social relations, and especially with the regeneration of deprived communities, that constitutes social work in this broader sense. Its practitioners have important values, commitments and methods in common, and would gain from sharing aspects of training and development. This is not an attempt to suggest that established social work 'take over' these other branches and occupations; rather it proposes a mutual identification and merging of approaches.

This is all the more necessary because of the 'divide and rule' policies of New Labour. Under the guise of improving training and setting higher standards, much is being done to deskill local authority social workers, to reduce their scope for judgement and interpretation of regulations, and make their work mechanical and administrative. At the same time, more power is being given to new enforcement counsellors, but within very focused, instrumental roles, cut off from the wider context of welfare issues, political and moral analysis. Finally, much front-line, direct work with service users, performed by employees of voluntary and community organizations, is drifting away from 'social work' (as defined by New Labour), and it too has much to lose from this potential isolation from other services.

In this chapter, we will consider the proposals for the reform of local authority social services departments, and the agencies which carry out the work commissioned by them under contract. Here we argue that these reforms do not address the central issues at stake, or model an adequate view of practice. We will use case examples to illustrate these points.

The modernization and management of the local authority social services departments is, as far as we are aware, the only area in UK public policy documents where the expression 'third way' is actually employed to capture a distinctive approach to governance. The sense in which it is used is much narrower than the Third Way of the title of this book (a completely new set of philosophical, institutional and cultural resources for politics) but it is nonetheless revealing of New Labour's attitudes to the public personal social services.

The White Paper *Modernising Social Services* (DoH, 1998a) defines this 'third way' as lying between the commercialization of care provision that characterized the period of the Conservative reforms, and the near-monopoly of local authorities in the field of social care during the 1960s and 1970s. It consists in applying the principles that

    i) care should be provided to people in a way that supports their independence and respects their dignity

    ii) services should meet each individual's specific needs ....(a)nd people should have a say in what services they get and how they are delivered

    iii) care services should be organized, accessed, provided and financed in a fair, open and consistent way in every part of the country

    iv) children who for, whatever reason, need to be looked after by the local authority should get a decent start in life....

    v) every person – child or adult – should be safeguarded against abuse, neglect or poor treatment whilst receiving care

    vi) people who receive social services should have an assurance that the staff they deal with are sufficiently trained and skilled for the work...

    vii) people should be able to have confidence in their local social services, knowing that they work to clear and acceptable standards, and that if those standards are not met, action can be taken to improve things. (DoH, 1998a, para. 1.8)

The first two of these principles link the agenda for modernizing social services with the other parts of New Labour's social welfare reform programme. They assert that this aims to 'strengthen family life, reduce social exclusion, tackle youth crime and reform the welfare state' (para. 1.12). The notions of 'promoting independence' and 'meeting each individual's needs' are in line with the achievement ethos of the whole reform package, and its emphasis on a targeted, focused and individualized form of social intervention – replacing *generalized* safety nets by *customized* trampolines. But this task faces a number of specific and distinctive obstacles in relation to personal social services, which the White Paper does not adequately recognize or address.

The rest of the principles of the 'third way' outline a programme for modernization by means of a characteristically Benthamite, regulatory and supervisory method, with the threat of heavy penalties for non-compliance. As Mitchell (2000, p. 185) points out, the proposals aim to make local authority councillors and managers more accountable for the quality, suitability and efficiency of the social services. 'This is an extremely prescriptive approach to policy making and implementation in the social services field, which has not been attempted on such a wide scale hitherto, and it remains to be seen how successfully this can be carried through.'

The White Paper puts forward specific statutory changes to improve protection of children, highlights continuing problems of co-ordination of housing, health and personal social services, outlines standards and measures for judging effectiveness, addresses inconsistency between different parts of the country, and identifies issues of inefficiency over costs. It also sets up new ways of enforcing reform in all these areas. The details of the programmes sketched in it are followed up in more detail in subsequent documents.

Our goal in this chapter is to provide a critical review of these proposals, and try to relate them to the more general principles, and central programmes set out in Chapters 2 and 3. In the next chapter we will show how the overall values and objectives of the programme are blocked by inconsistencies and contradictions in its content and by the shortcomings of its model of implementation. Detailed lists of standards and requirements are no substitute for an understanding of human motivation. In so far as this chapter deals in the government's language of modernization and management, it is pretty dry stuff, but we will try to make it more recognizably human by the use of real case examples, which are truer representations of complex, messy reality.

Adult Services: Independence, Consistency and Fairness

The White Paper criticizes the performance of social services for adults for failing to promote independence (DoH, 1998a, Chapter 2). Instead

> Because of resource pressures, councils are tending to focus more and more on those most dependent people in their community. For example, although there has been an increase in the overall level of domiciliary care supporting people in their own homes, that increase has been concentrated on those getting more intensive support, and the number of people receiving lower levels of support has actually dropped .... This means that some people who would benefit from purposeful interventions at a lower level of service, such as the occasional visit from a home help, or over a shorter period, such as training in mobility and daily living skills to help them cope with visual impairment, are not receiving any support. This increases the risk that they in turn become more likely to need much more complicated levels of support as their independence is compromised. (para. 2.6)

The claims that 'social services are for all of us' (para. 1.1) and that the proposals will 'support welfare reform and social inclusion' (1.9) are intended to reinforce this point, by trying to move away from management methods that target and prioritize the most vulnerable adult applicants for social care, putting financial ceilings on domiciliary care packages, and withdrawing low-level support (para. 2.7). Yet such approaches were precisely what was indicated by the ideas that inspired the NHS and Community Care Act 1990; any authorities that failed to focus care in this way were criticized (Audit Commission, 1997). Previously, more generalized help had been available to less vulnerable older people in particular. Research such as that of Challis and Davies (1985) had shown that many entered residential care for want of more individualized, flexible and *intensive* domiciliary packages. But they also pointed out that it was impossible to use these as a way of saving money. The best domiciliary supports (those most valued by the service users and – more ambivalently – by their carers) were those that allowed them to remain at home for longer, rather than enter residential care. But this *eventually* costs as much as the former methods, because service users lived longer, and were admitted straight to hospital, which was more expensive than residential care.

In rather the same way, since almost everyone experiences dependency at the very end of their lives, however support is offered, they will come to need looking after at some stage. More low-level support may delay this somewhat, but it will not prevent it; hence the claim that it will be 'good … for taxpayers' (2.6) is suspect. To provide *both* low-level *and* intensive social care will cost more, not less. The dilemma is captured in the White Paper's pledge to give a 'prevention grant of £100 million, to stimulate preventive strategies and effective risk assessment, so as to target low-level support for people most at risk of losing their independence' (para. 2.12, box 2). 'Targeting' and 'risk assessment' are hardly appropriate in providing for vulnerabilities that are so widespread as these.

Indeed, the whole attempt to make such services more generally available goes against New Labour's overarching principle of providing benefits and services only for those 'in genuine need', and excluding those with the resources and capacities to manage without them. It seems strange to be promoting low-level services in kind at the same time as cutting incapacity and disability benefits for those with less serious conditions – unless care services are supposed to be some kind of substitute for benefits. But simultaneously, the government wants to extend the practice of local authority social services departments giving 'direct payments' to service users – cash to buy their own care. 'One way to give people greater control over their own lives is to give them money and let them make their own decisions about how their care is delivered' (para. 2.14). The government is 'considering making it mandatory for all authorities to operate schemes, to ensure equality of opportunity across the whole country' (para. 2.16); it will also make people over 65 years old eligible for direct payments (para. 2.15). While there are good reasons for applauding these proposals, they are a very labour-intensive way of achieving the government's declared goals. Already the Benefits Agency has experienced great difficulties in implementing New Labour's pledge to give at least £75 a week to disabled elderly claimants of income support. The fact is, low take-up and complexity always bedevil means-tested benefits; help delivered through social work services suffers even more from these problems.

Box 13   Delivering means-tested benefits to elderly people with disabilities

The New Labour government is committed to improving the welfare of this group of 'deserving' claimants. But even when promises are made and goodwill is present, means-tested benefits are complex and time-consuming to administer.

The Mid Devon Citizens' Advice Bureau (CAB) was chosen to co-ordinate the Benefit Take Up Campaign with the Benefits Agency funded by Devon County Council as part of their anti-poverty campaign. Elderly disabled people were the main target of the campaign.

CASE 1:   TOM

The Benefits Agency promised to fast-track claims and the first submitted on 7 November 1999 for Tom was processed in three weeks. Tom had suffered shellshock on the beaches of Dunkirk, resulting in bad eyesight and uncontrollable shaking of the hands from that day in 1940. He worked for the local council until taking early retirement at the age of 60 to look after his severely disabled wife. She died in 1997 and now at the age of 79 he received only a retirement pension plus a small private one, totalling £89.06 a week in all. He had at no time received benefits to help with his disabilities, which are now so bad he cannot walk unaided. After he contacted the CAB, they applied on his behalf, and he now receives attendance allowance, income support and full housing benefit, a total of £165.27 a week. In Tom's own words, this gave him one of the best Christmases of his life.

CASE 2:   TAFFY

Contrast this with the experience of Taffy, a fellow member of the British Legion with Tom. His disability became acute two years ago and worsened recently when he had part of a foot amputated due to gangrene. His claim was submitted a week after Tom's. When nothing had been heard by the middle of December his adviser was told, on contacting the Benefits Agency, that due to pressure of demand, claims were now taking at least 10–12 weeks. Taffy couldn't understand why his plans to visit his relatives in Bristol for Christmas were going to be thwarted by lack of funds whilst Tom's life had been enhanced by his extra money.
On 6 January Taffy died from a heart attack. The week of his funeral a letter arrived from the Benefits Agency, telling him of the increase in his benefits.

New Labour is keen to standardize eligibility criteria for services, contribution rates and means test, so as to provide 'fair access to care; and consistency across the country' (paras 2.25–2.40). These goals require a great deal of central government monitoring, supervision and direction of local authority rules and practices. The variations now evident are a direct result of the decision in 1990 to shift responsibility for funding social care to local authorities from social assistance (income support). Such a decision was bound to result in variations, because of the different political complexion of local authorities, their fiscal capacities and resource holdings, and levels of need. It rather destroys the point of having services under local control to make detailed national rules on allocation of resources imposed from above.

All this implies a great increase in the regulatory role of central government, epitomized in the Fair Access to Care initiative (para. 2.36). The government will 'set out the principles local authorities should follow when devising and applying eligibility criteria' as a way of achieving consistency, clear objectives, a common understanding of risk assessment and regular reviews. It also seeks to standardize charging systems, and achieve 'greater transparency and fairness in the contribution that people are asked to make towards their social care' (para. 2.37). This means greater uniformity through new regulations, supervision and inspection. But the White Paper insists that services must be 'individually tailored' (para. 2.44), quoting from an Audit Commission report that

> Sometimes older people and their carers do not appear to have as much influence over their care as they should. In practice, care managers have limited choice to offer older people. Social services departments should ensure that care managers have greater influence over services by reducing restrictions on choice, introducing service-level agreements with in-house providers and delegating budgets. (Audit Commission, 1997)

Here again, the government displays its faith in a regulatory and enforcement-orientated approach to implementing its goals; greater flexibility and choice can be achieved through 'improved commissioning', the use of a 'self-audit tool' to review care management arrangements (para. 2.60) and strategic planning. These in turn will be reinforced by 'Best Value service reviews, Joint Reviews and SSI Inspections' (para. 2.60). The approach combines 'listening to people' with 'good commissioning' – based on assessment of needs within the general population, planning for strategic objectives, contract setting and market management (variable contracts) and contract monitoring, ensuing that specific conditions are met to acceptable standards (para. 2.60, box 2). This approach is supposed to deal with diversity and complexity of needs, including 'the specific needs of ethnic minority people' (para. 2.46), whose disadvantages and frustrations were recognized in earlier government and voluntary sector reports (CRE, 1997; SSI, 1998).

The shortcomings of this whole approach are signalled by the sections of the White Paper on the needs of carers (para. 2.22). These largely restate propositions that have been piously repeated for many years, before and after the reforms of community care (Jordan, 1987, 1990). The principle that family and other unpaid carers should be recognized, supported and empowered is familiar, but remains unimplemented in practice. It is difficult to see how yet another National Carers Strategy, due to be published in 1999, will do much to improve this situation.

These past failures reflect the fact that family and neighbourly relations are not easily sustained by official systems of care, surveillance and monitoring. It is a very old truism of the personal social services that the public welfare system has difficulties in meshing with the informal world of love and duty that constitutes family and neighbourly caring (Finch and Groves, 1984; Ungerson, 1987; Finch, 1989). The myth that sustained the NHS and Community Care Act 1990 was that this was because local authority social services were rigid and inflexible, that they responded to the needs of politicians and service providers, not those of service users and carers; and that all this would change if local authority care managers purchased flexible packages from voluntary agencies and commercial firms. Now that this has been tried, we know from research evidence that most of the same issues persist, along with new resentments about financial assessments and providers' non-compliance with the terms of contracts

(Hadley and Clough, 1995). The White Paper's reliance on yet more regulation and review does not make sense in this context.

The ironic fact is that here the Third Way does exactly the reverse of its attempt to ground citizens' obligations in community membership (see pp. 48–57). In its attempt to ground its concept of responsibility in an ethically relevant experience of belonging and an emotional commitment to mutuality, the Third Way tries to draw its moral messages from the 'blood-and-guts code' that regulates everyday interactions. But in its detailed implementation of principles and standards for social care, it tries to prescribe for the commissioning of services and the support of carers in ways that totally fail to take account of the way the blood-and-guts code works in practice.

Family and neighbourly care is the very stuff of the blood-and-guts code. People are moved to care for their partners, parents, kin or neighbours by ties of affection, gratitude, guilt, greed, interdependence, obsession, power or powerlessness – and usually by some mixture of these. Caring is sustained by processes of communication (of identity and relationship, as well as shared history and meaning), and not by specific rules, roles or contracts (Jordan et al., 1994, Chapter 4). Into this maelstrom of mixed feelings and often conflicting interests, a care manager arrives to assess resources and risks, and purchase a package of care. The success or failure of this in sustaining the relationships between carer and cared-for, in managing the transition to greater dependence and eventual 'social death' (Miller and Gwynne, 1972) – the loss of a viable life in the community, often long before physical death – and the parting itself, relies on complex understandings and skills, well beyond the reach of Benthamite regulation.

The following case example illustrates the complexities of caring relationships, and the failures of a rather mechanistic and unimaginative style of care management to take account of these. Unlike the extremely brief and dry case examples in the White Paper (see for instance para. 2.60, box 1), it is intended to show how the blood-and-guts code of family and kinship requires something more than 'better commissioning' and 'self-audit tools' to provide an effective service to those in need and their carers. What it requires is a sensitive but fair and committed response to passionate distress, anger, confusion, grief and bereavement (see also Chapter 1, pp. 23–5).

CASE EXAMPLE: NEVILLE FRANCIS

Neville Francis was 67 years old when he suffered a massive stroke. Only recently retired from a well-paid, responsible job as a supervisor in a large enterprise, Neville came from a close-knit family of six brothers, three of whom had already (like their father) died of strokes or heart attacks. He was left without the power of speech and paralysed down his right side, and remained in hospital, close to death, for several weeks. Eventually he revived sufficiently to be put on a rehabilitation ward, for his future care needs to be assessed.

Neville's relationship with his wife, Susan, had for many years prior to his stroke not been a close one; they had drifted into little more than co-existence in their comfortable house, each following their own interests. Their married daughter was closer to her mother than her father. Faced with the prospect that

Neville would need very intensive and intimate forms of care because of his helpless condition, Susan quickly made it plain to nursing staff at the hospital that she could play no part in the care he would need. Given the fact that she herself had health problems, and the lack of warmth in their relationship, this was an understandable decision, and well within her rights as a partner and a person who deserved to have her own life in her retirement. The prospect of caring for a large man (he had been a prominent sportsman well into middle age, and was still very fit at the time of his stroke) who was very frustrated by his new disabilities, was a daunting one.

However, Neville's brother, Tom, responded in the opposite way to the crisis, spending hours at his bedside in the hospital, and coaxing and challenging him to fight and to live. Although himself a very ill man (he had had a long-term heart condition for many years), and with a wife who was also ill, Tom rallied the rest of the family in support of Neville. He and his wife were shocked by Susan's refusal to play any role in Neville's post-hospital care, and determined to compensate for this by their own efforts.

The health service district in which they lived had a very small number of social service department stroke rehabilitation homes, with an impressive record of keeping patients alive and placing them either back in their own family homes or in ordinary residential care. In relation to the total number of stroke cases in the whole district, the number of beds in these homes was tiny; but Neville was assessed as needing one of these places, and prepared for placement there. He was also assessed as having no psychiatric problems or needs as a result of his stroke.

Obviously the process of negotiating the placement with Neville was not an easy one. Neville was angry that Susan and his daughter visited very infrequently, and that he could not go straight home. Only Tom was really able to get beyond his lack of speech, and communicate directly with him. But Tom strongly supported the placement, realizing that it represented far the best chance of full rehabilitation for Neville, and pleaded with him to accept this opportunity. A social worker was allocated to Neville's case, and discussed the plan with Susan and her daughter (who endorsed it), but did not establish rapport with Neville.

The events surrounding Neville's discharge from hospital were key for the subsequent tragedy, and are disputed, but certain facts are clear. Neville was transported to the rehabilitation home, where he was supposed to be met by the social worker, to help him settle; but the social worker did not turn up. Tom met Neville there, and found him restless and distressed – he wanted to go home, and did not accept that he needed rehabilitation. Tom stayed with him for several hours to try to settle him, and then went home for a meal. Later in the evening, he received a phone call from the home saying that Neville was still distressed, so he returned and spent the night with Neville in his room, to be sure that he slept. No staff were involved with Neville or Tom during the night. Tom went home in the morning, leaving Neville asleep.

That day a snap decision was made that Neville was unsuited to the rehabilitation home, and he was transferred to a private home for elderly people with mental infirmities – a mixture of those discharged from psychiatric care, and sufferers from dementia. Evidently Susan was consulted and agreed to the move;

Tom was not, and the decision was not made in negotiation with Neville himself. In effect, Neville was reclassified as in need of psychiatric care without reference to any medical opinion, and from this point onwards the rehabilitative services that he would have received as a victim of a stroke – physiotherapy, speech therapy, and so on – were completely denied him. In the new home he was totally isolated, because he did not identify with the other patients and did not accept being there. He became depressed and withdrawn, lost many of the capacities and skills he had regained in hospital, and deteriorated into a sad and dependent figure.

Tom was furious and frustrated by these developments – with Susan, whom he saw as colluding in Neville's exclusion and psychiatric imprisonment, and with the home, for failing to recognize Neville's individuality and identity, his needs as a stroke victim, and his vulnerability and despair. Tom visited every day as before, but came to be at loggerheads with the home owner over Neville's care; for instance, Neville's clothes were often lost, and he appeared in ill-fitting garments belonging to others. Eventually, when Neville's glasses were broken, Tom – who knew that his brother's eyesight was exactly the same as his own – brought him a pair and gave them to him: reading was Neville's only way to occupy himself in his isolation. The glasses were returned to Tom by Susan, with a letter saying that the home owner did not allow residents to use ones that were not prescribed, and that he must wait six weeks for an appointment with an optician. Enraged by this, Tom (himself a formidable physical presence) got into an argument with the home owner, who called the police. Despite the fact that Tom easily reached an amicable agreement to leave (and had in fact done so by the time the policeman arrived) he subsequently received a solicitor's letter requiring him not to visit his brother at the home in future.

By now, the pattern that had emerged was clear. On the one hand, Susan was very ready to accept the perception of Neville as a man with brain damage from his stroke so serious as to require psychiatric care. This helped justify her decision not to have him home, and not to visit him more than once a fortnight. Neville could not accept that he was not allowed back home – with access to his hobbies, his garden and his extended family of brothers, nieces, nephews and their children. Tom was angry that Neville was denied all these things, and became his champion, against Susan and against the authorities. He wrote frequently to the health authority, as the original purchasers of his care, protesting not only about what he saw as an unsuitable placement, but also about Neville's lack of stroke rehabilitation services. As original purchasers, the health authority were uncomfortable and defensive about Tom's letters of complaint. Even though the snap decision to place him in the private home was made without the involvement of the key health authority staff who knew Neville and had assessed him as in need of stroke rehabilitation, they felt it necessary to justify the decision as in Neville's best interests. Above all, they insisted that – as nearest relative – Susan was the person with whom they should consult over such issues, and that Tom had no status in issues of care and was not even required to be informed about them, except as a matter of courtesy. The fact that it was Tom, not Susan, who was closely involved with Neville, and able to communicate with him, was not taken as a relevant consideration.

Thus Neville's family was split into conflicting factions over his care, with Susan and their daughter on one side, and Tom, the other surviving brothers, the widows of the deceased brothers, and all the nephews, nieces and their children on the other. The health authority and social services were in uneasy alliance with Susan and the home owner against this mass of kin. It would seem obvious that what was needed at this point was a social worker to assess the *social* situation, and to try to mediate between the parties, as well as to consult with Neville about his wishes and feelings, and to investigate the possible need for rehabilitative services. No such referral was made, and the previous contact was not maintained.

Six months after he was admitted for psychiatric care, Neville was transferred back to the hospital unit. His condition had deteriorated rapidly, to the point where he was clearly sliding into total dependence and depression – losing weight, not attempting to communicate, and keeping entirely to himself. Once he was back in the unit, Tom at once resumed contact, and encouraged and cajoled him back into health. In a short time Neville was communicating and walking, and well enough to spend time (several days a week) outside the hospital with Tom, visiting various members of the extended family. Indeed, over one holiday he was at a nephew's home, enjoying the company of his great-nieces and great-nephews, and very much part of the family again.

However, when he was considered fit to leave the unit, it was to Susan that the authorities turned to discuss the placement, and, despite Tom's protests (and eventual formal complaint), he was again placed in a private psychiatric home, this time in a town some distance from his home. Tom continued to press for his reassessment, and for an alternative placement, and for rehabilitative services, but to no avail. Neville became frustrated and restless again, had spats with staff members, was injured in an unexplained fall, and took a swing at a fellow resident. After a series of such incidents, he suffered another massive stroke; but the decision was made not to admit him to hospital for treatment. Barely conscious, he was kept in his room and given liquid nourishment, as he was unable to chew or swallow properly. Tom protested frantically, requesting his admission for active treatment, but Susan was adamant that Neville should remain in the home till he died. After some weeks, during which Tom was constantly by his bedside, Neville died in Tom's arms, an emaciated and barely recognizable version of his old self.

Discussion

Whatever the rights and wrongs of Neville's final months, certain features of the situation facing the health and social services staff who were making decisions about his care stand out as particularly significant:

(a) the problem of communicating with Neville about his wishes and feelings. According to Tom, no health or social services staff made serious efforts to help Neville come to terms with his massive losses – of his physical health and strength, of his immediate family, his home, his possessions, his savings, and above all his control over his life decisions. As a result, Tom never accepted that he need rehabilitative residential care, and specifically rejected psychiatric care alongside others who were suffering psychoses or dementia.

(b) Although health and social care staff relied on Tom to communicate and care for Neville in many ways, and always called on him in emergencies (e.g. Neville's unsettled, conflictual or 'violent' behaviour), Tom was never used as a 'translator' or interpreter between Neville (who never regained the power of speech, but could readily make his feelings understood to those he trusted) and those making decisions about his case. And Tom was never formally consulted about any of the decisions over placement or treatment (including the decision effectively to let Neville die); indeed, he was often not even informed of these.

(c) The conflict between Susan's faction and the much larger group of Neville's kin became so hostile that no direct communication was possible, except through solicitors. At Neville's funeral, all the rest of his family and friends sat or stood on one side of the chapel, with only Susan and their daughter on the other. Yet, at no stage was any effort to resolve their differences or reach a compromise initiated by the health and social services staff. The notion that Susan had – as legally nearest relative – the sole right to make decisions about his care overrode the obvious anomaly that she had refused to play any part in this, whereas Tom and other relatives were active in caring for him and continuing to treat him as a member of the family, even long after Susan had decided he was 'socially dead'.

(d) These three factors made the notion of simply 'purchasing and providing appropriate services to acceptable standards' highly problematic. Neither Neville nor Tom ever accepted the premises upon which social care was bought for him – they insisted that he was a stroke victim, not a psychiatric case, and that his behaviour was explainable as the result of frustration with not being consulted, or even directly addressed, about choices of placement, the disposal of his property, or anything else. What was required to make the care package 'appropriate' and 'acceptable' was highly skilled and sensitive work with a man suffering grief and shock and family members in conflict and crisis. Such work was not even attempted, still less achieved.

(e) As purchasers of care, the health authority soon sought to transfer responsibility to the local authority social services department. In the event, the snap decision to transfer Neville to a psychiatric residential home saved the health authority a great deal of money in rehabilitation services, though they denied that this was a motive for the sudden change, made without assessment or planning. At least the health authority did hear a formal complaint by Tom, and conducted a reassessment by a psychogeriatrician, just before Neville's final stroke. The social services department was deaf to all Tom's complaints and pleas, until after Neville's death, when it dismissed a complaint about the manner of his passing. Whatever the supposed safeguards of the formal system, they left Tom utterly disillusioned, as well as stricken with grief, and with absolutely no support.

Although this example and the one on pp. 23–5 (John and Mary Ryan) are extreme in terms of their outcomes, they represent one end of a scale of human suffering and perplexity associated with illness and disability in old age: the management of physical and social care, and public support for informal, unpaid caring relationships. The White Paper lists many unsatisfactory features of present systems, and promises to undertake improvements. But its failure to recognize the importance of fundamental skills of social work, and to consider how they can best be deployed in implementing its (valuable and praiseworthy) values and objectives, leaves its proposals with fatal weaknesses. Benthamite methods of surveillance, control, reward and punishment of local authorities by inspectors and auditors will not achieve these goals.

Fragmentation of service responsibility, poor co-ordination and co-operation between health and social services, and an instrumental approach to purchasing have all been blamed for these recent failures (House of Commons Health Committee, 1998; Hudson, 2000). However, these examples indicate that, although they all contribute to the problems, the issues are deeper. Shifting more financial responsibility back onto health services, and away from means-tested social services as purchasers, would not resolve the difficulties identified in John and Mary Ryan's case, though it might have prevented Neville Francis' tragedy.

Box 14   'Involuntary euthanasia' in the NHS and social care

The tragic examples of Mary Ryan (pp. 23–5) and Neville Francis have been given topicality by a scandal in December 1999, when a consultant psychogeriatrician, Dr Adrian Treloar, alleged that elderly patients were being allowed to starve to death in the NHS (*Daily Telegraph*, 6 December).

Dr Treloar said, 'If the medical profession is going to move, as they have done, to a position where they accept the deliberate withdrawal of food and fluids from patients then it's very difficult for patients to trust the doctors.' He added that 'involuntary euthanasia is not too strong a word for it', when BMA guidelines allowed staff to withdraw nutrition and hydration by tube for stroke victims and the confused elderly who were not terminally ill. The article spoke of 'pervading ageism ... manifested in staff, cases of neglect, and allegations that elderly people are dying unnecessarily by being left untreated and uncared for in geriatric wards across the country'. An unnamed member of a health authority in the north of England commented: 'If we are sending elderly people into hospitals who have no life threatening illness but who in four or five weeks are dead, we must ask whether the treatment they received in that hospital was appropriate or inappropriate.'

The report provoked a new debate about medical ethics, NHS resources and professional power. Newspaper articles and radio phone-ins produced countless examples of relatives who were left powerless as staff withdrew food and fluids, or prescribed medication that left patients physically weakened and sapped their will to live.

This scandal was shortly followed, in January 2000, with fresh evidence of underfunding of the NHS, as intensive care beds ran out,

> and patients on waiting lists for life-saving operations were left untreated.
> The issue of medical ethics and euthanasia was raised in Parliament by a
> private member's bill (Anne Winterton, MP) on 28 January 2000.

Services for people with learning difficulties and for those with mental illnesses
make up smaller, but equally important, parts of adult personal social services. We
will consider these in the next chapter, when we will look at the overall direction
of change, and put forward an alternative approach to social care.

Services for Children and Families

Services for children and families have historically followed a slightly different
pathway from those for adults (Packman, 1975; Packman and Jordan, 1991;
Parton, 1991). In some ways they have been barometers of social issues in the
UK, giving advance warning of problems to be tackled later by the major policy
programmes, and used to experiment with and pioneer such approaches. For
instance, in the early 1960s, concerns about family poverty, lone parenthood and
their efforts on children triggered the provision of small cash payments to families in crisis under the Children and Young Persons Act 1963, prefiguring the
expansion of discretionary social assistance payments in the later 1960s and
the 1970s (Jordan, 1974, 1976; Hill and Laing, 1979). The child care scandals of
the 1970s and early 1980s, starting with the death of Maria Colwell, led to a
reliance on court orders and statutory powers in child protection work that anticipated many of the 'strong state' policies of Margaret Thatcher in issues of order
and social discipline generally (Packman et al., 1986; Parton, 1991). And the
more negotiated, partnership and voluntaristic spirit that informed the Children
Act 1989 and tried to move practice away from such reliance on statutory intervention was a forerunner of other attempts to soften Thatcherite toughness and
introduce elements of compassion into social policy under John Major's leadership (Packman and Jordan, 1991).

Thus the White Paper's proposals for modernizing and managing services for
children and families address a rather different set of structures, practices and
issues from the ones that are identified in services for adults. In many ways, they
are unresolved problems and repeated themes of the policy debates of the 1970s,
1980s and 1990s that have emerged from research reports (Packman et al., 1986;
Packman and Hall, 1997; Millham et al., 1986; Fisher et al., 1986; Gibbons et al.,
1995; Aldgate and Hill, 1996; Thoburn, 1994; Tunstill, 1996) and from inspections and parliamentary committees (SSI, 1998). The main priorities identified
in the White Paper are:

1 protecting children from sexual, physical and emotional abuse and neglect;
2 raising the quality of care of children in the care of local authorities, so that it
   is 'as close as possible to the care provided by loving and responsible parents';
3 improving the life chances of children, both those 'in need' and those 'looked
   after' by the local authority, by improving their education and health and the
   support they receive after they leave care. (para. 3.7)

In this section, we will review the proposals made under these headings, and argue that the Third Way in local authority services for families and children has little new to offer. It merely seeks new mechanisms for regulating and supervising the delivery of these services, and offers new resources for those who comply with the standards. The process of 'modernization' offers no new vision of how to resolve the tensions and contradictions that have bedevilled this branch of social work for a whole generation (Packman, 1975; Packman and Hall, 1997). In particular, it provides no clues as to how to balance the need to protect children exposed to widespread and diverse risks – not only as a result of pervasive poverty and the cultures of resistance among marginal communities (Campbell, 1993; Jordan, 1996a, 1997, 1998a), but also more generally in the fluid and unstable marital relations of current mainstream social life – with the need to promote their well-being and active membership of wider society. The constructive role of care and accommodation in achieving this balance is never really addressed, although this is central to that whole set of issues. We will argue that these omissions and evasions in the Third Way reflect its lack of vision about the role of children in society, and betray its authoritarian fears of young people as potential subversives and dissidents within its over-controlled and disciplined notion of communities.

PROTECTION OF CHILDREN FROM HARM

In line with the recent recognition of widespread abuse of children by those entrusted or employed to care for them away from their families, the White Paper extends its understanding of child protection to foster care, residential homes, boarding schools and other settings (paras 3.8–3.11). It criticizes inconsistencies and shortcomings in the quality of child protection services in local authorities, including poor assessment, recording and planning, failure to implement or review plans, failure to allocate children at risk to social workers, and failure of training and supervision (paras 3.12–3.14), leading in the extreme case to the death of children known to social services.

The White Paper's responses to these issues are purely regulatory and concerned with enforcement of standards. It proposes:

(a) a new regulatory system, separating inspection from purchasing functions;
(b) full powers of inspection and enforcement for all children's homes, including homes run by local authorities;
(c) new protective regulation of small children's homes, state boarding schools, residential family centres and independent fostering services;
(d) new national standards for regulation. (para. 3.16)

The White Paper lists a comprehensive and laudable set of responses to the *Review of the Safeguards for Children Living Away from Home* (DoH, 1997), including provision for complaints procedures, information, independent visitors, involvement in reviews and decisions, collective voice, standards for foster care, and guidance for the governing bodies of organizations (para. 3.17). It outlines measures for stopping dangerous people from working with children (para. 3.18), and promises new child protection guidance from the Department of Health, on assessment, records, planning and allocation (paras 3.20–3.23). However, none of this is located in a clear account of the overall processes, relationships and mechanisms (in family life, in school and in the community) by which children are protected from harm of all kinds, and how the official, formal investigative and interventive arms of the local authority can best mesh with informal systems of support, regulation and protection of children.

Implicit in all that is said about child protection is the notion that it is about providing a secure and loving *parental* (or substitute parental) setting, reinforced by monitoring, regulation and enforcement of standards. Although the government says elsewhere that child protection is 'ultimately the responsibility of the community' (DoH, 1997, preface), this really refers to the sanctions wielded by local networks against those who abuse children, and therefore to informal social discipline reinforcing formal rules and sanctions. But the protection of children requires a network of adults who are interested in, stimulating of, and committed to the child's development (Jordan, 1998c). An exclusive form of parenting, or roles for those *in loco parentis* (entrusted with or employed to care) is misleading, because it fails to recognize that children need a diverse set of adult influences, models and relationships to form a satisfactory identity and develop into rounded personalities and active, competent citizens. It is often outside the family, the classroom and the church that such adults are to be found – in sports and cultural clubs, among wider kin and neighbours, family friends, and so on. Escape from parental influences and pressures, as much as guidance or redirection of these, is an important part of the development of children and young people. Statutory services may not so much be substituting parental care as providing this diversity of models and roles, including those of champion, advocate or supporter of the child who is in difficulties or crisis (Hazel, 1982). Where no such models, guides, confidants or supports are available in an adult network, a needy child or young person may seek them, and in the process be more vulnerable to abuse.

CASE EXAMPLE: MICHAEL BROWN

Michael Brown came into local authority care at the age of three, in tragic circumstances: his young mother committed suicide, and his father – always a somewhat remote figure in his life – was unable to care for him. He was offered a home by distant relatives, who already had five children and two foster children of their own, and were barely coping with the emotional, physical and material demands of a family of this size. Michael's adult memories of his pre-school years with his foster (later adoptive) parents were happy, and he made a good start at school. However, when he was about eight years old, the family situation began to deteriorate, as the parents had difficulties handling their teenage children and foster children, the mother turned to drink, and the father was preoccupied with earning enough to provide for the family. Michael (who has subsequently obtained his social services department file) began to get into trouble at home and school, mainly because his intelligence, imagination and liveliness were not sufficiently stimulated and channelled in an increasingly fraught home environment. He was befriended by a neighbour of the family, who started taking him to his house, and sexually abused him there. Michael saw this relationship as an escape from the parental home, as personal attention and reward (e.g. presents, toys), but obviously also as distressing and confusing; it contributed to his attention-seeking and delinquent behaviour, which drew punishment from the father. Here is his social worker's report for a review when he was 12 years old:

> There is a great bond of loyalty within the family, and Mr and Mrs Brown's commitment to the family is unquestioned. They could be described as two of 'life's givers' which unfortunately has led to much of their difficulty. With such a large family, there is a lot of competition for attention, and it is impossible to meet everyone's needs. On reflection they have probably taken on too much over the years. They have admitted that, had they known how much time and attention Rosalind (younger natural daughter of the family attending special school) would need, they would not have taken Michael.
>
> A few years ago problems with Michael began to emerge. Money and articles began to disappear from the house. This continued over the years, but recently it would appear to have stopped .... As a result of his behaviour, Michael has been physically punished, had his pocket money stopped, been stopped from taking up interests outside the home, and searched before leaving the home. Mr and Mrs Brown sincerely want to help rather than punish, so we agreed that he should be allowed to join the Cadets. We felt Michael needed outside interests and company; it would also show Michael that his parents do care about him and want to try to help; his pocket money has also been resumed.
>
> Michael ... is a friendly, likeable boy, intelligent and a good talker; he seems eager to talk, but is less comfortable when the subject is 'misdemeanours'. He seems to understand and appreciate the difficult position his parents are in having to look after such a large family and give each member a fair share of time and attention. I think, however, that Michael does feel rather 'the odd one out'; there is a fairly big gap between him and the youngest of the older members of the family, and Rosalind needs special attention. Also because of his stealing much of the attention he has received has been negative. (Case file, 1981)

Discussion

In this report, the social worker shows awareness of most of the factors in Michael's behaviour, but fails to make the connection with possible abuse. Other signals – short concentration span, restlessness, over-anxiety to please – might have signalled the possibility of abuse, and the fact that the parents were not protecting him. Above all, the acknowledgement that the parents could not meet all Michael's needs, and that he required the attention, stimulation and challenge of outside activities, was important, but not sufficiently acted upon when Michael was younger, or developed at this stage of the social worker's contact with him. The example shows that it is difficult to recognize all the signs of abuse, even when a social worker is in regular contact with a child (as in this case), and that only sensitive and imaginative supervision is likely to lead to the awareness of the need to protect a child, where the social services department and the child her/himself have much invested in the security of a family placement, and the stability of a set of relationships sustaining several vulnerable children.

RAISING THE QUALITY OF CARE

The second goal of the Third Way programme of modernization is to raise the standard of care given to the 55,000 children in England looked after by local authorities at any one time – a total of 88,000 in any year (para. 3.24). Here some of the changes in practice promised are similar to those for child protection (improvement in the poor assessments leading to frequent changes of placement, lack of clear eligibility criteria, especially for children with disabilities, lack of a range of residential and fostering options); others are rather different, and relate to the *culture* of social services departments. These include treating adoption as a last resort, and the overall quality of decision making and management (para. 3.24).

The first part of the programme is again largely concerned with systems of regulation and enforcement. The Quality Protects initiative is a three-year plan to spend £375 million from the Social Services Modernization Fund, in response to satisfactory action plans by local authorities (paras 3.25–3.27). Such plans should demonstrate the improvements listed above, as well as 'dissemination of research relevant to the management of children's services' (an echo of evidence-based services), and identifying centres of good practice to act as beacons for spreading excellence in children's services (para. 3.28) – see also Box 11, p. 69.

The attempts at cultural change are more original. In particular, adoption is presented as a positive option, based on research evidence of good outcomes. The aim is to 'break down prejudices against the principle of adoption' and 'challenge rigid attitudes in the transracial placement of children for adoption if they are carried to the point of withholding the potential benefit of an adoption from a child simply because it cannot be matched with parents from the same ethnic group' (para. 3.29, box).

This latter point is especially contentious. The movement among social workers for placement of children from minority ethnic groups with adoptive parents from the same group arose in the USA, and spread to the UK during the early Thatcher years, when large numbers of black children were being taken away from their parents under court orders, and placed with white adoptive parents. The context for these practices, not mentioned in the White Paper, was that black parents were facing severe economic and social disadvantage at the time, and there was a shortage of children for adoption by white couples. The positive findings of research on transracial placements (Gill and Jackson, 1983) specifically did not attempt to assess issues of black identity and long-term adjustment, focusing instead on educational and occupational achievement, and short-term acceptance of adoptive status. Although black people have made great strides towards prosperity and upward mobility, and their cultural contribution to British society is now more widely recognized, it is far from clear that this signals a stage when 'race' and racism are no longer relevant to the issues of policy and practice in adoption (Ryburn, 1994).

It should not be forgotten that in the case example, Michael Brown was an adopted child. Furthermore, his experiences of the quality of care received by those taken away from their parents were very mixed.

CASE EXAMPLE: MICHAEL BROWN (CONTINUED)

During his teenage years, Michael was constantly involved with social services through complaints made by his adoptive parents about his behaviour at home, incidents at his secondary school, petty thefts and running away. All these were recognized as 'cries for help', and Michael complained about the lack of warmth in his relationship with the parents, the father's punishment of him, and their unfairness towards him (in comparison with their own children). Michael was taken away from home under court orders on three occasions, and spent time in an assessment centre twice. Finally, he was sent to a community home with education on the premises, where he remained for two years. Even though several reports recognized that it was inappropriate for Michael to be sent home after this, and he had no desire to go back to his adoptive family, he was in fact discharged to the parents' care at the age of 16.

Michael's educational achievements in this period were impressive; he was sent to an ordinary secondary school from the home, and made good progress in a number of subjects. He also made a promising start in work, where he demonstrated alertness and initiative. However, Michael's relationship with staff members was sometimes conflict-laden. One female staff member hit him with a horsewhip, and later briefly throttled him after he had called at her home when she was at work.

Discussion

Michael's case illustrates the problems of pinning down and implementing the notion of 'quality of care'. The fundamental flaw in all plans for Michael, and the way he was supervised, assessed and placed, was that none of those involved asked themselves more fundamental questions about the origins of his attention-seeking behaviour and 'cries for help'. The whole story is one of occasionally kindly, sometimes irritated and frustrated reactions to his wayward and provocative behaviour. Issues of Michael's identity, his early experiences, his natural parents (especially his mother), and his brother (who was placed with another family), were never touched upon. Although the situation in his adoptive family home was seen as far from perfect, its specific deficiencies for Michael's needs were never addressed.

His experiences of the community home were mixed. On the one hand, he respected the head, who recognized his intellectual potential and supported him in his early experiences of work and independence. On the other, he had problems with some members of staff, and particularly the woman who assaulted him twice. He complained about the second incident, but this remained unresolved. Above all, Michael's emerging identity as a young gay man was not recognized or supported, and the decision by his social worker to send him back to his adoptive home, out of apparent lack of imagination over alternatives, nullified much of the progress he had made in the home.

IMPROVED LIFE CHANCES

The White Paper criticizes the outcomes for children who have been cared for by local authorities. Access to health services is problematic in many cases; around 30 per cent have special educational needs (cf. 2–3 per cent of the general population with such needs); in some authorities as few as 25 per cent leave care with any educational qualifications; one in four aged 14–16 either do not attend school regularly or have been excluded from school; 67 per cent have identifiable mental health problems. Between 14 and 25 per cent of young women leaving care are pregnant or have a child; up to a third of young people sleeping rough have been looked after by a local authority; and 39 per cent of male and 22 per cent of female prisoners under 21 have been looked after at some point in their childhood.

It is good that the government acknowledges and faces up to these issues, and wants to improve educational and health services for these children, to extend parental responsibilities of local authorities to 18 years, and make more efforts to help these young people achieve independence on leaving care. However, these problems have been identified and publicized for at least fifteen years (through government-commissioned research). There is little evidence of new thinking about how to tackle them in the White Paper. Instead, as in so much else in the government's relationship with local authority social services and the social work profession, it focuses on compliance with its guidance, and on enforcing standards set by the centre. This is not a new approach, and even if it is more rigorously followed it is unlikely to make much impact on the situation of young people leaving care.

The fact of the matter is that the UK is a country in which young people have very unequal life chances. Mainstream middle-class and skilled working-class parents devote considerable resources and energies to giving their children advantages in competition with others (Jordan et al., 1994, Chapter 5). Furthermore, schools with devolved budgets are increasingly competing with each other to achieve high grades in exam results, and follow overt or covert strategies to attract high-achievement, low-cost pupils, and repel or exclude high-cost low achievers (Jordan, 1996a, Chapter 5). Both parents and schools are involved in strategic 'games' to maximize their returns on educational inputs, and this works to the disadvantage of those least able to compete; the Prime Minister and Harriet Harman provide clear examples of these processes at work in their choice of schools for their children. Something similar occurs in relation to health care facilities, now that budgets have been devolved for these services also.

By definition, children in the care of local authorities are those with least parental support; they often have the most psychological, behavioural and emotional problems. Local authority staff cannot use the same strategies (such as moving to a more favoured area) that better-off parents employ, nor can they drive children miles each day to find better facilities; nor would such places be likely to accept their children. The fact is that, in a very unequal society like the UK, the children of the least advantaged are likely to have their disadvantages reinforced in schooling and health care.

All this implies that the success or failure of policies to improve the life chances of children in care depends more on the fate of New Labour's broad programme for social security, employment, social inclusion, housing and health than on the specifics of how these measures are implemented, regulated and enforced. This is, of course, a truism in any society; in so far as those who receive personal social services are always the most disadvantaged, their welfare will be more influenced by their relative position *vis-à-vis* those on higher incomes, and more equality of resources will improve their life chances. New Labour has recognized this in its promise to abolish child poverty in a generation (Darling, 1999), and some of its programme is already having an effect, albeit a limited one (Grice, 1999).

However, there are other respects in which the modernization and management programme for local authority services outlined in the White Paper is a missed opportunity. Its lack of any originality of vision betrays its limited conception of the role of personal social services, and the potential of social work. It neither clarifies the role of local authority care and accommodation in policy for supporting the families of children in need; nor locates a strategy for such support within the wider context of its conception of 'community', or the place of children in it; nor reveals a notion of social work *practice* that is sensitive or subtle enough to sustain either of these.

In the 1990s, it was recognized that there is a fundamental tension between the tasks of child protection and family support (Parton et al., 1997). The Children Act 1989 attempted to shift the balance away from court decisions about care towards voluntary agreements, partnership with parents and shared responsibility; and away from care as an expression of the power of professionals and officials, towards accommodation as a supportive service for families and children in need (Packman and Hall, 1997). It also tried to promote a more flexible range of supports (day, after-school and holiday care, childminding, and so on) to allow children to continue living at home under stressful conditions. However, research shows that the effects of those measures are strongly counteracted by the consequences of social polarization. In an unequal and divided society, with an excluded 'underclass' (Auletta, 1980), the child protection system becomes a repository for allegations of abuse from mainstream citizens against minorities – lone parents, minority ethnic groups, poor people and people who behave in unorthodox ways generally (Thorpe, 1997). Hence the number of *investigations* of such allegations rises over time, even though the level of cases judged to merit removal of children from their parents, or identified as constituting 'abuse', may stay exactly the same (ibid.).

British researchers have found similar outcomes to those reported by Thorpe in Australia; the proportion of allegations that lead to court orders is about 4 per cent, and those resulting in any kind of service being given almost 20 per cent (Gibbons et al., 1995). But the high and rising number of contacts with child protection services by mainstream citizens means that a large proportion of professional social work resources is used up in investigations (Parton et al., 1997). The conundrum for child care policy in the 1990s has been how to shift resources towards family support, and out of these investigative interventions. The White Paper has nothing to say on this whole topic, which is central to the quality of services to children in need.

More fundamentally, the question for child care policy since the 1960s has been the role of the local authority's facilities for looking after children (fostering, residential care, training and education) in the wider context of services for families. If too much emphasis is placed on family support, with care defined as *failure* and a last resort, then this is reflected in stigma for parents and low quality of provision in accommodation for children. If too much emphasis is given to compulsory protection and substitute care, then parents feel unsupported, and may feel able to get help only by rejecting or hurting their children (Jordan, 1979, 1983). They may even believe it is in their children's best interests to be in care, especially if they are depressed or in extreme poverty. Policy must therefore seek a balance between these polarities, that supports but offers respite, relief and rescue as alternatives to parental care – as the Children Act 1989 attempts to do (Packman and Hall, 1997; Packman and Jordan, 1991).

The Third Way should, on the face of it, have something valuable to offer in all this. Its concept of *community* seems potentially important in striking this balance (Jordan, 1990, Chapter 5). After all, children are the future members of society, and all share the responsibility for their education, socialization and well-being. If a community cannot express its concern for its future members, and try to teach them how to contribute to its quality of life, then it is probably not sustainable in the long term.

So it is surprising that, for all the rhetoric about responsible community in so many of New Labour's pronouncements (see Chapter 2), there is little or nothing in the White Paper on this topic. Above all, there is nothing to show how statutory services for children and families relate to the bigger picture of *children as citizens*, except for the usual clichés about better co-ordination of education, health, and social services. This seems to be partly because, in relation to children in need, the Third Way cannot see beyond an attempt to hold parents responsible for their upbringing, and to enforce this responsibility through a rather unimaginative, oppressive, Benthamite kind of approach. There is nothing to indicate what the Third Way has to offer beyond propping up the creaky structure of family life; the social work experienced by Michael Brown in the case example might serve as a metaphor or microcosm for its model of social policy in this domain. New Labour would be more interested in the kind of community that would control Michael's delinquency through strong traditional ties of social discipline than in the kind of supportive network that might have prevented him from being abused, or helped him once he had been abused.

Above all, the White Paper seems to accept that local authority social services will focus on *changing parenting behaviour* rather than making communities more child-friendly (NSPCC, 1999) or giving children better access to enabling adults and older children. Historians have emphasized that the notion of childhood as a period of protected development within the confines of a nuclear family is peculiar to European (and especially the North European) culture, and to the modern view of society and the family (Pinchbeck and Hewitt, 1973; Aries, 1983). In earlier societies, and in non-European cultures, children played an active role in all social interactions, and in economic life. Sociologists now take seriously the idea that this afforded them better opportunities for development, better status as members of society, and better protection against abuse. If it is part of the rights of adults to be included as full members in the active life of productive co-operation and collective decision-making, it seems unlikely that the status and significance of children will be enhanced by excluding them from these spheres. Leading children's charities now emphasize that children should be consulted and involved, in social work decisions about them, through Schools

Councils, and perhaps even through a Youth Parliament (NSPCC, 1999). New Labour should be looking at policies for involving children in the community *as members*, rather than always protecting them from specific predators, inadequate parents or hostile neighbours, or protecting property and persons from them.

Instead of focusing on investigating allegations of abuse, a more positive and proactive approach would be to improve access to adults who would raise the quality of their lives by introducing them to a range of alternative perspectives, experiences, stimulations and possibilities, as well as allowing family and school life to become less claustrophobic, pressurised and stressful. Although this approach was considered in Michael Brown's case, it was not systematically pursued. It is well recognized from research on sexual abuse – the most difficult and taboo kind of abuse, of which only around a third is reported (NSPCC, 1999) – that the best protection is afforded by a wide circle of aware adults (Pringle et al., 1997; Pringle, 1998). But there is a wider point: if abuse is to be minimized, and the quality of children's lives improved, then children must be aware of wider possibilities and different standards, and they must know as much as possible about society, and not be confined to their particular family and school. This applies especially to children from families that are poor and excluded, or have special problems, or from stigmatized minority groups.

If one reads autobiographical accounts of how disadvantaged children have escaped the constraints of their families and neighbourhoods, what stands out is the role of inspiring adults from outside the family, who have stimulated, nurtured and supported higher aspirations. Another factor is mobility – such as during wartime evacuation and fostering – that gave children access to a wider range of interactions with adults and other children, and hence greater confidence and social skills. This implies a far more positive, proactive approach to fostering and the recruitment of foster parents, not as substitute family carers, but as providers of lively and outward-looking environments and new experiences.

Conclusions

This chapter has reviewed the main thrust and substance of the Third Way's programme for modernization and management of the personal social services, as set out in the 1998 White Paper. We have argued that, in the case of services for adults it fails to do justice to the complexity of the tasks and the conflicts of interest they involve; and in the case of children and families it reflects a blinkered vision of the role of children in communities, and hence a missed opportunity.

Above all, New Labour's crude view of social identities, interactions and cultures, and its mechanistic, Benthamite approach to policy implementation, limit its scope for designing an innovative programme for the personal social services. But the White Paper also reflects fundamental mistrust of local authorities' capabilities as instruments of Third Way policies, and ambivalence about the future of local authority social services; and it reflects doubts about the value of social work as a professional arm of social policy, and about the training and supervision of social workers as autonomous professional practitioners, exercising independent judgement based on knowledge and experience.

There have been some very positive elements in the government's programme. For instance, Sure Start, an interagency initiative to help very young children and their parents in the most deprived districts, will spend £450 million over three years to build on existing provision in health, education, social services and the voluntary sector (DoH, 1998a), and there have been excellent projects under the Quality Protects initiative (DoH, 1998d). These demonstrate the progressive potential of the Third Way.

In the next chapter we will turn to some of New Labour's ideas about social exclusion, incapacity, disability and vulnerability, and the contradictions between its policies on participation, inclusion and empowerment and the detailed implementation of its policy programme. In Chapter 6 we will return to the White Paper, and examine how its visions about regulating professional practice in social care relate to the real-world situation in personal social services.

5

Capacities and Empowerment:
The Contradictions of the Third Way
over Exclusions and Disabilities

In this chapter we will look at how New Labour's rhetoric on social inclusion, enhancing the capacities of sick and disabled people and empowering the excluded, are implemented. There is a fundamental contradiction at the heart of the Third Way on these topics; the targeting of benefits on those in 'genuine need' requires them to demonstrate *in*capacity and *dis*ability, so they must pass tests that rule them out of most of New Labour's programmes for inclusion, which are based on formal employment. Hence the values of participation and empowerment are greatly fettered by the mechanics of welfare-to-work policies.

However, this is not the whole of the story. People with disabilities are particularly active in organizations in pursuit of their collective interests and purposes, and the effectiveness of their lobbying was part of the reason why the Labour Party rebellion against the Welfare Reform Bill focused on these issues. Activism of these kinds is empowering, and defends the interests of these citizens. Paradoxically, the rhetorical goals of the Third Way are often achieved more by those who oppose its measures than by those who comply with them.

Furthermore, aspects of policy and practice in local authority social services departments favour the inclusion and empowerment of these groups. In the 1980s, against the trend of policy towards reliance on formal power (court orders) and arm's-length methods (reports and contracts), social work with people with learning disabilities, long-term mental illnesses and physical handicaps moved in the direction of 'normalization' – treating service users as citizens, whose primary need was for access to the enabling facilities and resources by which all citizens sustain their lives as members of the community. Such ideas – coming initially from the USA – promoted a style of social work that was more informal and supportive, and that focused on service users' capacities and potential rather than their disabilities. Indeed, it was these principles that largely inspired the positive part of the Third Way's programme for inclusion and empowerment of these groups of citizens; the language employed by New Labour is largely that of this movement.

In the 1990s, those ideas are still strong in social work practice (as principles and values guiding the spirit of day-to-day work), but they are always in tension with the momentum of actual policy and management of services for adults. The programme of closing large institutions for people with learning disabilities and mental illnesses, which got under way in the 1980s, had built into it many boundary problems and administrative difficulties, as well as a massive budgetary challenge – how to relocate a large population of often long-term residents of huge and remote institutions into reluctant and resistant local communities, and how to shift responsibility for their care from one large service with strong central government constraints on its budgets (the NHS) on to another smaller one with even stronger constraints on it (the local authorities). In this process, many of the high ideals of the movement that inspired the policies were compromised or lost.

After 1990, an additional pressure came from the new management, financial and administrative structures of the NHS and Community Care Act, and the strong injunctions the Act contained to use the commercial voluntary sectors for provision of social care. This in turn redirected the thrust of the programme from normalization and inclusion towards giving priority to sheer numbers placed, and minimizing the per capita costs of these placements, putting service users at risk of being reinstitutionalized in small commercial homes, where they were as isolated from the normal facilities and opportunities of citizenship as they had been in large NHS hospitals.

In this chapter, we will start by analysing the concepts of exclusion and inclusion, and how these are applied to people with incapacities and disabilities, in the Third Way's policy documents. We will see how New Labour's thinking on this subject is incomplete, because it does not sufficiently address issues of how inequalities of income and wealth influence exclusions, and how the actions of mainstream citizens who cluster around the best health and welfare facilities exclude those without the resources to follow such strategies.

We will then turn to a more detailed critical examination of the Third Way's plans for including and empowering people with incapacities and disabilities. Although there are many positive and valuable ideas in these programmes, they all stumble on one or both of the problems we have identified – the requirement either to demonstrate total incapacity to take formal work or to engage in labour-market activities, however unfulfilling; and the exclusions associated with low income. Yet the empowerment gained by participation in movements for people with incapacities and disabilities can in part compensate for these policy deficiencies, and may eventually lead in a new direction from the Third Way. In the final section of the chapter, we will begin to analyse how social work can contribute to and support such movements.

Social Exclusion

The notion of social exclusion comes from the Continental European, and especially the French, schools of social theory (Paugam, 1998). It is the part of Third Way thinking that owes most to Europe, rather than the United States. In Continental theory society is seen as a hierarchy of collectivities, bound together by mutual rights and obligations. This social order implies that at every level any individual is included as a member of such a collectivity (for instance, a trade union), which has reciprocal relations with other organized interests, such as employers and the state. This tradition most strongly emphasizes the common interest of all members of society in order and harmony, which finds its expression in corporatist institutions, through which top representatives of capital, labour and the state reach agreements which are then benevolently imposed on their members, for the sake of the common good. This approach to economic management and social distribution sustained the long success of Germany, Austria and the Scandinavian countries during the period from the Second World War until the 1980s (Cawson, 1982), but it has now largely fallen into disrepair.

New Labour has no desire to revive corporatism of this kind, but it does claim to represent the *whole* nation, and appeals to all sections of the community to make a common effort for the sake of 'national renewal'. This is brought into the programme for welfare reform in Tony Blair's plea for a 'new social contract': 'Reform is a vital part of rediscovering a true national purpose' (Blair, 1998b, p. iii). Social inclusion contributes to the rationale for this redirection of national energies, because it aims at healing the wasteful and harmful divisions and conflicts of the Thatcher–Major years. According to the Continental theory of social exclusion, it occurs when members become detached from the systems of mutuality and reciprocity that constitute the social order, and hence lose their bonds with the rest of society. Since the Continental corporatist version of the welfare state was based on employment (through which men became part of the public order of social relations) and the family (incorporating women and children), this fits well with the Third Way's vision of increasing labour-market participation and strengthening the family unit.

However, this analysis provides no explanation of how collectivities change, grow or shrink, how they coalesce, regroup and interact; or how individuals leave one collectivity and join another, or how they come to be active or passive members within them. It tends to assume an enduring hierarchy of organized interests, giving rise to stable institutions and relationships, out of which individuals may fall (for instance, as a result of unemployment, homelessness, long-term illness or alcoholism), and into which they should be reinstated. It fails to capture the fluidity and evanescence of many present-day social phenomena, or the processes of decomposition, fragmentation and reconstitution that have overtaken the larger structures of societies – especially UK society – in recent years. It tends to see European history as a story of progressive *collectivization* (Swaan, 1988), whereas the recent trend has been towards the break-up of large collectivities, and especially those constituting welfare states, into smaller mutualities, based on narrower perceptions of shared interests (Jordan, 1996a; Breuer et al., 1996).

In the individualist tradition of American and British thought, and especially among economists and the school of social theorists who take their inspiration from rational-choice and public-choice theory, the fundamental questions are about why individuals should act together in collectivities at all. In a market economy and a competitive political environment, there are always incentives to leave the hard work of organizing and maintaining the solidarity of groups to others (the free rider problem), to resort to competition rather than co-operation (the temptations of opportunism), and to exploit shared resources rather than conserving them (the tragedy of the commons). Collective action *can* overcome these problems, but only by enforcing the rules of mutuality and membership and excluding those who cannot or will not contribute, or who break the rules of solidarity, conservation and co-operation (Olson, 1965, 1982; Taylor, 1987; Ostrom, 1990).

Hence exclusion is part of the rule of collective action, and not the exception. Like inclusion, it is an inevitable consequence of the dynamic between rules of membership that restrain competition and conflict between members for the sake of mutual advantages, and mobilization of members for competition with other groups (Jordan, 1996a, Chapter 2). Except in large campaigning organizations, the general rule is that the benefits of collective action must be conserved by restricting membership and enforcing co-operation with rules (as in cartels or trade unions), otherwise these advantages are simply competed away or – if no one makes their contribution to common efforts and funds – there are no benefits to distribute. Exclusion is not an unfortunate consequence of unusual circumstances; it is of the essence of collective action of all kinds, from families, through associations, firms and communities to nation states. Benefits stem from *exclusive* co-operation; collectivities mobilize members for competition with other groups.

During the postwar period, in all advanced capitalist societies, collective institutions for organizing employers and workers were able to reach agreements about the restraint of competition and the rules of co-operation between them needed to achieve rapid growth of national incomes, and to distribute the benefits of this growth to all members of each nation state – even those unable to contribute to the formal economy (Scharpf, 1999). Increased mobility of capital between states, the growth of trade and the gradual weakening of these restraints and rules have forced governments to allow more and more unrestrained competition both between and within economies, further eroding these systems, and especially their capacities to raise revenue for redistribution (Jordan, 1996a, 1998a).

These changes made it possible for individuals to seek advantage by combining in smaller collectivities, by leaving state schemes in favour of private ones, or by pursuing strategies for getting the best out of public systems. In the UK, this was partly the intention of Margaret Thatcher's policies – to encourage better-off citizens to leave the NHS and the state educational systems in favour of private provision, to join occupational or commercial welfare schemes, to form new mutual societies and associations (Green, 1993), and to move to better-favoured residential districts. But this in turn led to greater awareness in mainstream society of possible strategies for gaining competitive advantage over fellow citizens, in just the ways that postwar welfare states tried to block. Either by moving house, or by driving considerable distances each day, mainstream parents clustered around the schools with the best examination results, which found new ways (such as opting out of local authority control) of attracting such pupils. As budgetary devolution gave medical practices and hospitals more scope for strategic action, to attract patients giving better cost–benefit returns, this afforded opportunities for mainstream citizens to get the best from health services. It was as much by these actions by advantaged citizens as by the policies of the Thatcher and Major governments that the poor were excluded from decent schooling and health care, and their residential districts became concentrations of social disadvantage of all kinds (Jordan et al., 1994).

The point of all this is to show that social exclusion does not simply stem from global economic change and neo-liberal politics. Poor people, and especially those with incapacities and disabilities, cannot afford to move in search of competitive advantages, or to pay the contributions that would give them the best facilities. Their carers are similarly barred from strategic mobility of this kind, because their caring obligations tie them to a specific location. As a result of new forms of collective and strategic action, a process of social polarization occurs (Jordan and Redley, 1994) and concentrations of disadvantaged people get the worst housing, health and educational facilities. But they do not remain passive: they take whatever opportunities for collective action present themselves. We have already analysed the resistance practices of able-bodied poor people, who have used cash-in-hand undeclared work, dealing, petty crime, and other informal economic activities to compensate themselves for the disadvantages stemming from their exclusion from mainstream economic and social life (see pp. 31–3). Such strategies have not often been open to people with incapacities and disabilities, so they are more likely to be involved in other forms of collective action.

The Third Way has a whole battery of policies to combat social exclusion. In this chapter we will focus on those that aim to include people with multiple social problems, incapacities and disabilities, to show that New Labour's blind spot over the strong association between income inequality and exclusion greatly weakens what are otherwise valuable and relevant policies. Because the Third Way focuses always on such people's ability or inability to contribute through formal employment, and on addressing what it sees as barriers to this contribution, it is tied to an approach that can realize only a part of the potential of these groups of citizens. It also forces voluntary organizations and community groups for and of these citizens into certain kinds of 'partnerships' with government agencies (including local authorities) that distort their purposes, or limit their empowering potential.

These limitations affect the process of 'inclusion' in two main ways. On the one hand, the 'choices' exercised by people with serious multiple problems, with incapacities or disabilities, are extremely constrained, and are shaped by the government's perceptions of their needs, their degree of dangerousness or risk, and their potential contributions. Its programmes require them to comply with these perceptions, or drop further into poverty and marginality. Voluntary organizations and community groups in turn are offered 'partnerships' that are aimed at fulfilling the goals of the various programmes, zones and initiatives and give them little room for manoeuvre in their attempts to involve their members in democratic participation, in setting their own collective goals and objectives, and in mobilizing them for action in their own interests. Even the forms of resistance to New Labour programmes that they can adopt are – in this sense – framed in terms of the budgets, rules and priorities of such programmes, zones and initiatives.

To illustrate these difficulties, we have chosen the example of homelessness. This is the target of several Third Way programmes. The Social Exclusion Unit's report, *Rough Sleeping* (Social Exclusion Unit, 1998), identifies drugs, alcohol and mental illness as factors in this social phenomenon, along with inability to get health care, leading to mortality rates twenty-five times higher than the national average. The report outlines a strategy for cutting the numbers of people sleeping rough by two-thirds by 2002, including better co-ordination and planning services. Meanwhile, the New Deal for Communities also addresses homelessness, but within a broader context of helping deprived communities to improve their economic and employment prospects and gain control over problems of order and social discipline (DETR, 1999). Finally, the government is promoting supported housing schemes and issuing guidance to social services departments, housing authorities and other housing providers, including voluntary agencies, on how to provide for the needs of vulnerable people (such as young people leaving care), as well as a revised Housing Allocation and Homelessness Code of Guidance from the DETR (DoH, 1998a, para. 6.22).

The general thrust of all these programmes is to require homeless people to form an orderly queue for accommodation, regulated by officials who direct them to appropriate housing, based on professional assessment of need. The Third Way is first and foremost preoccupied with clearing the streets of menacing, dirty, sick or homeless people, beggars and drinkers. New Labour's policies for being 'tough on crime and tough on the causes of crime' gives precedence to reducing offending and the fear of criminality over any concern for improving the prospects for homeless people. An array of punitive measures, from police raids on projects working with homeless people to suspension of the benefits of non-compliant claimants, have been developed to herd them into rehabilitation programmes, job clubs, and training schemes offering no immediate prospects of employment. New Labour places an additional premium on payment to private sector employment agencies, operating under New Deal and Employment Zone rules and contracts, for placing long-term unemployed people in work, on pain of loss of benefit for the claimant and loss of profit for the agency. It remains to be seen how far these measures genuinely help homeless people to secure a job of their choice (rather than simply bullying them into one which leaves them worse off), and how far it drives them off the unemployment statistics and further into informal survival strategies and criminality.

The following case study of an alternative approach to meeting the needs of homeless people illustrates some of the paradoxes of voluntary agencies attempting to operationalize concepts like 'empowerment', 'activation', 'inclusion' and 'community' against a background of the Third Way's programmes and initiatives.

CASE STUDY: THE BRIGHTON AND HOVE EMMAUS COMMUNITY

The Emmaus communities in the UK were inspired by the longstanding movement in France, founded by a Catholic priest, Abbé Pierre. A wartime Resistance hero, and now an octogenarian, he started the movement in war-torn Paris in the 1940s, where the destitute and marginalized, victims of a fractured society, abounded. Using principles derived as much from the French Resistance as the Church, this charismatic leader based his thinking about the communities on ideas of self-help and mutual aid; they were highly democratic in structure and had an anarchic tendency to challenge authority and bureaucracy. This was evident from the way that the movement appropriated land and property, completely disregarding bureaucratic rules; it was able to do this with impunity because of Abbé Pierre's Resistance record and his skilful manipulation of the media. In its early days, the movement lent its weight to squatter encampments under motorway overpasses which were accepted as Emmaus communities. At that time, no politician or bureaucrat would dare to challenge the authority of Abbé Pierre for fear of the adverse media attention they would attract.

The fundamental principles of the movement are rooted in Christian belief and are the same in all Emmaus communities world-wide. They are most simply expressed in the statement: 'All are expected to work for the benefit of those in greater need than themselves.' This variant of 'from each according to his or her abilities, to each according to his or her needs' owes as much to the Continental concept of solidarity as it does to Christian values. Its main expression is through projects which make the Community economically self-sufficient, such as recycling; the Brighton and Hove Emmaus Community has a very successful recycling unit for furniture and household effects. However, the Abbé Pierre himself retains a more radical interpretation of the principle as applying to all in need, including those outside the Community itself. The Companions (residents) were alarmed to hear him proclaim on a recent visit, 'Whenever I visit a comfortable new Community like this one, I want to smash the glass in the windows, so that we can hear the cries from outside.'

In France the movement has a fiercely independent attitude to the state, turning down all state benefits on the basis that to accept the state's money might allow it to interfere in the running of communities. The movement tends to argue that 'the state did nothing for us when were down and out; therefore we owe it nothing and seek nothing from it'. This attitude is not quite the same in the UK, where communities formally charge Companions rent, and they in turn claim housing benefit. This pragmatic measure is justified by UK communities on the grounds that it enables them to establish themselves more quickly, helping them to reach the point of supporting the formation of other communities at an earlier stage. Emmaus France frowns on this argument, maintaining that it is the thin end of the wedge. They have some reason to disapprove, given that increased delays and conflicts with local authorities over housing benefit have driven communities to become more complicit with the benefit authority in harassing Companions for information related to disputed claims. The Brighton and Hove Community also receives some funding towards the costs of employing a Leader from the DETR for the 'resettlement of homeless people', and has received capital funding from the government under the Single Regeneration Budget.

However, in almost every way, the Emmaus Community's terms of membership are diametrically opposed to those envisaged by the Third Way for organizations providing accommodation for homeless people. All Emmaus communities have a policy of accepting anyone who arrives at the door wishing to live there, subject to availability of a free room. There is no needs assessment to select the most deserving or needy, nor is there a requirement for the Companion to reveal any part of the personal history which led them to the Community's door. Provided that he or she accepts the basic rules and is prepared to work, each is welcomed unconditionally on a first-come-first-served basis. (In France,

Companions are not even required to reveal their identities but in the UK this is necessary, because of claims for housing benefit, though there are contingency arrangements for the admission of those without proper immigration status, who can stay rent-free.)

This goes against the overwhelming direction of this form of social housing provision by voluntary agencies under contract to the state. In general, homeless people are also unemployed and therefore do not have the security of income to afford to choose accommodation in the private rented sector. Social housing for homeless people is a scarce resource, which is financed by a mix of public sector and private money. As a condition of funding, the state generally requires the social landlord to set further conditions on the allocation of such accommodation, which prioritize need rather than choice. Homeless people are subjected to a rigorous assessment of their individual circumstances and, after further investigation of their resources, offered such accommodation as the assessor considers suitable. The homeless person will be expected to reveal all manner of intimate personal details to the state's intermediary, generally some form of social worker. The more desperate the applicant's circumstances, the more likely he or she is to score points based on need. The more compliant he or she is, the more likely to score points based on the probability of a successful outcome. The more intractable the problems, the fewer points awarded.

Many homeless people are unwilling to subject themselves to this process. Others who have tried it have failed to secure an offer they considered acceptable. Since the state holds a monopoly of access to such social housing, there is no way to circumvent the process. Emmaus offers an alternative way of addressing homeless people's needs, based on the principle of voluntarism. Although the rules of the Community are restrictive, work is compulsory, and decisions to exclude can be summary; people enter by choice, can leave when they choose, and can return again without explanation (even if excluded, after a set period of time). Although the choice that homeless people exercise in opting to be housed in such accommodation is of quite a different order from that exercised by an autonomous individual choosing accommodation in the marketplace, it nevertheless increases the options available to them, and allows them to use the facility on their own terms, according to their own interpretation of their situation and needs.

The Emmaus Community as a response to multiple social problems is analysed further on pp. 131–2.

Discussion

This example shows how concepts such as 'inclusion', 'exclusion', 'participation', 'community' and 'empowerment' are open to very different interpretations and implementations in practice. According to the Third Way, homeless people are socially excluded by virtue of their lack of formal employment, a settled lifestyle and family relationships. The route to inclusion lies through assessment for social housing, resocialization and retraining for work. The homeless person must comply with official definitions of his or her needs, and be compulsorily 'reintegrated' into a 'community' of these professionals' choice.

For Emmaus, no inclusion is possible without a positive act of will by the Companion (the request to enter the Community as a member) and the active welcome of that Community, accepting him or her into full, democratic, participatory membership. Work for the community in the informal economy is a condition of membership: this is not seen as fulfilling an obligation to the state or the taxpayer (as in the Third Way), but as the expression of active membership and commitment to that (micro) Community.

At one level, an Emmaus community in the UK could be seen as a privatized form of indoor poor relief – a workhouse, operated according to strict rules, with informal systems of surveillance amounting almost to a blood-and-guts Panopticon. It offers accommodation to destitute people in an institutional setting. Their basic requirements for subsistence – food, shelter, clothing and a very modest weekly allowance – are met in exchange for work, which is obligatory. Companions (inmates) have no employment or housing rights – they can be ejected at the drop of a hat (or more often a can of lager). Their 'earnings' from the institution are specifically excluded from the provisions of the legislation on the minimum wage. Governance is vested in a Board of Trustees, drawn from the professional and property-owning classes, who hold the property and control the finances. Their policies are mediated through the Community Leader – a trained social worker – who has autocratic powers to exclude on the spot, without appeal. Companions are not allowed to receive any income beyond the subsistence allowance they receive from the institution; they must relinquish any existing claim to a state benefit other than housing benefit; all pensions, private earnings or tips are expropriated by the institution. Individuals caught with additional income, whether or not legitimately earned or claimed outside, are deemed guilty of 'theft from the Community' and immediately sanctioned. Companions are expected to lead a sober, industrious and orderly lifestyle. Alcohol and unprescribed drugs are not allowed on the premises. Violence, threats, and nuisance to others are not tolerated.

It must be doubtful that many people would accept such a regime, were it not for considerable discomfort and unhappiness in their current existence, and strong revulsion against the official alternatives. In this sense, the Emmaus Community thrives because these other alternatives are so bleak, cheerless or hyper-authoritarian that its regime seems liberal by comparison. Once accepted, however, Companions do have a good deal of latitude in making what they choose of what is on offer – from very temporary respite to a permanent home (see below, pp. 131–2). In contrast to the prescriptive formula set down by the bureaucratic official services, Emmaus accepts the individual uncritically without enquiring about his or her needs or goals. Help is given when requested, not imposed in order to comply with some wider policy agenda about regulating society.

One key way in which Emmaus tries to reconcile institutional authority and individual autonomy is through face-to-face, participatory democracy. Although procedures and principles of collective decision-making vary between communities, all are committed to giving Companions a direct voice in the running of their enterprise, within the overall manifesto (constitution) of the movement. Whatever the precise methods of participation, it is the face-to-face nature of these processes which gives the Community meaning to the participants, who long since have ceased to see themselves as stakeholders in the political economy at large. The importance of this democratic principle will be further discussed in Chapter 8 (see pp. 179–82).

The point of this example is that inclusion is achieved (if at all) in Emmaus through a self-generated blood-and-guts code *within* the Community, and in explicit *rejection* of official attempts to include, integrate and enforce membership of civic society, through social housing provision and employment training. Unlike a state-run Panopticon, Emmaus can offer personal, emotional support through love, affection, care, toleration and understanding of individuals with many and varied needs, and this invites a response in like kind. But equally it can regulate members' behaviour through harsher attitudes and codes of conduct. Many people living in Emmaus communities learned about 'community' in other institutional settings, such as prison, the forces, mental hospitals and children's homes. Such institutions tend to generate their own 'counter-communities', where members regulate one another's behaviour, away from the official gaze of those in authority, through forms of bullying, baroning and blackmail (whose cruelty is often in direct proportion to the oppressiveness of the 'official regime'). Left entirely to its own devices, an Emmaus community is as open to such cultural forms as any other institution. The skill of the Community Leader's professional (social work) role is to know when and how to confront the Community collectively with the destructive crosscurrents of the blood-and-guts code, yet leaving it to determine the outcome.

The other positive aspect of democratic self-regulation relates to the economic activities of the Emmaus Community as a self-supporting enterprise. Participation derives a special meaning when it extends out of the politics of domestic life (as in most therapeutic communities) and into the economics of earning the Community's collective livelihood. Debates in Emmaus community meetings are not focused on washing-up rotas, pecking orders and rules on smoking at mealtimes. Important though these things may be, they assume a lesser significance when compared with the imperatives surrounding the successful organization of a communal business. The changing membership of the Community requires it to cope with a permanent revolution, reinventing its organizational processes to accommodate the different skills and preferences of people who happen to be working together at any given time. To achieve this places considerable normative pressure on Companions to participate in the decision-making process for the sake of the common good, accepting collective choices and contributing to shared purposes.

All this is in stark contrast with the implementation of official policies on social inclusion through economic participation, where getting claimants off the register and into paid work usually takes precedence over any sense of individual self-development, let alone the sense of belonging, influencing and contributing to a community whose collective quality of life is at stake. The relevance of economic activity to new forms of social work practice will be discussed more fully in Chapter 7, pp. 154–77.

Mental Health

Mental health might seem an obvious target for New Labour's policies on social inclusion, empowerment, improving capacities and realizing potential. Research has repeatedly revealed the skewing of statistics on mental illness towards subordinate and relatively powerless members of social units. Married women's high rates of mental illness of almost all kinds, of psychiatric treatment and hospitalization, point towards patriarchy and gender-related inequality of opportunity as factors in such problems (Brown and Harris, 1978; Goldberg and Huxley, 1980). High rates of compulsory treatment orders on young black men indicate the power-laden, differential perceptions of psychiatrists and other mental health professions in crises, especially those involving disturbances of public order (Mezey and Evans, 1971). Working-class people in general are more likely to be diagnosed as psychotic than are middle-class (Middleton and Shaw, 1999). For these, and many other reasons, people who have suffered mental health difficulties might be seen as a priority group for the enabling and capacitating aspects of the Third Way's programme.

In reality, the government has focused its reforming zeal on attempts to resolve the remaining administrative and professional problems of the previous government's reforms. Notoriously, mental health services were an instance of the gaps left when responsibilities were divided between the NHS and local authority social services departments. The Care Plan Approach of 1991 required the two agencies to collaborate in developing a co-ordinated framework for assessment, care plans, appointment of key workers and reviews. However, the complexities and costs of closing down old mental illness hospitals and arranging suitable placements for large numbers of long-stay former patients have defeated most of these aspirations. Often the large public institution was replaced by a small, commercial one, with fewer facilities or opportunities for individual autonomy and group interaction. Patients placed in mainstream or up-market districts encountered hostility and fear from local populations. Support services were limited, and day care sparse; above all, there was a lack of imaginative, creative provision and stimulating therapeutic or care environments. A series of reports by the Audit Commission (1994), the Mental Health Foundation (1996), a House of Commons Select Committee (1994) and other bodies criticized all these aspects of arrangements, identifying lack of co-operation between health and social services as a major problem.

At the same time, another set of issues was identified concerning threats to public safety. The closing of hospitals gave a minority of patients more autonomy and scope for non-compliance with professionals plans and prescriptions. Under community placements it proved more difficult to monitor medication and maintain surveillance over behaviour (Shaw, 2000). Issues of dangerousness began to surface in the media, surrounding such high-profile cases as the murder of Jonathan Zito on the London Underground, and the death of Ben Silcock, who climbed into the lions' den at London Zoo. Although there was no hard evidence of an increase in homicide by people with mental illnesses, the higher visibility of inner-city concentrations of homeless ex-patients led to calls for new measures to contain such threats.

The New Labour government has continued in the direction set at the end of the Major regime. Instead of focusing on the lack of support and stimulation leading people discharged from hospitals to drift away from placements and treatment, it has been concerned with the medical management of dangerous patients. Frank Dobson announced that 'Too many confused and sick people have been left wandering the streets and sleeping rough. A small but significant minority has become a danger to the public as well as themselves' (Dobson, 1998). The safety of the community was recognized as a justifiable priority in the review of mental health services announced in *Modernising Mental Health Services: Safe, Sound and Supportive* (Department of Health, 1998b). In July 1999 the provision of an extra 221 secure places in mental health services was announced (Department of Health, 1999b). The promised Green Paper, published in November 1999, confirmed that patients arousing concerns for public safety could be told where to live and given a care plan to comply with; if they failed to do so, they could be taken to a treatment centre and forcibly treated. While these measures reflect little other than a more determined approach to implementing the Mental Health (Patients in the Community) Act 1996, they indicate the importance of dangerousness management in the government's thinking.

The rest of the Green Paper reasserts the need for health services to go to the roots of mental illness, treat quickly and guarantee high standards of care. On the social services side, it restates the goals of promoting independence, improving protection and raising standards, along with new methods of regulation through Regional Commissions for Care Standards. Co-operation between health and social services is meant to improve risk management and provide an assertive outreach service, to make provision safer and more supportive.

The main thrust of New Labour's concerns in mental health policy is therefore towards the efficient provision of first-line medical assistance to people in distress, and discipline and surveillance of the minority who pose a threat to the public. This reflects a certain blindness to the very obvious social factors that skew mental illness statistics, and is a missed opportunity for more radical thinking. Amongst the broader population there is an increased awareness of emotional and psychological issues in personal development, of the significance of power in relationships, and of the need to balance productivity, consumption and achievement by measures supporting identity, meaning and consciousness. This is shown by the proliferation of counselling and counsellors in society, and the growth of various kinds of groups and associations promoting well-being and emotional security. The role of public policy in this field might be to try to link three different elements in social welfare – the state's medical and social services, the economic and social interactions which generate emotional and psychological suffering, and the informal and commercial resources for managing that suffering generated by civil society. The fact that treatment within the state's systems (from primary care to secure units) correlates highly with roles of subordination and relative powerlessness in the family, in the economy and in the community should be seen as a challenge. More advantaged citizens now recognize the need for help in dealing with everyday stress and intimate relationships, and the publicity surrounding Princess Diana's problems highlighted the fact that mental suffering is not confined to the underprivileged. Yet the broader *social* factors in such problems – gender and racial inequality, stress in the workplace, consumerism, lack of exercise and recreation – are seldom addressed as issues for public concern or collective action. Third Way policies do little to make these lost connections, or provide the missing links.

CASE STUDY: THE CLUBHOUSE MOVEMENT

The clubhouse model of psychiatric rehabilitation grew from Fountain House, established in Manhattan in 1948 by ex-patients from Rockland State Hospital. It provided both immediate refuge and help for residents to resume a normal life. Fifty years later there were 340 Fountain House clubhouses around the world, linked through the non-profit International Center for Clubhouse Development (ICCD), which provides training and certification.

The clubhouse model (Flannery and Glickman, 1996) is a voluntary therapeutic community made up both of people who have a serious mental illness and of employed staff. Residents are called members, and the regime is primarily a club with rights of membership, including choice over work activities and whether or how much work to do, choice of key worker, access to all records, lifelong re-entry rights and community support services. These are balanced by responsibilities, for undertaking essential tasks in the house and ensuring that clubhouse standards are sustained. Members can also work outside the clubhouse.

Originally set up in protest against neglect of ex-patients, the clubhouse movement has expanded in recent years partly because several US states fund clubhouses as part of managed care programmes, because it is supported by service users and families, and because it is a relatively low-cost model of care (Macias et al., 1999). However, most clubhouses maintain budgets separate from their public funding. Average membership is just over 100, comprising residents and others who go to the clubhouse for services. Activities focus on the running of the house and support for outside work to provide meaningful activities and a bridge to the wider world. Above all, staff work to the agendas set by members, whether in counselling or in work activities, and therefore serve the membership rather than vice versa. Real power is given to members; staff are not allowed to hold closed meetings, no clinical practice is allowed (members attend outside clinics, if at all), and voluntarism over entry and exit is the rule.

The movement adapted in the 1980s in line with the US government's new emphasis on employment, and took advantage of transitional employment programmes to advocate for fuller participation in the labour market by people with serious mental illnesses. The movement insisted that staff be properly trained in its principles, which emphasized peer support as a means of rehabilitation, genuine partnership between members and professional staff, and involvement of family. The movement campaigned for funding on the principles of empowering a large group of people with psychiatric disabilities by providing expanded employment opportunities, while meeting their personal, social and everyday needs through clubhouse membership (Dudek and Stein, 1999).

Discussion

This example has some similarities with, and many differences from, the Emmaus Community. Also founded on self-help principles, but less defiant of the state's services and methods of provision, it has adapted the basic therapeutic community model to emphasize the empowerment of people with serious mental illness, and the enhancement of their capacity to be autonomous and contribute to wider society. This involves a trade-off; since the US government shifted in the direction of policies to promote formal employment (anticipating the Third Way), the movement has stressed its ability to sustain members in work outside the clubhouse, in exchange for increased public funding and the support of main-stream mental health programmes. In this respect, it has accommodated itself to the main thrust of policy, both in the US and the UK.

Yet in another sense it does challenge the stereotype of people with serious mental illnesses. These conditions are usually regarded as giving citizens valid reasons not to take part in the formal economy or hold jobs. Equally, they give the state the excuse to put them away in various kinds of care, out of sight of the mainstream, whether in large old-style hospitals, or new, small commercial homes. The clubhouse movement advocates for social inclusion on a range of access issues, including reduced fares on public transport, and so is active in promoting the right of people with mental illnesses to participate as full members of the community. It combines many of the features of face-to-face, voluntary, blood-and-guts community with a greater involvement in the formal worlds of work and welfare, with far higher staff ratios than Emmaus, and without the emphasis on economic self-sufficiency. For the purposes of this chapter, its main interest is its insistence that mentally ill people should have a stimulating, involving, active and participative life, with power to make the important deci-sions over how to live it; and that this should include access to formal employ-ment, rather than an assumption that they need forms of care and control that exclude them from this sphere.

People with Disabilities

Benefits and services for people with disabilities provide the clearest example of policies pulling in opposite directions. Under the Thatcher–Major administrations, two different tendencies were obvious. On the one hand, the number of claimants of various incapacity and disability benefits grew enormously. This followed a European trend of the 1980s, especially in the Continental, Christian Democratic countries (Esping-Andersen, 1990, 1996). By 1998, the number on incapacity benefits had risen to 1.75 million in the UK, three times more than in 1979 (DSS, 1998, p. 54). This expansion reflected government policies that allowed firms to 'shake out' older workers, people who were less productive or less quick to adapt, and many low-skilled employees. Because high unemployment figures were embarrassing for governments, these benefits supplied a fig leaf for this process, and allowed those made redundant, and with no prospects for re-employment, to be given a kind of compensation and security. Various eligibility tests were relaxed, and a whole cohort of former workers in their forties and fifties were allowed to adapt to a new status outside the labour market, on benefits which, though by no means generous, allowed them rather more favourable terms (for instance, by disregarding partners' earnings) than unemployment benefits.

In the mid-1990s, as first the Major and then the Blair administration began to experiment in policies for increasing labour-market participation and cutting expenditure on benefits, this tendency was put into reverse. A new 'All Work Test' was introduced for claimants of incapacity and disability benefits, involving a huge review of millions of individuals, to see whether they were capable of *any* work. The test was crude, carried out using bureaucratic procedures, and meant the sudden reversal of previous decisions, sometimes over deteriorative or progressive conditions. Government targets involved large savings in benefits. When New Labour's plans for the New Deals were first announced, in November 1997, there were immediate and effective protests by disabled people, causing hasty redrafting and presentational changes. The eventual Green Paper (Department of Social Security, 1998) included much new rhetoric on empowerment and access in its New Deal for Disabled People, but the message was still much the same. At the same time as introducing a new Disability Credit (on the lines of Working Families Tax Credit) it also proposed means-testing of incapacity benefit, using some of the savings to uprate benefits for the most severely disabled people. This provoked two backbench revolts by Labour MPs against the Welfare Reform Bill in 1999. Meanwhile, the process of applying the All Work Test to claimants was continuing, reducing the new claims for incapacity and invalidity benefits from 337,000 in 1993–94 to 128,000 in 1996–97 (DSS, 1998, table D1.14).

On the other hand, the Thatcher–Major years witnessed a growth in the numbers and membership rolls of organizations for disabled people (including people with learning disabilities), an increase in their confidence and effectiveness, and in their organized campaigning and lobbying potential. Partly inspired by the American principles of normalization (O'Brien and Tyne, 1981; Brown and Smith, 1992), and partly generating their own programmes for independent living and self-help, these groups and organizations challenged the traditional conceptions of social care, with their assumption of the need to protect and exclude people with disabilities.

The local authority social services departments played an important role in this cultural and professional shift, which involved a change from a medical to a social model of support and care (Hudson, 2000). This is most obvious in the case of people with learning disabilities. In 1979, the Jay Report, influenced by the ideas of the normalization movement (that such citizens should be in the community, make choices about their lives, develop competence as service users, be respected and encouraged to participate in the community), recommended that long-stay hospital care be wound up and new services developed. By the late 1980s, hospital closures were taking place and new forms of housing emerged, so that between 1981 and 1990 the numbers in NHS long-stay institutions fell by almost half, and by an even higher proportion in the 1990s (Department of Health, 1998b). Recent research on the increasing proportion of older people with learning disabilities cared for by family members has shown that they received less consistent and reliable as well as quantitatively less support than those in care homes (Walker and Ryan, 1995), as did their carers (Walker and Walker, 1998). Thus the improvements brought about by the policy of community care, which are recognized in official reports, were not always carried over into the whole population with learning disabilities, nor were the principles of empowerment and inclusion always consistently applied. There was scope for the development of advocacy and campaigns by groups of people with learning disabilities and their families, as occurred in the 1990s.

Similarly, for people with physical disabilities there has been a battle of ideas about the significance of these conditions and the appropriate response in terms of support and care. Organizations of people with physical disabilities have struggled to overthrow notions of 'impairment', 'abnormality' and 'lack', which are quasi-scientific and point towards medicalized institutional care, and to substitute versions of the issues that focus on the limitations of the physical and social environment (Oliver and Barnes, 1998). But policy changes have not been so marked as in the case of people with learning disabilities (Nocon and Qureshi, 1996), and spending has remained low in local authority social services (Hudson, 2000). The bulk of expenditure for people with disabilities of working age goes towards day care, with more spent on home care packages per capita than for older people. The Independent Living Fund supplements such packages by an average £190 per week. However, research suggests that local authorities are casual about planning such services or registering people with disabilities, and that these younger people endure longer periods of dependence on parents, more limited leisure and social opportunities and higher rates of unemployment than their able-bodied counterparts (Hirst and Baldwin, 1994).

New Labour announced its intention to raise standards of care, to improve housing for the disabled (Department of Health, 1998a, sects 6.16–6.21), and to promote independence. Local authorities are reminded of their responsibility to help service users and carers of working age, and to participate in the New Deal for Disabled People. The White Paper gives examples of deaf people taking part in a project for work experience in Lincolnshire, and a scheme in Kensington and Chelsea in which social services work with employers and people with disabilities to place them in regular paid employment; this emphasizes support from a professional job consultant and improving skills (sect. 2.18 and box). Social services have also been given a role (albeit a small one) in the Single Gateway under which access to welfare for all claimants of working age is organized.

There are obvious tensions between the parts of this programme. The All Work Test is a way of policing access to incapacity benefits, and results in many decisions that claimants regard as harsh and unfair, as well as unrealistic about their chances of gaining suitable employment. It sorts the previously large mass of claimants into three categories – those who get no benefits or support at all, those who are eligible for Disability Credit but are required to work, and those who receive incapacity and/or disability benefits. Among the last group will be some who are made substantially worse off by the means-tested nature of what they are now allowed to claim. But this third category is a residual one, and those viewed as incapable of all work may lose out in other ways. Since they have been deemed unfit for 'activation' (in the Third Way's sense, i.e. formal labour-market participation), they may become even more identified with passivity and a stereotype of dependence. Since 'independence' according to New Labour is largely synonymous with working and earning, it is not at all clear that this group, in many ways the most disempowered and excluded, will be the focus of policy efforts to improve access to the facilities for self-development, cultural and social participation, and personal autonomy. Their eligibility for benefits depends on their maintaining a posture of helplessness and inactivity, which locks them into passive and excluded roles. The Green Paper recognizes this dilemma; it acknowledges that the All Work Test writes off some people and is 'all or nothing', classifying people as either fit or unfit for work. It says the government is 'examining the scope for a more effective test in future' (DSS, 1998, p. 54) – but one has not so far been forthcoming, and the contradiction persists.

CASE STUDY: ORGANIZATIONS AND MOVEMENTS FOR PEOPLE WITH DISABILITIES

The 1980s and 1990s have witnessed a change in the nature and strategies of organizations of claimants and service users in the UK. In the 1970s, such movements tended to emphasize the economic factors which united all such citizens (oppression due to crisis of capitalism, need for common liberation struggle), and to link their protests with each other, and with wider movements (e.g. for women's emancipation, against racism or for nuclear disarmament). In the 1980s and 1990s they were more specific, stressing the identity and needs of people with disabilities as citizens, and focusing on the welfare state. While the former mass organizations and movements tended to decline, the latter flourished.

In part, this reflected the changed situation under the Thatcher and Major governments, where most marginal and excluded people would expect very little advantage from mass political action, and when protest risked police action followed by punishment. As the returns on collective struggle were so small, many turned to individual or covert small-group resistance of an instrumental kind, in the shape of informal economic activity, undeclared cash work, and so on (see pp. 31–3). But whereas able-bodied men had strong incentives and opportunities for such practices, many lone parent women and people with disabilities had none. Hence they turned mainly to mutual support and self-help associations, and to movement involved in long-term campaigns around the significance of and appropriate response to their situation by public services.

The emergence of movements of service users of these kinds has been documented by some writers (Oliver, 1996; Campbell and Oliver, 1996; Campbell, 1996), but has seldom been noted in literature on social work and social policy (Beresford, 1997). Yet the movements have developed new political discourses and strategies (Oliver and Barnes, 1998), which have proved effective in subverting some of the New Labour government's attempts to stifle opposition to welfare reform. People with disabilities have managed to combine lobbying and campaigning with direct action and very photogenic street protests, such as the mock-bloody scenario staged by a group in wheelchairs outside Parliament in late 1997. Above all, they insist that service users should have a voice in the development and implementation of social policy, as active participants rather than passive recipients of welfare, as well as an active role in designing and carrying out research and the evaluation of services. Such claims are based on assertions of civil and human rights, and the ethical analysis of the consequences of exclusion (Barnes, 1991; Oliver, 1996).

These movements demonstrate a wider and deeper understanding of the concepts of 'participation' and 'inclusion' than that promulgated in the Third Way. New Labour ministers have shown little willingness to include service users and carers in the policy-making process (Lister, 1999). Their methods are prescriptive and top-down, with a strong authoritarian tendency, focused on improving economic performance, limiting public expenditure, and getting better value for taxpayers' money. Their narrow conceptions of work and independence preclude considera-tion of many of the aspects most significant for people with disabilities. Welfare service users face a battery of assessments, paternalistic packages of help and com-pulsory 'inclusions', and strong pressures to comply with these categorizations.

The movement of people with disabilities promotes a social model of inclusion and independence that focuses on the barriers, discrimination and oppression practised by mainstream institutions. It claims the right to independent living in the sense of adequate support, under the control of (or at least accountable to) the person receiving it, and appropriate social conditions for living a life on equal terms with non-disabled people. Activists point to the costs of denying people with disabilities these rights, in terms of wasted potential and unnecessary depen-dence. They also draw attention to the gap between New Labour's rhetoric of partnership and empowerment, and the reality of being a service user.

Discussion

Movements of service users generally provide opportunities for identity-building, activating and morale-boosting experiences. They foster mutuality, solidarity and self-help. They are open to the accusation that they exploit marginal citizens, by making them responsible for their own welfare and forcing them to rely on each other rather than the resources of mainstream society. However, history seems to show that, without the previous experience of identifying with others and becoming active in pursuit of collective interests and purposes, it is difficult for public policy to inspire and motivate such citizens, or improve their self-esteem.

From an economic perspective, small associations and groups have incentives informally to produce and exchange commodities and services, which can greatly improve their quality of life and enhance their long-term employability. The Third Way seems blind to such possibilities in its emphasis on immediate formal employment or training of those capable of any work. Service user empowerment depends on a wider understanding of activation.

Social workers have always been ambivalent about collective action by service users. In principle they support it, and a minority of professionals are very active in promoting it. But many fear 'contamination' of compliant clients by more stroppy ones, or argue that groups demanding participation and a voice for service users are 'unrepresentative' and partisan. Working with service user organizations is a small or non-existent part of social work training. Only Bob Holman among leading social work writers consistently advocates this approach (Holman, 1981, 1988, 1998).

Conclusions

This chapter has presented a number of different examples of Third Way approaches to the issues of social exclusion of people at the margins of society, and alternatives from practice. The common themes have been New Labour's rigid perceptions of the bases of exclusion, its mechanistic methods of implementing its efforts at reintegrating and activating such citizens, and its lack of understanding of their need for identities, bonds, supports and activities that they generate for themselves, together, and in negotiation with the public authorities.

The alternative approaches analysed in the case studies have in common an emphasis on direct democracy – giving the members a strong voice in determining their collective decisions. This helps transform them from objects of social policy to subjects who are able to give their own meanings to freely chosen activities (Halverson, 1999). There are indeed dangers in the creation and maintenance of such groups and associations. Strongly oppositional ideologies, rejecting élite definitions of needs and deserts, developing into cult- or sect-like closed societies with strict and repressive blood-and-guts regulatory codes, or discriminatory terms of membership, are all risks. But this risk is a reason for social workers and others to try to participate, engage and link with such groups, since most of these dangers spring from isolation and the sense that no-one is listening or heeding.

The case studies illustrate a general weakness of Third Way notions of citizenship and empowerment. If the goal is activation and self-responsibility, this cannot be achieved by paternalistic prescription, still less by compulsion. Claimants and service users must have autonomy; they must be given opportunities to choose between alternative activities, and decide how to combine them. In the next chapter we will turn from the alternatives for service users to the alternatives for professionals. As social work has been transformed by the Thatcher years, and now again by New Labour, there have been new developments in social care and support, which open up other paths to many of the values and aspirations of social work in the 1970s.

6

Social Work and Street Credibility

The personal social services have a double agenda – to serve the policy purposes of government, and to be credible and relevant factors in the lives of those they encounter. This chapter investigates the emerging tensions between these elements. As 'tough love' requires social workers to be more demanding of their clients (asking them to contribute more and behave better), it must – to do its business – also become more meaningfully involved in their lives. It is not enough for social services to be more efficient and effective by government standards; they must also ring true in terms of the ways in which service users make sense of their worlds.

A large part of the White Paper *Modernising Social Services* (DoH, 1998a) is concerned with raising standards of practice. Chapter 5, 'Improving standards in the workforce', is given over to a full review of the registration, qualification and training of practitioners in the field of social care, and how standards can be sustained and enforced. But it conceals a set of basic assumptions about what practice *is* which are very restrictive and stifling. Social work practice cannot break out of its present poor performance (much criticized by the government) if it accepts the Third Way's limited vision of its nature and purposes.

Built into everything that New Labour's policy documents say about training and supervision is a view of local authority personal social services as concerned with policing the community to forestall breakdowns in its informal caring functions, and with stepping into the breach to provide care of various kinds when such breakdowns occur, or shortcomings are identified. For all the rhetoric about 'promoting independence', this boils down to various financial payments, material services and moral exhortations, mainly for the sake of promoting either employment or family living. What is missing is a vision of a quality of life, a richness of conviviality, or a culture of civility that could be improved by imaginative and supportive methods of partnership and service. More than this, *practice itself* remains entirely shadowy, portrayed either as anxious monitoring or decisive protection, or even as tough enforcement, but never as sensitive, aware, dialogical and flexible negotiation about the kinds of complex messes that constitute ordinary crises in ordinary lives.

This does not imply that social work is universally reduced to the kind of stiff formalism and unimaginative provision that seems to emerge from the government's policy documents. In the 1990s a new trend was recognizable – the development of a range of intermediate projects, units and homes, between the formal world of the local authority services, the big voluntary agencies and the commercial sector, and the everyday world of citizens' lives, and in some cases as aspects of, or outposts of, those major agencies. These provide a link between those two worlds, supplying the flexibility and imagination that is lacking in much formal provision, and giving some street credibility to the policies and goals that government agencies represent. With the structure of formal services dominated by ideas about regulation, commissioning, contract and management, they get alongside service users, enter their interactions, and operate in a fluid, provisional and *ad hoc* way to help them cope with social change, economic insecurity and the demands of tough love's harbingers.

The difficulty about this development is that these practitioners – project workers, street workers, support workers, and so on – are seldom employed as qualified social workers, and often do not think of themselves as social workers at all. Indeed, there is really no recognized qualification for the kinds of work they do, and although many are highly educated and motivated, and have a variety of qualifications and experience, there is no unifying rationale for their practices, or way for them to share their experiences as professionals. This is partly because they do, in a sense, represent a new kind of practice, perhaps even a new profession, of street-level worker, face-to-face worker, or social mediator. It may be that, over time, new training courses and new professional organizations will emerge to cater for their needs. However, in the meanwhile these things are largely missing, because the emergence of this new kind of practitioner goes largely unrecognized in the literature of the personal social services (Parton and O'Byrne, 2000).

Simultaneously of course, New Labour's broader policy programme is generating another very large number of practitioners (enforcement counsellors) of something a bit like social work, but in the formal, public sphere. New Deal counsellors, Single Gateway officers, and many other such public service roles have been spawned by the Third Way's raft of legislation and provision. Much of this has to do with the goals of social inclusion through participation in employment, training or education; much of the rest is about social discipline and the enforcement of rules; and there is a good deal of overlap between the two. New Labour's programme relies heavily on individual counselling and 'personalized packages of help' (DSS, 1998), but there is up to now no systematic training or method of supervision and professional development for such people.

This is not to say that we would recommend that such new workers – either the street-level, project and support ones, or the official enforcement counsellors who staff the reformed welfare programmes – should be trained as social workers on courses like the ones that exist at present for people who will be employed in personal social services. This would be far too limiting, especially given the Third Way's very restrictive views of what social work is, and how people should be prepared for practising it. However, what we are arguing for is a recognition of the commonalities between all these activities – street-level work, formal social work, and the work of the new agencies and programmes. All are ways of implementing social policy through direct, face-to-face interventions in citizens' lives, and all rely on interactive skills in negotiating, influencing, mediating, advocating or challenging, for the sake of changing social outcomes. There is a strong case for an attempt to identify these common elements and devise methods of training, supervision and professional development which rely on the systematic application of certain principles and learning approaches. Indeed, we would go so far as to say that the successful implementation of the Third Way's policy programme (suitably modified in the ways we will outline in the following chapters) largely depends on the identification and application of such principles and methods, since it relies so heavily on the effectiveness of individual interventions aimed at behavioural change.

In this chapter we will look at the prospects for the emergence of such approaches. We will examine New Labour's prescriptions for raising standards in local authority services, then show how new projects and new kinds of workers are emerging, with special reference to programmes for youth justice. Next we will look at the pattern of new services for 'tough love's' programme, by examining provision for asylum seekers, including the enforcement of benefits restrictions. Finally we will try to identify common themes, principles and methods that could inform future training, supervision and professional development.

Training and Standards in Practice

The White Paper *Modernizing Social Services* (DoH, 1998a) acknowledges that of the one million people working in 'social care' (mostly in residential homes, and most of these commercial), 80 per cent have no recognized qualifications (sects. 5.1–5.3). The more that they are working face-to-face with vulnerable people, the less likely they are to have educational or professional qualifications. New Labour seeks to 'set and enforce standards of practice and conduct' (sect. 5.3). The priority is 'to give those working in social care a new status which fits the work they do' (sect. 5.6).

New Labour's approach to this aim is to focus on the specific tasks done by staff, and equip them with the technical competences they need to perform to the required standards. As might be expected from the Third Way's limited conception of human motivation and action, and its instrumental approach to governance, this has a strongly mechanistic and managerial flavour to it. Staff are to have clear definitions of their roles and the way they are to be deployed; individual objectives related to service objectives; better supervision and management; and improved education and training which is geared to the new agenda of promoting independence, protecting children and enabling people with disabilities (sect. 5.5).

To these ends, the government will set up a General Social Care Council (GSCC) to replace the Central Council for Education and Training in Social Work (CCETSW). It will regulate training, set conduct and practice standards for social services, and register those in the most sensitive areas. The government will also develop a new training strategy through a National Training Organization for social care staff (sect. 5.6). The GSCC will be a 'lean and effective body', accountable to the Secretary of State, consisting of about twenty-five people representing all the key interests. It will therefore be an instrument of governance, deployed by the state, rather than a professional body; service users and lay members will have a majority (sects 5.8–5.10). It will regulate personnel so as to protect the public, and ensure a coherent, developed and regulated training system. Standards of conduct will be published as codes. Practitioners will be personally accountable for their actions, based on the code, and required to sign up to these as conditions of employment that are enforceable (sects 5.16–5.17). Individuals will be registered on satisfactory completion of approved training (sect. 5.20).

Whether one finds these Benthamite visions sinister or comic is a matter of perception, but they perfectly capture the Third Way's version of the relationship between policy and its implementation. It is the role of the Panopticon minister (the Secretary of State) to preside over institutions that regulate and enforce the public good. Those who work directly with the public are trained and mandated to do so on behalf of the minister, thus applying his rules, acting according to his standards, in ways he approves. The scope for professional judgement or practice-experienced creativity is deliberately narrowed to a minimum in this version. Social work is not an art or even a science, but an instrument of ministerial will.

Of course, this is not unique to social work (though it is a particularly strong version of the methods deployed throughout the public sector, and especially in education). It has been argued that the Thatcher revolution was to use the disciplines of the market to regulate society *indirectly* (through the internalized constraints and rules of responsibility and efficiency that individuals adopt from commercial ethics as their own standards of behaviour) rather than relying on the state's direct laws and rules to constrain behaviour. In this way, first in the UK and then in Europe (through the market-making and competition-enforcing role of the EU), the power of the state over its subjects has been re-established after the erosion of welfare-state collectivism by global economic forces, and governments have begun to regain sovereignty over their populations (Fernandes, 1999). Thus states have been able to give up much of their regulation of mainstream society and economy, relying on the market to provide the necessary disciplines. But if this is so – and the case is quite convincing, when one looks at New Labour's cosy relationship with business and commerce – then it certainly does not imply that new-style governance abandons direct regulation. Instead, it focuses this, and all the moralizing rhetoric that goes with it, on two groups: public sector staff and service users. Direct regulation in the manner of the White Paper is all the stronger because New Labour has been forced to abandon this preferred instrument in the fields of economic planning and management. Like claimants of social security benefits, public sector staff feel the full force of Benthamite zeal, since the more mobile and evasive holders of capital can now escape collective restraints.

The rest of this chapter of the White Paper describes the government's training strategy, through the National Training Organization for Personal Social Services

(NTO). This is responsible for maintaining standards underpinning recognized qualifications, carrying out workforce analyses, and ensuring that identified training needs are met (sect. 5.34). A Training Support Programme, with an appropriate grant of £19.7 million, will sustain it in these tasks. This will allow 7,000 child protection social workers to get post-qualifying awards, and 9,500 residential child care workers to attain an NVQ level 3 (sect. 5.38). Managers will also be trained for the Quality Protects programme.

The version of training foreseen in these developments is, of course, now well established. It relies on the notion of 'competences' that are appropriate to each level in a hierarchy of roles and tasks connected with care and its management. It is largely taken for granted that the Qualifications and Curriculum Authority and awarding bodies for NVQ-level training will be able to identify appropriate occupational skills and standards, and train people in competences appropriate for their work. However, this conceals a number of uncritical assumptions about how individuals learn to practise. As we will see later, it is by no means certain that this kind of learning is the best way to acquire the kinds of aptitudes and attitudes that inform sensitive and effective practice.

The 'competence movement' appeared in a recognizable form in the United States as early as the mid-1970s. It represented a healthy reaction against some of the more pretentious and exclusive aspects of psychodynamic training, and the vaguer and more esoteric claims of counselling and therapy. It has now become such an established orthodoxy, has gained such hegemony over training in social care, and fits so well with the Third Way's general philosophy of social regulation, that it is now seldom questioned as a basis for learning. The fact that training in competences on this instrumental and task-specific model has failed to improve standards or generate more reliable and flexible forms of care, despite an extended trial period, does not seem to have discredited it in any way. If anything, its hold on training seems stronger than ever.

The structure of NVQs is well adapted to New Labour's hierarchical and meritocratic vision of society, with incremental additional qualifications allowing lifelong learning. This is fine, so long as what is learned is really what is needed for adaptable and effective practice. If one accepts the Third Way's conception of social work as protecting vulnerable individuals from harm (often from predatory or neglectful fellow citizens) and providing substitute care after social death, then it probably is – but that is a very unimaginative and restrictive version of what social work is, and might become. Furthermore, it does not reflect the needs of many of those working outside the structure of local authority social services departments and the voluntary and commercial providers from whom they purchase care. It is to those new projects, units and systems, and the workers who staff them that we now turn.

Street-level Practice

It is precisely because social work had already been developing in these directions before the advent of New Labour that such new projects, units and systems have emerged. As early as with the NHS and Community Care Act 1990 the essential features of the new approach were clear. The strong emphasis on management and accountability, together with budgetary rectitude, was clearly discernible (Clarke et al., 1994), while the purchaser–provider split allowed the emphasis on assessment and matching instrumental solutions to superficially defined needs to be established. The rise of evidence-based practice, using quantitative research methods and evaluation procedures, enabled the centre to direct practice as an arm of the 'scientific' approach to human problems, without questioning the assumptions built into this style of service provision.

All this meant a growing gap between the forms of social intervention available under such a regime and the actual needs of service users. Practice under this dispensation was firmly rooted in managerial perceptions and categories, with almost no flesh and blood. Qualified social workers spend most of their time either investigating allegations of abuse and writing reports, or assessing people to fit them into such categories. Care itself was supplied by agencies with one eye on the cash register, and the other on recruiting staff at the lowest possible cost. All the projects, movements and groups identified and analysed in the last chapter can be seen as reactions against this style of implementation, as much as against the policies they implemented.

The essence of these alternative approaches is that they involve getting far closer to the service users than the arm's-length, official, formal and rule-orientated systems allow. They require staff to *share in* the lives of service users, to participate with them in activities, to enter into dialogue about the significance of such activities for their lives, and to be open to other meanings of their choices and actions than the standard interpretations of official categorizations. More frequent and more informal interactions lead to fuller understandings of service users' cultural practices, and more opportunities to influence them. Far from seeing this approach as less challenging of irresponsible or predatory behaviours, exponents argue that it provides better opportunities to recognize, focus on and change them. In a sense, the moral credit and credibility gained from closeness and practical support gives the practitioner the basis for making these challenges; without this, they seem too much like hectoring, moralizing, preaching, or any other form of communication *de haut en bas*.

The space created by the withdrawal of official social work behind a wall of managerialism, budget control, form filling and report writing, into office-based practice of assessment and rationing, has quickly been occupied by a range of such projects, units and support systems. One has only to glance at the *Guardian* Society section on a Wednesday to appreciate the variety of such operations, in the fields of housing, mental health, youth justice, drugs, delinquency, alcohol and so on. Although content and philosophy may vary considerably, the basic approach of all these street-level or informal support groups is similar – to get alongside service users, to be available for them, to work with them on their definitions of their current problems, and to give them lots of influence over processes of deciding on and progressing towards solutions.

The irony of all this is that this approach comes much closer to 'tough love' than the one promoted by New Labour does. By working informally, by giving masses of support, by getting to know intimately the thoughts, feelings, dreams and fears of service users, such practitioners are much better placed to be tough with them – in a loving way. More formal methods, based on drier, scientific or bureaucratic classifications of human distress, tend to make fewer demands. It is quite easy for resourceful or experienced service users to press the buttons that release basic services. One need only adopt a certain posture of deference, compliance or desperation, or make the slightest hint of something worse, to trigger the provision of a (usually fairly useless) facility or placement. A few muttered words are often enough to satisfy the professional with a clipboard and a dangerousness or risk assessment form to complete. As a result, the requirements of such formal methods are seldom tough – and almost never loving.

By contrast, the alternative approach has a flexibility that comes from its willingness to allow service users to determine their own agendas. For example, in the Brighton and Hove Emmaus Community, several quite different patterns of use of the Community emerge. Some Companions see Emmaus as a stopgap solution to their immediate problem, providing respite from the trials of their immediate circumstances. It offers a safe, clean, dry place in which to shelter and a place from which to launch themselves back into the wide world. Most Companions' first visit tends to be of short duration, a few weeks or months, and this suggests that their purpose was of this kind, though amongst them there must be some who decide to give it a try and find that it does not suit them. Most respite-seekers return to the chaotic circumstances of their arrival, but a high proportion return at a later point, sometimes several times. Subsequent stays tend to be of longer duration. A very few Companions use Emmaus as a stopgap before they return to mainstream society as successful citizens, living in conventional housing and participating in the mainstream economy.

In terms of motivation, the second category of Companions may be characterized as people who are explicitly seeking a safe place in which to address some aspect of their life that has been troubling them. It may be to do with drink or drugs, loneliness, aggression and violence, a mental health problem or personal loss. The Community offers an accepting place in which they can devise strategies for dealing with these sorts of issues in their own way. In many cases, their expectations of themselves and of the Community prove to be unrealistic, at least on a first visit. Where this happens, it is sometimes possible for the Community to help them negotiate a better deal from the 'needs assessment' system than they had been able to obtain on their own. Such Companions are helped to move back into the state-approved care and rehabilitation system of detoxification, dry houses, etc., and sometimes to alternative schemes and projects. Again, many of those who leave the Community in a mood of disappointment or disaffection return for a second spell at a later date.

The final group consists of those who choose to join Emmaus for life. Because Emmaus is not a state-approved scheme, there is no limit to how long anyone may stay, nor any attempt to 'move people on' to prevent 'silting up'. Companions who choose to stay are free to do so for as long as they like. Joining a Community for an indefinite period or for life is actively encouraged. Clearly, with only a limited number of places available, not many of this group are found in any Community; but because the movement is growing in the UK, there is an increasing availability of places in other Communities. Some Companions who have chosen Emmaus as a way of life move from one Community to the next, settling for as long as it suits them. Some more enterprising individuals move abroad to Communities in other countries.

Box 15   New Labour spending priorities

ENFORCEMENT COSTS

The New Contract for Welfare promises mainstream citizens that expenditure on social benefits and services will give priority to work, order and social discipline. This implies that people and behaviour which cause public anxiety, or represent highly visible reproaches to their comfortable status, are given 'zero tolerance' – whatever this costs. Crime and homelessness are therefore high-priority spending targets, irrespective of the 'success' rates of provision.

Here is a list of the costs to taxpayers of:

- one place in prison – £25,000 per year (more than 50 per cent increase in places since 1993)
- one place in a hostel or other accommodation for rough sleeper – £24,000 per year (extra 2,000 places planned under New Labour)
- one place in school education (average) – £2,000 per year
- one place in New Deal programme (average) – £3,000 per year

(*Guardian*, 17 December 1999, p. 23)

TRANSACTION COSTS

Another rising cost is spending on monitoring. In addition to the National Audit Office (750 staff in Great Britain), New Labour employs a growing army of watchdogs – auditors and inspectors to check expenditure and standards in central and local government departments. These include:

- Health and safety executive (GB)   3,930
- Audit Commissioners for local government and NHS
  (England & Wales)   1,349
- Accounts Commission in Scotland   157
- Planning Inspectorate (E & W)   644
- Office for Standards in Education   460
- Parliamentary Commissioner for Administration (UK)/Health
  Services Adjudicator   200

(*Guardian*, 18 October 1999)

Another field of intervention, youth justice, illustrates how the issues identified at the start of this section work out in this policy domain. Youth justice has been contested territory in social policy in the UK since the 1960s. At that time the battle was between the conservative forces associated with the juvenile courts (the magistracy and the probation service) and the reforming zeal of the Labour government and the local authority children's departments (Packman, 1975). The latter succeeded, in large part, in transferring initial responsibility for young offenders to the system of supervision and care by the new social services departments. But by the mid-1970s it had become clear that young people were entering care, community homes, detention centres and borstals in far higher numbers than before these reforms, which had been designed to protect their welfare (Thorpe et al., 1980). Accordingly, a movement for juvenile justice, taking its inspiration from the USA, argued successfully that strict principles of proportionality and retribution were more appropriate for youth offenders than more open-ended welfare principles, which tended to draw them into a net of care provision and to lead to an adult criminal career (Giller and Morris, 1981).

New arrangements for juvenile justice bureaux, involving police, probation and social services, allowed the development of strong policies for diverting young offenders from the courts, substituting community penalties and activities for care and custody (Raynor, 1985). Very large numbers of minor offences were dealt with by informal or formal cautions. The success of these measures, and of the local authority youth justice teams which were credited with achieving them, led to high status and the attraction of more generous resources. Relationships with services for families and children became strained, because the principle of non-intervention in welfare problems of offenders left parents desperate at times, and demanding that something was done to relieve their stress and protect wayward youngsters. Above all, these policies became very unpopular in deprived neighbourhoods, which were required simply to consume their own smoke. These communities' quality of life was damaged by young delinquents on the rampage, perceived as left to cause mayhem by an uncaring local authority social services department. Instances of juveniles with huge lists of offences evading custody were taken up in the media. With the murder of James Bulger, and the moral panic that followed it, the tide turned again (Franklin and Petley, 1996). The Major government introduced measures to tighten up youth justice practice and restrict the autonomy of youth justice teams. Ideas from the USA, such as 'zero tolerance' and 'three strikes and you're out', began to influence policing and government thinking. Above all, the Labour Party in opposition saw a political opportunity, which it has since exploited in government.

Under the Crime and Disorder Act 1998 the focus in youth justice is shifted from that of keeping young people out of care and custody to *community safety*. Specific measures provide for curfews, and for keeping unaccompanied children under 10 off the streets at night. The role of the police and probation service in the development of community safety initiatives is again emphasized, with duties on the local authority to co-ordinate plans. The White Paper comments:

> The Government has undertaken a comprehensive review of youth justice issues .... Multi-agency youth offending teams are to be established in local authorities with social services and education responsibilities, in partnership with health authorities, the police and the probation service. A draft inter-departmental circular *Establishing Youth Offending Teams* explained the important role that social services and health authorities will have within these teams. Pilots of these teams began on 30 September, 1998 in

selected areas and will run for a total of eighteen months, with a view to implementing them nationally by April, 2000. A new national body – the Youth Justice Board for England and Wales – has been established to advise ministers on setting standards for service delivery and to monitor performance across the youth justice system, including youth offending teams. (sect. 6.30)

Behind this typically dry and bloodless system building lie some important developments. The ideological shift towards a community safety approach that is 'tough on crime and tough on the causes of crime' cannot, of course, rely solely on formal measures like curfews, or arm's-length expressions of toughness. It demands negotiation with local people, mediation between victims and offenders, and sensitivity to local tensions and conflicts. Here co-ordination between large public sector services has little to offer, and the participation of intermediate groups or organizations becomes essential. The space for practice based on something closer to the alternative principles identified at the start of this section becomes obvious, because young people are in and of these communities, and their actions reflect the social relations of these neighbourhoods, with all their blood-and-guts elements of bonding, loyalty, fear, loathing, violence and reconciliation – the solidarities and the feuds of the informal, local order. It requires practitioners far closer to the ground, and far more intimately involved in local communities, to work in these ways.

Here New Labour's ideas about partnership with voluntary agencies come into play (sect. 6.30, box). This can cover anything from large, national and highly professionalized organizations who contract for mass service provision, to small community groups with a strong stake in a local neighbourhood. In this field, a number of new organizations of all kinds have sprung up, and can play a part in linking the formal world of community safety initiatives to the lived experience of deprived neighbourhoods. The following case study illustrates both the opportunities for such projects, units and agencies, and the trend for new kinds of workers to emerge, without affiliations to or training in social work.

CASE STUDY: YOUTH JUSTICE

Jacqueline is 33 years old, and now works for a small mediation and reparation agency, which forms part of a pilot Youth Offending Team in a city in the South of England. She has been working there for almost a year.

Jacqueline graduated in natural science, and went on to take a doctorate in the same subject. However, she found the routines and social relations of laboratory and academic work stifling, and decided to make a complete career shift into working with people. She gained some part-time voluntary experience, and then pondered what further study to pursue. Jacqueline says that she never seriously considered social work training as an option, because she saw the work of the social work profession as too tied up in bureaucratic processes and formal methods. Instead, she took a two-year diploma in counselling, before applying for her present job.

Jacqueline finds her work stimulating and challenging. She has had in-service training in principles of mediation and reparation, which represents a very different approach to the main ideological underpinnings of the Youth Offending Team. However, in practice there is substantial space for this approach, which tackles the actual relationships between offenders and victims, who often share the same set of disadvantages and deficits, and have a common stake in improving the quality of life in their communities.

She finds plenty of scope for using the skills she developed on her course, but worries about her lack of experience in the field, the lack of consistent supervision, and above all the absence of any broader contextualizing framework in which to understand these teams' work. As in all Third Way 'pilots', little attempt is made to gather systematic data or draw conclusions from experience; the blueprint for the development of a new set of institutions has already been drawn, and results are selectively used to justify a predetermined model for that programme.

Jacqueline is uncertain whether she will continue to develop her counselling skills with the aim of becoming a senior practitioner in this field, or branch off into management. One thing is certain: she will not study on any kind of social work programme.

Discussion

This example illustrates the strengths and weaknesses of the Third Way's approach to a number of policy domains. Jacqueline is a very bright, motivated and skilled worker, with plenty to offer to her work. Yet she feels – and is – somewhat isolated, in a small, specialist field, accumulating experience on which she has few opportunities to reflect with peers or more experienced practitioners. She is on a steep learning curve, but her potential for gaining new competences and insights is limited by the restricted chances for exploring new methods and linking her practice with other approaches to comparable problems. Above all, her training has not given her a policy perspective, or contextualized her work within the social relations of present-day UK society. The relative isolation of her project denies her learning opportunities and developmental pathways that might help her more fully realize her potential as a practitioner.

Juvenile delinquency and adult crime are two obvious fields where principles of 'tough love' could appropriately apply. In terms of public policy, the Third Way is largely unimaginative about how to achieve this. The probation service, now transformed into an arm's-length, corrections-orientated agency – whose officers are ostentatiously *not* trained alongside social workers, and some of whose senior managers are to be drawn from industry and the armed services – may look tough, but is unlikely to scare offenders. Its new methods are by no means strategy-proof, because they are so stereotypical, merely confirming that authority is stupid and archaic. But this leaves an open field for work that is quite different in its methods.

New Labour's policies perhaps signal an overdue recognition that social relations in the UK's most deprived areas have deteriorated beyond the reach of traditional social work methods, and that the influence of drugs and organized criminality on behaviour has made offending a different problem from the one tackled by the postwar probation services. What seem to be needed are charismatic figures who combine authority with street credibility, and challenge with real compassion and concern. Exactly the same qualities are in demand for the classrooms of sink schools, on the beats of high-crime police divisions, and even perhaps in the training programmes of some welfare-to-work New Deals. But role models are in short supply. We do not really know where to find such people, or how they can best teach their skills to the many others (project, unit and support workers) who need them.

It is true that professional social work training does not select or nurture these workers or these qualities, any more than teacher training does. The creation of a largely graduate profession ensures that recruits tend to come from the other end of the polarized society from the clientele, and that empathy is conveyed in culture-bound ways that restrict the expression of moral demands and physical challenges. Furthermore, the arm's-length nature of office-bound practice in probation and social services involves workers more in the authoritative imposition of conditions and sanctions (community punishments) than in directly confronting the emotional and physical phenomena of crime. In other words, they are more into bureaucratic sympathy than tough love – and sometimes not even much of that. A senior probation officer tells of a report on an offender brought back to court for breach of conditions: 'Jenkins told me that he had missed three appointments because his son was in hospital, his mother had died and his wife had had a car accident. I told him that I was not here to listen to his problems, but to enforce the order ...'. So much for the 1948 Act's injunction to 'advise, assist and befriend'. Beyond befriending or past caring? (Arnold and Jordan, 1995).

The difficulties of finding a way to operationalize tough love beset New Labour's policy initiatives across a wide range of issues. All the measures to activate the dependent, motivate the apathetic, include the excluded and challenge the disaffected need doses of it. But its front-line public sector troops are tired and dispirited members of a welfare army that has been under fire from both sides during the Thatcher revolution. They have been fully occupied in trying to defend their budgets and their autonomy from managerial incursions, and their professional effectiveness from the erosive consequences of poverty and underclass strategic resistance. Worldly-wise and somewhat cynical from this campaign, charismatic and energetic they are not.

Yet there are success stories – from abroad, and from particular projects in the UK. Tough love is most convincing when it is expressed either by strong authority figures with exceptional communications skills (such as some black women Drugs Court judges in the US, who can project both challenge and empathy, and mobilize peer group pressure and peer group support to change offenders, in what amounts to a secular 'prayer meeting'); or by those who have been relatively successful deviants and have 'changed sides' (as in some residential drug rehabilitation programmes). Grassroots movements everywhere also tend to rely on charismatic leadership to mobilize both the reforming zeal and the mutual support of sufferers and perpetrators. Finally, there is the inspiration that comes from sheer dedication and altruism. In Bob Holman's case (Holman, 1981, 1988, 1998) this comes across more as love than tough, but he must be tough to have lived his principles all these years.

The raw enthusiasm of young, new semi-trained or untrained recruits can go some of the way to supply the needs of tough love; but there is a danger of burnout and disillusion if these are not reinforced by further training and supervision, and by links with a wider movement for progressive improvement in social relations.

The New Authoritarianism: Tough Love in a Cold Climate

A new style of practice is evolving in the agencies spawned by the more authoritarian side of New Labour's programme. Obviously it is difficult to write about this, and to capture its essentials, for two reasons. The first is that many of the agencies and services are still in a developmental or pilot stage; even if there are some publications about their results in quantitative terms, there is as yet nothing in the way of qualitative research about what they are doing. The second is that they are extremely diverse. One of the features of New Labour's programme is to devise a number of very specific organizations to deal with the issues it regards as having policy priority. Within these organizations, enforcement counsellors, advisers or officers are appointed to perform quite specific tasks, to published standards, with the aim of achieving policy targets – such as getting people into work, catching and removing immigration offenders, detecting benefit fraudsters, placing rough sleepers in social housing, or whatever. There is no commonality in the methods they employ or the training they receive, except that they are all Third Way (in a Big Way). Indeed, if they have anything in common it is the specificity of their tasks, the narrowness of their focus, and the isolation of their work from other similar – yet quite separate – official practices.

This makes it very difficult to write in a convincing way about the dilemmas that they face, or the opportunities for good practice that their roles afford. Although many of them (New Deal counsellors, social housing assessors) are engaged in formulating 'individual packages of help' and 'care plans' – much in the manner of local authority social work – others are more concerned with investigative tasks, rationing and surveillance. What unites their practices is the legal and moral authority they are given to be tough on their clienteles, their power to give or withhold, to reward or punish, to support or withdraw. They have the discretionary authority, based on judgements formed in face-to-face interactions, that characterizes a public service profession, without the kind of training, supervision and practice environment (concerning ethics, sensitivity, empathy, accountability and so on) that does or *should* prevail in professional settings.

As it happens, one of us has done research in just such an environment and policy domain: immigration and asylum issues (Düvell and Jordan, 1999, 2000). New Labour has published its plans for reorganizing provision for asylum seekers, and its controversial new legislation has made its troubled way through Parliament. However, all the issues and many of the practice dilemmas have already been reverberating around the public sphere, turning up in the press as scandals and moral panics, even though neglected by the social science research community and the professional journals. In what follows we will set the policy background of the practice issues that will later emerge as two case studies on practice in immigration control and enforcement and provision for asylum seekers. In these case studies, the dilemmas over toughness and street credibility within the kinds of agencies that the Third Way favours – tailor made for specific groups, but isolated from mainstream local authority or central government social services – will become clear.

In recent years, the management of immigration has – both nationally in the UK, and internationally, in all the OECD countries – come to be focused on asylum seeking. This is because, during a period of very rapid economic transformation (due to global economic forces) and political instability, migration flows have increased. In Western Europe, the rise in numbers of asylum seekers has coincided (partly contingently) with the collapse of the Soviet and East Central European regimes, and the consequent increase in migration from that region, including those fleeing conflicts in the Balkans and Caucasus. Issues of asylum and issues of 'economic migration' have become intertwined and confused, and policies, especially in the UK, reflect this confusion.

Paradoxically, within the European Union, this is also a period when – following from the establishment of an area in which workers gained the right to move freely between member states – there has in fact been 'a fall in legal entries by permanent or seasonal workers' (European Commission, 1997, p. 21). This strong and universal trend has been masked by a number of factors, and especially by large but variable numbers of asylum seekers; member states acted, individually and with some co-ordination, to tighten their policies and practice on asylum, following examples already set by Australia and Canada (Adelman, 1991). The UK was relatively late in its decision to reform asylum law and practice, as numbers of applicants varied dramatically in the 1990s – from 73,400 in 1990 to 32,300 in 1991 and up to 41,500 by 1997 (Home Office, 1998, figure C). The Asylum and Immigration Act 1996 began the process of restriction, and New Labour took office as it started to be implemented. The White Paper of 1998 commented approvingly on the fact that the Conservatives' abolition of the right to social assistance benefits of those who apply for asylum after entering the country had led to a 30 per cent fall in applications (Home Office, 1998, para. 8.20). New Labour aimed to adapt and 'modernize' asylum procedures and provision for asylum seekers by taking the same logic much further.

The structure and analysis of the White Paper reveals the ways in which illegal immigration, economic factors and asylum claims are related to each other in Third Way thinking. The framework for its analysis is an attempt to relate overall numbers seeking settlement in the UK to patterns of international migration. It argues that 'economic migration' to all OECD advanced countries has increased because of better communications and travel facilities, which create 'opportunities for those who seek to evade immigration control' (Home Office, 1998, para. 1.3). It notes that there have been no recent increases in the numbers of spouses and dependants gaining settlement to join their families, or in tiny numbers coming for authorized employment purposes (para. 1.2), and goes on to argue that increases in asylum claims must therefore reflect economic migration. In effect, it argues that most claims for asylum are attempts at disguised economic migration, and conversely that most economic migration is carried out through the medium of 'bogus' asylum claims, concluding that welfare benefits are part of the attraction for people from regions 'where relative poverty is combined with political instability' (para. 1.4).

The White Paper's analysis fails to prove this connection. The 'smoking gun' of rising asylum claims from poorer countries does not indicate the true source of most economic migration. Instead, we should look to the vast and increasing number of 'passengers' entering the UK (from a total of 44 million in 1988 to 80 million in 1998) for the bulk of economic migrants. Although the White Paper characterizes these as 'people travelling abroad for legitimate purposes including business, study and holidays' whom 'the Government welcomes and wishes to encourage' (para. 1.6), most economic migrants are in fact drawn from this huge influx, and not from the tiny (by comparison) group of 80,000 asylum seekers. Research interviews with seventy-five Brazilian, Polish and Turkish citizens who admitted working in the UK without proper immigration status showed that all but one of the first two groups, and a substantial majority of the third, entered the country as tourists, students or au pairs, though several Turkish citizens subsequently applied for asylum (Jordan et al., 1997; Jordan and Vogel, 1997; Jordan, 1999c; Düvell and Jordan, 1999, 2000). The flawed conceptual framework in which New Labour addresses the notions of 'illegal immigration' and 'bogus asylum seeking' lead to confusion and cruelty.

In particular, the equation between economic migration and asylum claims is used to justify further measures to deter applications. Clearly a 'fairer and faster' process of determining such claims is needed, but the government goes on to set out measures for establishing a new welfare service under the Home Office, providing accommodation and other services for asylum seekers, under public–private partnerships that are right outside the structures of local authority social services or the major health and welfare agencies of the UK state. What is coming into existence is a kind of authoritarian Panopticon state within the welfare state, a Poor Law style of provision aimed at deterrence rather than respect for the rights and dignities of those fleeing political oppression.

It is not our purpose here to try to anticipate the exact form that such provision will take (though advertisements for staff indicate that toughness rather than love will be the key value). Rather, we will look at home developments in public services that have prefigured these policy directions, and how social work staff in local authorities have been the unwitting pioneers of such provision. It is instructive to see just how tough enforcement rationales and deterrent principles influence *practice*, when people who have had professional social work training work as rationers of minimalist services, or new recruits from educated, decent backgrounds, often from minority ethnic communities, are required to implement tough rules.

CASE STUDY: ASYLUM TEAMS IN SOCIAL SERVICES DEPARTMENTS IN NORTH-EAST LONDON

The research project interviewed six members of four teams in social services departments in north and east London, all set up in 1997 to deal with the aftermath of the High Court judgment that local authorities were obliged to provide shelter (under the 1948 National Assistance Act) for in-country asylum applicants who were no longer eligible for social assistance benefits. Two of the interviewees were managers, the rest social workers. The restrictions on the amount and form of help they were mandated to provide meant that such teams were operating well below the standards seen as acceptable for UK citizens: in other words, these social workers were, by some criteria, violating human rights. The research question might have been formulated as something like: given your professional ethics and training, and having regard to the service you provide, how low are you willing to go? (Düvell and Jordan, 2000).

The managers and social workers were actually aware of the shortcomings of the work they were doing, and found it extremely stressful. Yet they felt obliged to try to justify it in terms of their professional code, and to account for it by the standards of professional practice. The interviews therefore provided a case study of the cognitive and narrative survival codes of a profession practising under very adverse circumstances – for themselves and their clients (Satyamurti, 1980). But from another perspective they illustrated the fact that social workers will volunteer to do the 'dirty work' of social policy, even when this involves intentional and systematic deprivation by official agencies of the means of dignified existence.

Three of the four teams appeared to be in very temporary, *ad hoc* accommodation, in corners of large offices, or in cramped spaces, giving a provisional air to their work and reflecting the organizational response to the asylum crisis, and the low status and priority given to the team's clientele. They assessed applicants' eligibility for accommodation and food vouchers, and referred them on for any other needs. In this sense, it was more like the work of the prewar Poor Law relieving officer than anything in the postwar welfare state. Team 1's manager said it 'concentrated almost wholly on ... a very basic minimal service ... at the lowest cost to the council'. Team 3 gave fortnightly vouchers for food, and staff tried in addition to give information about access to NHS and drop-in centres. One interviewee commented: 'you don't need social workers to do the job we are doing' (Team 2).

Even so, these staff strove to do something more, to be able to give a morally adequate account of themselves to someone like the interviewer:

'in the afternoons when we do reviews, social work with clients ... to talk about other problems they have ... that is the moment I feel I am really doing social work .... This is the first time I am seeing the client as a person, as a human being.' (Team 1)

'... getting people registered with doctors, getting children into school and helping people find community groups, so they can link in with English classes, places where they can get cheap clothing. And then in a small number of families I might actually feel concerned about the children ... whether they are being cared for adequately.' (Team 3)

Caseloads varied between averages of 30 (Team 4, counting financial assessors as staff) and 400 (Team 2, excluding the financial section), but these were very approximate, reflecting the reactive, crisis nature of the work. The manager of Team 1 explained that his staff 'have no control over the numbers of people who can walk through the door at any time'. From all this need, social workers evolved *ad hoc* rules of priority, with little consistency of application, to do with perceived vulnerability – those who were 'genuinely homeless and destitute', 'who don't speak English', or feared contact with their own community. Good appearance and grooming were negative indicators: 'we tend to prioritize those we think are genuinely sleeping rough'. 'At times we have to be quite harsh and brutal about it'.

Staff lacked preparation for and guidance in their tasks. Work with refugees was not part of their professional education or previous experience, and there was little in the way of policy interpretation from central or local government, so they were forced to rely on 'learning by doing'. Inevitably in such a situation, practice is guided by bureaucratic rules of thumb. Staff normally had extra-professional (life-cycle or relationship-orientated) reasons for accepting short-term contracts, and were surviving in these posts temporarily; they sought defences against the unease they experienced in their exposed and stressful position by developing a kind of *esprit de corps*, based on limiting their focus to provision of immediate 'solutions' to the most desperate emergencies.

Like the social workers in Carole Satyamurti's classic study *Occupational Survival* (1980), they resorted to stereotyping their clients, creating distance from them, and defining their cultural practices in terms of problems and deficiencies. But they still did try, despite all the contradictions and anomalies of their work, to give a social work service, and to protect the most vulnerable individuals from abuse by an uncaring authority. In this they were helped by being able to blame central government (and specifically the Home Office) for the worst aspects of their clients' situation, rather than blaming the asylum seekers themselves. They could also portray themselves as struggling with the twin pressures of a state authority that had dumped all its ethical problems and their practical conse-quences on to local authorities, and a clientele that lacked a developed sense of civic competence.

The social workers said that the applicants sometimes tried to convey them-selves as more needy than they were; some had friends and were not actually sleeping rough, but wished to have 'accommodation where they are fairly inde-pendent and self-contained' (Team 1). Hence the task was to distinguish between these ineligible and low-priority cases, and others who were 'quite socially iso-lated, who find it very hard to cope within a foreign country'. A social worker for Team 4 said that asylum seekers had 'very high expectations' and 'tend to think that we could provide more than we can offer', adding that 'when they don't have the service they expect to get they get very angry and frustrated'. Another reported complaint and aggression, and yet another 'people screaming at the counter', while a third spoke of 'emotional threats'.

The social workers accounted for such behaviour as resulting from the asylum seekers' backgrounds and cultures, rather than the inadequacy of their own ser-vices, the rationing process, or the lack of interpreters and explanations that was intrinsic in their interactions. Two argued that applicants were from educated or professional backgrounds, and so had high aspirations. One social worker acknowledged that applicants might find the process of claiming assistance bewildering, but not that they might be traumatized by being homeless and stateless persons, or by what had happened in their home countries. Not one interviewee speculated on how those refused service survived. It seemed to be assumed that they must have access to some sort of alternative resources in the family or community.

Discussion

In many ways, the work of asylum teams prefigured other aspects of New Labour policy developments in enforcement counselling – systems for replacing both cash benefit rights and social services by in-kind provision, offering no options, and giving officials complete power over applicants (Home Office, 1998, paras 8.20–8.23). Ironically, in Third Way rhetoric this return to nineteenth-century principles is justified as 'modernizing' immigration control systems. In a wider context, some authors have seen it as part of a transformation of welfare regimes, from solidaristic principles to an achievement orientation, from social rights to rights-and-responsibilities, and from uniform rules to a case-by-case basis (Cox, 1999, p. 19). If this is so, social workers will be in the vanguard of public officials who negotiate with individuals over the terms and conditions on which services are given or refused – and asylum teams were the pioneers of this approach.

Although they tried hard to soften the brutality of what they did, and to find ways to use professional skills, they were aware of the shortcomings of what they offered, and recognized why asylum seekers were critical of their service. Team 1's social worker distanced herself from negative decisions by saying to clients, 'It's only the system, it's not us, not the individual person who is responsible for what happens.' Team 2's commented, 'It's like responding as a sort of Red Cross crisis centre … in a war zone …. We are just responding to crises as they occur.' They also skimped on checking papers, turned a blind eye to discrepancies, and gave applicants the benefit of the doubt – 'we have to rely almost wholly on their own word … we have to take things at face value' (Team 2). Against the expectation of being detectives, they asserted, 'we are here to provide a service' and 'we are not an investigative branch'.

Their narratives were reinforced by an emphasis on the provisional and contingent nature of the legal framework within which their tasks were being done, in contrast to the professional discourses (in terms of service users' 'rights and needs'), which usually inform social workers' accounts of practice. The law 'is constantly being challenged, the way it is interpreted is shifting, sometimes in a big way', so 'you are dealing with something you can never quite understand … you are never quite sure whether you are right or wrong'. This is a classic recipe for anomie (Durkheim, 1933; Hilbert, 1992; Jordan, Redley and James, 1994, Chapter 4); respondents felt accountable as individuals for their practice, but no professional principles covered the situations they encountered, so any interpretation or action seemed equally valid or invalid.

However, from another perspective these social workers were in many ways carrying out assessments and rationing services according to a hierarchy of risks and priorities, in ways which were extreme versions of the standard practices of the 1990s. In this sense, they could feel justified in undertaking these tasks, especially when they were willing to overlook certain checks and ignore some anomalies in applicants' stories. Social workers acknowledged that they were assessors and rationers rather than counsellors – but this was not so far out of line with the work of their colleagues in child protection and adult services, especially in hard-pressed boroughs like these. So they echoed the unease, guilt and resentment felt by the whole profession, simply taking to the extreme the tendency of staff and teams to become trapped in a downward spiral of compromise between client need and resource scarcity – always pressed, rushed and conscious of their shortcomings, but never able to draw a firm line where falling standards have sunk to unacceptably low levels.

It was also interesting to see how social workers picked up the managerial and budgetary jargon of mainstream social services to justify their practices. They said they had 'a duty to be responsible to those [who provide] money', and to be 'careful with money ... because this is council taxpayers'' (Team 3). Another said, 'if you are giving the money to someone who is not entitled to a service it restricts the amount of money that goes elsewhere' (Team 4). More subtly, restrictions were justified by the argument that an unconditional, open-handed approach would lead to bad publicity for asylum seekers themselves. 'The client group as a whole tend to be blamed' for individual fraud and 'any bad publicity tends to take a long time to repair', so checks were justified as being 'very protective of them as well' (Team 3).

All this illustrates how practitioners in such restrictive and deterrent agencies come to internalize the standards and rationales of policy makers, and somehow fuse them with their professional ethics and methodologies, even when aware that they are falling short of what is decent. Once rights are removed (as with asylum seekers), service users become highly vulnerable to any practices that fall short of outright abuse, because these can always be seen as somehow shielding or saving them from an even harsher fate.

During the Thatcher era, local authorities, the public sector in general, and social services in particular, stood as a buffer between the government and unpopular but vulnerable groups like these. New Labour's populism, and its large majority, make this government harder to resist. It is determined to break this barrier, turning to new organizations to implement its programme – as with the new Home Office services for asylum seekers. These will increasingly work on the 'take it or leave it' basis pioneered (albeit reluctantly) by asylum teams, using the threat of destitution and the power of material dependence to enforce compliance.

Box 16   Dispersing asylum seekers

Because New Labour is committed to withdrawing cash benefits from all asylum seekers – even though voucher schemes have been admitted by Home Office Minister Lord Bassam to be more expensive and to help fewer applicants (*Guardian*, 12 August 1999) – they must now either find accommodation and support with relatives or friends, pay for their own keep, or be sent to a reception area in a peripheral region of the country. The aim is to disperse them from London and the South East, where services are 'overstretched'.

The new model policy relies on a variety of types of accommodation, and of providers:

- In Cambridgeshire, a new secure 'reception facility' will provide 'fast track' processing of applications from new arrivals. It is expected to take individuals and families who are without papers. This blurs the distinction between the 800 or so places in detention (for those considered to be absconding risks) and applicants who are at liberty. Inmates (up to 400) will be allowed to leave the 'facility' (a former army camp) for specific purposes and periods (*Guardian*, 22 October 1999).
- In Norfolk, an entrepreneur has had his bid to house 1,000 asylum seekers (in addition to the 200 already accommodated by him) refused, as a result of allegations of assault, racism, overcrowding and inadequate food. His home for people with mental illnesses and learning difficulties had already been closed down, following a severe accident to a resident (*Guardian*, 16 December 1999).
- A private security company has bid to accommodate asylum seekers on a 'barge' on the Mersey – a multi-storey vessel similar to ones used in Germany. Another company said it preferred the term 'floatels' to 'hulks' (*Guardian*, 18 December 1999).

CASE STUDY: CO-OPERATION BETWEEN
THE IMMIGRATION SERVICE ENFORCEMENT DIRECTORATE
AND THE BENEFITS AGENCY BENEFITS FRAUD
INVESTIGATION SERVICE

In the course of the same research project, Franck Düvell had the opportunity of interviewing seven staff (from managers to front-line officers) in the Immigration Service Enforcement Directorate (ISED), who covered the north and east of London. He also accompanied them on 'raids' of workplaces suspected of employing immigration offenders. This was a chance to see internal immigration control work in action, and in particular to observe the practices of an agency which is at the cutting edge of New Labour's tough enforcement policies. In two of the 'raids', ISED officers were conducting a joint operation with officers of the Benefits Agency Benefits Fraud Investigation Service (BABFIS), another front-line Third Way organization. New Labour is pledged to 'modernize' immigration control (Home Office, 1998), and to put more resources into the control of benefits fraud (DSS, 1998). Both agencies are therefore now high-profile actors, thrust into the forefront of the Third Way's programme for social reform. These particular operations were of obvious relevance for the attempt to re-regulate work, increase formal labour-market participation, and clamp down on shadow, informal economic activity (see Chapter 7).

The legislative and organizational background to these operations is important to understand. By long tradition, UK immigration control policy focuses on checks within the country of origin (visa requirements) and at the port of entry (air or sea), and not on internal processes. Compared with European countries, the UK Immigration Service has a tiny number of officers involved in internal operations. The ISED has 564 staff in all, but most of these are in administrative work; the Ports Directorate has 2,425 officers. All this reflects two aspects of the UK political tradition, reinforced by policy in the Thatcher years. On the one hand, individual liberty is highly prized, there is no requirement for citizens to register with local authorities (except as voters and taxpayers), and no internal identity document. Some of this spills over on to immigrants, and racial equality laws give some protection against forms of official harassment that are common in European countries (Düvell et al., 2000). Secondly, the UK labour market is much less state-regulated than its European counterparts, and the Conservative governments removed most remaining protections. Interviews with undocumented immigrant workers showed that most were able to get work and accommodation in London within a week, even if they spoke no English. The Asylum and Immigration Act 1996 section 8, provided for the first time for employers to be prosecuted for hiring workers without proper checks on immigration status, thus bringing the UK slightly more into line with European practice. However, two years later not a single prosecution had been brought, reflecting the persistence of the cultural tradition, and the fact that ISED staff, who are very overstretched and practise in a reactive way, do not give such offences priority, and lack the organizational capacity to follow prosecutions through.

In research interviews, undocumented immigrant workers spoke of a general anxiety about their irregular status (they could have been removed from the country if caught), but most of them recognized that in practice they were in little danger from internal controls. Most knew someone who had been removed, and a few had actually escaped by hiding or fleeing during raids, or been tipped off by employers to stay away from work on a particular day. Among the Brazilians and Poles in London, fears of denunciation by fellow nationals far outweighed fear of other means of detection and removal by the authorities, or denunciation by UK nationals. The ISED interviewees said that many of their 'target' offenders were immigrants who had been denounced, and that most informants were members of UK minority ethnic communities – often citizens who resented competition for jobs and wages by 'illegals' (Jordan and Vogel, 1997; Düvell and Jordan, 1999). This kind of unrestrained competition between legals and illegals was not evident among more solidaristic Turkish and Kurdish interviewees, most of whom belonged to political associations and followed collectivist principles (Düvell and Jordan, 1999).

One ethical doubt about the research project was the extent to which we might discover strategies for evading capture among immigrants of which the Home Office was unaware, and might be quizzed by ISED interviewees about these. In fact almost all strategies were known, but only certain offenders could be targeted by ISED staff, because of scarce resources and reactive organizational systems. In the UK, immigrants enjoy legal protections which make it difficult in practice to remove them, and ISED staff have an almost 'sporting' attitude to their work, preferring a good chase to an easy capture, and criticizing incompetent immigration advisers for failing to tell their most vulnerable clients to abscond. This is an appropriate defence mechanism since, as we shall show, many of their operations go almost comically wrong because other agencies do not support them or co-operation degenerates into recrimination. Out of five 'raids' which Franck Düvell accompanied, not a single removable immigration offender was apprehended.

This case study selects two of these operations, which were planned to be carried out in co-operation with the BABFIS, the only agency with which the ISED has been able to sign a memorandum of understanding over such co-operation for intelligence and operational purposes (it tried all other public sector services, and was turned down; interviewees in NHS and local authority posts were openly hostile to ISED). Enforcement officers gave varying accounts of the motives for such co-operation, one senior manager saying that they accompanied BABFIS staff on raids at their request, mainly to protect immigrants' rights, the other that it was an important initiative of the ISED, to clamp down on massive shadow activity stemming from the use of false National Insurance numbers by immigrants.

In this instance, the joint aspects of the operation were immediately aborted when the prior visit to the local police station revealed that no police cells were available, because of another local event where trouble was expected (this typifies the low priority given by some police divisions to immigration offences, partly conditioned by the death during her arrest of Joy Gardiner, and by informal accountability to local minority ethnic community groups). At this point the ISED staff withdrew, one commenting, 'If we can't bang them up, it's not worth going there.' The BABFIS team then checked a Turkish-owned factory with a Turkish workforce. The factory was exceptionally clean and apparently very efficiently managed. The operation concentrated on computer-assisted checks of National Insurance numbers, contributions and claims. It was carried out in a professional, correct and polite manner, while staff – almost all of whom had relevant social security documentation to hand – remained calm and apparently unconcerned, continuing to go about their work, and answering questions readily. No obvious irregularities were picked up.

The second raid targeted an Asian-owned textile factory where conditions came close to those associated with a sweatshop. It had a much smaller, ethnically mixed workforce of Asian, African, white and black British workers. Several of the employees did not produce any papers and withheld all co-operation; they stared blankly in front of them without saying a word, like statues, not even giving their names and addresses, and seeming not to understand what was happening. The BABFIS officers' reaction was completely different from their behaviour in the previous raid: they took no further interest in benefit fraud, but shifted completely to immigration offences. The same officers were quite rude, aggressive and tough; they shouted and even tugged at employees. Repeated phone calls to the ISED asking them for support were refused due to shortage of staff there, causing some anger among BABFIS staff. The police officers present on the periphery of this scene appeared completely unaffected, aware that they could not in any case make arrests. In the end, the only realistic course was to insist that five immigration-offence suspects leave the workplace immediately, which is what happened.

Discussion

Many of New Labour's new policies and organizational structures raise issues of civil rights and accountability. This is especially obvious in the case of new agencies and legislation on juvenile delinquency, drugs, rough sleeping and employment-related conditionality of benefits (e.g. Employment Zones: see Chapter 7). We have chosen to illustrate these problems through the ISED and BABFIS, two agencies which are little known to the public, and isolated from the mainstream of the public sector's culture and informal practices.

The Third Way raises the priority and status of enforcement activities, and interviews with ISED staff showed their awareness of this, though they were justifiably critical that this was not reflected in increased resources. ISED staff were also conscious of racial equality laws and civil liberties issues; in this sense, they were more aware and scrupulous than their counterparts in countries like Germany. However, the fact that relations with other agencies are strained, and liaison is carried out only through sporadic contacts, often informal, and by the individual efforts of local officers, means that the ISED culture is not directly influenced by those of other public sector agencies. It has a characteristic tough enforcement flavour, more like the prison service or police, but softened by a sense of irony about the hopelessness of their tasks and the intractability of the problems they tackle – only the Marriage Abuse team, which conducts raids on suspected bogus weddings of immigrants at register offices, had any missionary zeal about it, or seemed to believe it was near winning the battle against irregularity.

New Labour favours such specialized agencies, keeps setting up new ones, and seems to prefer to isolate them from the Old Labour cultures of local authorities and the NHS. To have been involved in guerrilla war against Thatcherism (as the latter were) is to be the object of Third Way disapproval, and to risk losing tasks and resources to these new-style enforcers. New Labour wants staff who implement their policies not to shrink from tough action, and regards much of the culture of the public sector as lily-livered in this respect.

The problem is that local authority and NHS attitudes do not stem from professional ethics and experience alone, but also from formal and informal accountability to service users and to local community groups, especially those from minority ethnic communities. Even the police are far more accountable in these ways than new or old-but-newly-favoured enforcement agencies like these. The ISED is aware that it needs to improve this aspect of its service to the public, and its co-operation with the research project was a sign of its growing openness and transparency. But the behaviour of the BABFIS officers in the second raid showed that this process still has some way to go. Triggered by frustration, they acted in a way that indicated a lack of awareness of the requirements of professional ethics and accountability – even in front of an outside observer. Furthermore, although the most senior officer on this raid was very willing to take part in the research, repeated requests to his manager to allow him and others to be interviewed were simply ignored. This is not a very good indicator of willingness to be publicly accountable.

Two other aspects of this story are interesting. Neither the ISED nor BABFIS felt comfortable with their regulatory role in relation to employers/entrepreneurs, as opposed to employees. By tradition, and in line with the culture of previous Conservative governments, enterprise and ownership are allowed extensive liberties that public regulatory agencies limit only in extreme cases. Later interviews with undocumented immigrant workers revealed that the first (efficient, spotless) factory raided was practising a very serious form of irregularity, involving its whole workforce. The BABFIS officers did not query an anomaly in the payroll and wages record of this employer that was picked up by the researcher, even before the interview with the undocumented worker. In the second raid, the 'sweatshop' employer was given only a mild warning.

There is a paradox over a co-operation between agencies that New Labour structural reforms, and its strategy for creating new agencies, completely misses. Although ISED and BABFIS had overlapping interests, methods and cultures, both depend on the police for implementation of their tasks, and the police are not always willing or able to act as they require them to. This can cause resentment and recrimination between ISED and BABFIS staff, as occurred in this case. Across a range of policy issues, new agencies with an enforcement ethos in practice rely on old-style public services, either because of funding structures, or because they are needed in order to carry through their work to its final outcomes. Favouring tough organizations over ones seen as unnecessarily tender may even be counterproductive in terms of Third Way policy goals, if the latter are either too dispirited or too exhausted to play their parts. Changes in one part of the system can be effective only if there are compensating changes in others; otherwise all kinds of inefficiencies and perversities are generated. For further discussion of this see Chapter 8, pp. 194–8.

Authority and Street Credibility

For New Labour's policy programme to achieve its goals, implementation methods must translate the greater demands it wants to put on citizens into terms that make sense to their clienteles, making them into plausible reasons for acting in the ways they are required to act. Tough love is only going to be effective if citizens see the caring and concern behind the new conditions, rules and regulations, understand what is being required of them, and recognise that it is in their long-term interests to co-operate. Replacement of rights by rights-and-responsibilities will only work if service users carry over surface compliance with what is being asked of them by officials, face to face, deep into their everyday lives, so it becomes part of the lived culture of their interactions with family, kin, friends and neighbours. The alternative is that they find ways to feign co-operation, while actually pursuing strategies that are completely at odds with Third Way policy goals, and defeat New Labour's best intentions.

Margaret Thatcher's revolution in the cultures and practices of UK society, and especially the public sector, foundered on this step in the implementation process. It was one thing to make all individual and collective actors more cost conscious, more enterprising and more self-interestedly ambitious, but quite another to get them to keep the rules of intensified competition. In a polarized society, where the mainstream 'insiders' with wealth and secure jobs held all the advantageous cards, 'outsiders' had no motives to play the game by these rules (Jordan, 1995, 1996a). Instead, they invented their own, compensating themselves by informal (often illegal) means for lost rights and protections. In the end, the costs of this were obvious, in the crime statistics and the degenerating social relations of poor districts. Mainstream citizens who shut out issues of social justice in voting for Margaret Thatcher found that they returned (literally) by the back door, in the shape of break-ins, fear and insecurity, and higher insurance premiums (Jordan et al., 1994). This necessitated an attempt to remoralize society by exploitation (John Major's failed Back to Basics campaign), a return to retributive criminal justice (a rise of over 60 per cent in the prison population since 1993) and eventually Tony Blair's election on a platform of populist and paternalist enforcement policies.

In the public sector, a parallel story was unfolding. Staff in departments such as social services were caught between the budgetary requirements of the Conservative governments, and the growing needs and disaffection of service users. Trying to find a strategic balance between the two, they implemented the letter of the reforms, and the new managerial ethos; but at the front line workers tended to resist the harshest consequences of restrictions, and to bend the rules in favour of their clienteles. In the end, with the poll tax revolt, this shaky equilibrium was shattered. Poor people resisted the new tax by the most effective means: Can't Pay, Won't Pay. Along with spontaneous demonstrations, organized protests (outside the political mainstream, mainly through Militant), it was this resistance by defection and default (Scott, 1990) that contributed to the breakdown, leading to the fall of Thatcher – the 'Revenge of the Poor' (Hoggett and Burns, 1992). Local authorities and the main political opposition parties were left stranded in the middle, along with public sector staff, deploring non-compliance yet unable to control or channel resistance. Failure to implement an unpopular and unjust measure caused the eventual collapse of the political movement that had ushered in the whole reform process, and sowed the seeds of the Conservatives' subsequent troubles.

New Labour cannot afford to have a similar disaster. But it has put its faith in a particularly ambitious and untested method of carrying its programme into action. Nothing in the record of social work or similar professional activities suggests that individual interventions in citizens' lives to change their attitudes and behaviour can produce durable changes. Rather all the evidence indicates that short-term successes are likely to be followed by long-term diminishing returns. Medicine and education illustrate the same phenomenon. Breakthroughs occur through quite other factors – rising standards of living, greater social and economic equality, more effective public health and better public libraries (Moroney, 1976) – not new cures, more spending on health care (Lenaghan, 1999) or new educational methods (not even, as we are daily reminded, new principles for *organizing* health services and schools). The latter may show a temporary improvement in standards, but this quickly plateaus out, or slides backwards. For all their pretensions and claims, professionals can seldom identify a crucial difference they have made that shows up in the statistics.

A lot hangs on the success of tough love – far more than should, for a government that constantly emphasizes the need for prudence. If the programme is to be successful, and not deteriorate through the kinds of unintended consequences, negative spillovers and costly sequelae that dogged Thatcherism, then reliable implementation practices must be discovered, and quickly. The worst that could occur is that citizens (who are not persuaded of the justice or viability of the shifts in behaviour and culture required) discover strategic ways of using new systems for quite different purposes, defeating the whole thrust of the reforms, and throwing the delicate balance of a complex set of interactions out of equilibrium. The promising starts made in some policy domains (e.g. over youth employment) would then be in jeopardy, along with the remaining parts of the programme.

There is both good news and bad news about the risks involved in all this. The good news is that some of the unintended consequences might, in fact, be beneficial in the long term. The Third Way is rather paternalistic and authoritarian in its methods; this is probably justified as a short-term response to the legacy of Thatcherism – its excessive economic individualism and unrestrained competition (see pp. 31–3) – but it is not desirable in the longer term. If new systems allow strategic action that is against the aims of legislators, but actually liberates and empowers citizens, this is a potentially advantageous aspect for the future development of good governance. Throughout this part of the book we have argued that Third Way values are not successfully translated into policies in the programme. Much of the rhetoric of empowerment and inclusion is verbose, unconvincing and even hypocritical. Paradoxically, if citizens adopt liberating and empowering strategies of resistance to paternalistic and oppressive measures, this actually strengthens the long-term resilience of new systems (see pp. 178–9 and 193–4), so long as these do not frustrate each other's intentions, as they did under Thatcherism (Jordan et al., 1994, Chapters 7 and 8).

The bad news is that strategies will tend to have the latter undesirable effect, if reforms are perceived as differentially affecting life chances. The danger is that, as under Thatcherism, society will divide into two halves, insiders and outsiders, with members of each following strategies that are individually rational but defeat the purposes of the other, or of fellow members of that group. This is most likely to occur if New Labour's over-regulation of the public sector and the poor comes to be too much of a contrast with its *laissez-faire* approach to members of the mainstream. None of the rhetoric of remoralization and inclusion through compulsion applies to those who do not have to rely on state benefits and services, who need take no notice of either the morality talk or the rules and conditions. Poor people and public sector workers may come to resent their constraints and mainstream actors' freedoms, and turn to strategies that are costly for taxpayers, while the latter in turn start to resent the rising costs, and resist contributing to revenues. This is the classic remedy for an impasse, as under late Thatcherism, and the breakdown of a reforming movement.

For example, what are mothers on income support or in-work benefits like Working Families Tax Credit (WFTC) supposed to make of the new condition that they are required to attend child health and welfare clinics to qualify for higher maternity grants? Other mainstream mothers are free to use such health and welfare facilities as they choose. If nurses and health visitors are able to practise tough love in a way that convinces 'welfare mothers' that they can gain useful resources (in terms of advice and assistance) from such contacts, then a virtuous circle of income transfer and better services is completed. But if 'welfare mothers' feel demeaned and stigmatized by the process, encounter what they experience as high-handedness, condemnation or discrimination, they will act strategically and manipulatively to maximize their returns on these contacts in ways that are costly to the Exchequer, but do not benefit children. Then taxpaying families will criticize the transfers and the services, and vote against the government on such issues. A vicious circle of costly unpopularity and wasteful expenditure will be complete.

What do we know about how to work effectively in services which try to combine elements of conditionality or compulsion with care? The research answer is probably that we learn to be pessimistic, at least in the longer term, about the chances of such services achieving positive change. Public sector social services tend to revert to type, either as rather bleak Poor Law style provision, or as mainly investigative and enforcement-orientated branches of social control. This is particularly the case in polarized societies, where such services are reserved for the poor. It is less the case in more egalitarian societies, like the Scandinavian countries, where they are used by almost the whole spectrum of the population.

We also know quite a lot about *the kinds of practice* that stand the best chance of being effective in such agencies, or indeed in any agencies giving personal social services. These have repeatedly been shown to be ones where the social worker combines genuine empathy and communication of support with good listening, and the capacity to challenge service users in an honest, personal and human way, which may be sensitive, humorous or tough, but is always straight and not evasive or manipulative (Sainsbury et al., 1982; Howe, 1993). Service users value fairness and honesty, and recognize when social workers are willing to invest something of themselves in the relationship, to risk something, and to make themselves a bit vulnerable. Service users then feel that they are not the only ones who are bearing the costs of the relationships, being asked to open themselves to change and new perspectives, or being expected to give up the security of familiar ways of coping. They need to feel respected and valued, and that their defences and cultures are recognized as what they are (survival skills) rather than seen as obstacles to professional purposes. Then they can trust and be available for influence and change (see also Chapter 9).

In some ways this is a taller order than it sounds, especially if such practice has to be maintained over a long career. Bob Holman (1981, 1988, 1998) is probably the only publicly recognized UK example of someone who has sustained a life of street-credible service to poor people in rough areas, based on sharing their joys and sorrows, crises and triumphs. He is widely regarded as a saint. It is difficult to train people for sainthood.

Nevertheless, the research literature does give plenty of clues about how something less noble than sainthood, but more effective than everyday average local authority social service practice, might be sustained. Unfortunately, most of the research literature of the 1990s does this in a very dry and partisan way, conveying what is required as a technical approach to policy issues, communicable through checklists and a minute breakdown of detailed operations (see pp. 64–77). Something of this scientific, top-down approach is obviously an important part of the recipe for success, but it is a necessary and not a sufficient condition. Such bloodless positivism cuts little ice unless it is combined with the more human qualities that we tried to capture in the previous two paragraphs.

The sad thing for social work is that the literature that used to attempt to convey these qualitative aspects has almost entirely dried up. Only a few research accounts (such as Hall, 1997; Packman and Hall, 1997; Parton and O'Byrne, 2000) give the kinds of vivid, blow-by-blow versions that provide credible models of practice. Meanwhile, research into the qualitative elements of effectiveness have (like much of the best in what used to be social work practice) migrated to the field of counselling. For example Howe (1993), who teaches social work, has published a detailed and comprehensive review of the qualitative factors in effectiveness – but in counselling, not social work. Yet what goes round comes round; no doubt the turn of the cycle of fashion and preference will before long change all this and allow practice to be written about in a human way again.

CASE EXAMPLE: THE SCOTT FAMILY

Recently, Brian Scott made contact with his former probation officer, almost twenty-five years after they last met. At that time Brian was in prison, and now he wanted to bring his former probation officer up to date with news of himself and his family. A successful businessman, he lived in another part of the country, owned a large and comfortable house, and had two young children. He is now in his mid-fifties, a substantial and respected member of the community.

Brian Scott followed a career of crime for twenty years, after being sent to an approved school at the age of 10, for a trivial offence, committed with his 8-year-old brother. The local police and the then probation officer for the town (a former policeman) decided that the family were trouble, and that Brian (the biggest and ablest son) should be put away. He became a determined, accomplished and knowledgeable burglar, who made a lot of money but served several long sentences. His first marriage ended while he was in prison.

His mother died when he was 18, leaving the care of her family to the new, and then young, probation officer, who was supervising several of them. All of them – the other three sons and the daughter – were in contact with the criminal justice system, either directly or via their spouses, so the probation officer was at one time working with all of them at once, even though they were all either married, living independently or in prison (only one other brother served time, for offences of violence).

Brian Scott remembers more about these days than his probation officer does, though the latter has a good memory. He recalls his probation officer as 'always on our side', as taking risks with his own career and reputation, 'putting something of himself on the line'. He remembers the fact that he always received regular visits in prison, as did his wife and children at home; that his probation officer came to family weddings and his mother's funeral; that he kept the family in touch with each other after his mother's death; that he respected and listened to Brian's point of view, even when he was justifying his criminality; that he was not afraid of getting into political discussions about the class origins of criminal justice systems (he was a political activist), or about the economic origins of injustice and oppression.

All the family and their spouses have now turned their backs on crime; all are settled and have good jobs, except the one who has been forced to take early retirement through poor health. None of their children has been in trouble with the law, and perhaps more strikingly, nor have any of their twenty-six grandchildren.

Discussion

The Scott family was regarded as one of the 'worst' two or three in the town, and targeted by the police and the magistracy. But they were remarkably energetic and positive in their outlook on life, if sometimes unorthodox in their methods. Their probation officer found them rewarding company, if a bit exhausting at times. One of his wry memories is of taking the youngest brother back to court for breach of his probation order (the only time he ever did this), for failing to lead an industrious life – he always got into trouble when actually unemployed but pretending to work. The probation officer coached him so well in how to rebut this charge that the young man quite easily sustained his defence against the action. He never got into trouble again.

It may be a complete coincidence that the whole family, even Brian, who was committed to criminality, have done so well by any standards. Their former probation officer would like to think that he made some contribution to this outcome – and certainly not by methods that are fashionable or even tolerable in today's new model probation service.

Conclusions

Street-credible social work is not easy to practise in statutory settings, because it is a prerequisite of effectiveness that the social worker gets alongside the service user, invests something positive in the relationship, and somehow makes it worth his or her while to participate, trust and persist, even if not in the short to medium term to change. It is far easier to do this in settings where the social distance between practitioner and service user is small, as in street-level, support or project work, in community groups and some voluntary agencies. This is why the number and scope of all these has grown, as most local authority social work and probation have gone into a self-protective shell of formalism and relied on arm's-length methods.

In spite of these difficulties for statutory practice, the Third Way has expanded the number of agencies and practitioners with authority over citizens' lives and choices and the power to enforce compliance of various kinds. New Labour is running a big risk in relying on these forms of individual intervention, because there is little in the history and record of such methods to indicate that it is safe to build a whole policy programme around them. Tough love may work, given both intelligent and subtle practitioners, using both strategic thinking and good communication skills and investing a lot of themselves in their work. But this will depend on the organizational context and policy thrust of their work, as much as their sophistication and commitment. It is to these that we turn in the next two chapters.

PART III

7

Social Work and Economic Activity

In this final part of the book, we will develop the alternative approach sketched in the previous three chapters, and argue that it could provide a very different theoretical and organizational basis for practice. Such a shift would not necessarily involve huge changes in the kinds of face-to-face support, interaction and challenge that occur between givers and receivers of services, but it would require a reconceptualization and reorganization of these activities. Above all, it would seek to break down the growing distinction between social work (as an official practice, concerned mainly with assessment and provision of social care for vulnerable people, and the control of dangerousness in society) and a whole swathe of other activities involving counselling, support, the provision of alternative living opportunities, social inclusion, advocacy, economic activation and so on.

Here we are concerned with one fundamental source of that distinction – the exclusion of social and community work from the sphere of economic activity. We will argue that this can be traced to the origins of the Keynesian era of welfare state development, when 'the economy' was strictly separated from 'society' as an aspect of governmental regulation and management, and local authority social services were allocated the role of regulating 'the social' (Parton, 1991).

Because social protection relied on revenues from a kind of economic growth that used restraints on competition as the main feature of its 'truce' between national organized labour and national capital, in the advanced industrialized countries – unlike less developed countries, which make no such rigid distinctions – it was seen as essential to exclude part of the population from economic participation, and part of the real economy from the formal economy. Older people, people with disabilities, children and (in many countries, especially in Continental Europe) married women, were discouraged or barred from the labour market, mainly in order to allow labour organizations to limit their membership and exclude outside competition that might drive down wages. The informal economy of the household, the smallholding, the co-operative, the association and the community was marginalized, and its activity and output excluded from official economic statistics. Work was defined as employed labour, in what Guy Standing has called 'the Century of the Labouring Man' (Standing, 1999, p. 337).

Conversely, the growth of state-funded personal social services relied on the notion of a sphere of interactions that was 'private', in the sense that it had an enabling function in relation to economic production, but was essentially one of *social reproduction*. In Continental Europe the concept of 'subsidiarity' implied that this sphere should remain largely beyond the scope of public power (Badelt, 1990), and hence personal social services – which tended to be underdeveloped in these countries – were provided by voluntary agencies (Jones and May, 1992) and funded by local, not national, governments. In the UK and the Scandinavian countries (especially) greater involvement of married women in employment implied that the state had some responsibilities to supply services for child care and the care of other 'dependent' family members; in Scandinavia in particular, this led to the very extensive development of such services, which did not occur in the UK.

But one consequence of this rigid division into public economic sphere and private social sphere was that social work could play no role in economic development, and have no relevance for production and exchange. As we shall show, no such distinction held in the less developed world. Social work there was part of *community development*, and both involved stimulating the informal economy of non-market activity (communal gardens, village water supplies and irrigation schemes, mutual aid and co-operation over provision of machinery, raw materials, seeds, and food supplies) and the social infrastructure that sustained it (Batten, 1957). There were always problems in the relationship between such aspects of the informal and traditional economy and the formal economy's developmental trajectory (and indeed between the traditional structures of communal social relations and capitalist or colonialist ones), but these were sites for political debate and collective action, not rigid separation and exclusionary regulation.

The relationship between the Third Way and social work crucially concerns these issues. What is distinctive about the Third Way, as we saw in Part I, is its attempt to redefine the boundaries between the economic sphere and the social sphere, and between the public obligations of citizenship and the private moral duties that citizens have towards each other (Jordan, 1998a). Through its efforts to increase the labour-market participation of claimant groups, including lone parents (mainly women), and its focus on creating new employment in the sphere of social reproduction (especially social care of all kinds), New Labour is raising important issues about the division of labour between the formal and the informal economies – between the world of employment and the work done by household members, family and friendship networks, neighbourhood support systems, community groups and associations, volunteers. These programmes, and the redefinitions they involve, create new issues about the role of social work in society, at the boundaries between the economic and the social.

On the one hand, we see the creation of a range of new public sector jobs along this boundary, concerned with shepherding, cajoling, pushing or driving claimants into formal employment or training, but using means that owe something to social work practice. On the other (as we saw in Chapter 6, pp. 144–8), there are whole new agencies concerned with managing those excluded from the formal economy, or from some aspects of society (such as asylum seekers), or policing the rules of the boundary (such as Benefits Agency fraud investigation staff). Consciously separated from both of these we have local authority social services departments and the big voluntary agency service providers, along with the commercial sector of social care agencies, seen as having the narrowly defined function of meeting the residual needs of those who fall into the category of being in 'genuine need' of services, and most of whom fall outside the sphere of the formal economy. Between all of these move the new and assorted, uncoordinated ranks of project, street-level and support workers, who are of the social sphere, but often – as in the case of the Emmaus Community (see pp. 111–16 and 131–3) – also involved in stimulating and supporting informal economic activity, some of which directly challenges the categorization and the strict divisions enforced by the Third Way.

Box 17   Regeneration and social inclusion

Job Advertisement

Corporate Resources Group
GROUP ACCOUNTANT (REGENERATION)
£33,450–£34,797

Applications are invited for the post of Group Accountant – Regeneration in the Central Finance Division of the Corporate Resources Group.

This is a new post and the successful applicant will provide the finance lead across a range of regeneration initiatives in Ealing …

Ealing   Investor in People   An Equal Opportunities Employee
(*Guardian*, 1 December 1999)

The field of regeneration and social inclusion is now awash with new schemes, units and organizations. In homelessness alone, 'The available funding is a giant web of interweaving allocations for specific projects and initiatives, often over three years and usually through at least two agencies, working with numerous other organizations. It is no wonder that critics claim that homelessness has become an industry employing almost as many people as it helps. Most initiatives are operated by professional full-time staff working for charities and church groups …. They receive funding from a wide range of sources, including central government, through the rough sleepers' unit and through the benefits agency, from local authorities, housing associations, the housing corporation, other national charities …. There is a huge overlap of work, but each organization insists that they maintain their own area of expertise, whether that be outreach work …; counselling for drug or

---

addiction problems or mental health problems; training and employment
programmes; or long-term resettlement projects.'

Julia Hartley-Brewer, 'Tangled Web of Competing Charities',
Guardian, 16 December 1999

We will argue that this programme, and the assumptions it conceals, sets up a
range of tensions and potential conflicts that threaten its own success. The informal economy (of care, and of the social reproduction of a convivial, convenient,
comfortable and civilized social environment) is a crucial element in the quality
of life we all enjoy. It cannot be replaced by a commodified, commercialized
set of paid activities – or if it is, the costs of all kinds are very high. The informal
economy should be nurtured and conserved, as much as the formal should
be stimulated (Holman, 1998; Donnison, 1998). Deprived areas need social
regeneration, as part of economic regeneration (Ginsburg, 1999). There are
glimmers of recognition of all this in New Labour's policy documents, but only
glimmers.

On the other hand, formal social work (the work of voluntary agencies as well
as that of the local authority social services departments) cannot afford to get
locked into the very restrictive roles that the Third Way has conceived for it.
Compared with the 1970s, when ideas about community work and the political
dimensions of social work were at their height (Jordan and Parton, 1983), the
profession has allowed itself to become confined to a very narrow instrumental
and individualistic conception of social intervention. But even in those days,
when it was fashionable for social workers to be involved in collective action,
campaigning, advocacy and consciousness-raising, this view of its role in society
was too narrow, because it excluded *economic* issues. Indeed, because it was
equally fashionable then to deplore the work ethic, and to show something
like contempt for those who toiled in the productive sector, these versions of
community work even reinforced the barriers between the economic and the
social. Such a position is no longer tenable, if social work is not to become a
marginalized ghetto of restrictive, formal, standardized, regulated social care,
attracting few gifted or creative practitioners and giving an undesirable service to
its recipients.

The key to avoiding this fate is the informal economy. We will show that social
work ignores this at its peril, because it will become the site of all the potentially
creative and productive debates of the next ten years. New Labour's obsession
with creating employment in the formal economy has built-in limits and contradictions. At a certain point, these will manifest themselves in conflicts on the
boundaries between the formal and informal economies, about how the tasks of
social reproduction are to be done and how the work roles of informal carers and
volunteers are to be valued. At this point, social work can either become part of
the problem or part of the solution. If it takes the Third Way uncritically, it will
be part of the problem. If it takes the alternative path we will indicate, it can be
part of the solution.

Social Work in the Shadow of the Market Economy

In both the welfare states of the advanced capitalist countries and the state socialist command economies of the Soviet Bloc, the gains from industrialization and urbanization in the third quarter of the twentieth century were turned into gains in the welfare of citizens by Keynesian and Marxist-Leninist economic management. What these two systems had in common was the relegation of informal and communal activity to the margins of social life and their exclusion from the public sphere. In this way, in welfare states the 'insiders' of the formal economy – mainly men who were members of trade unions, professional organizations or public service agencies, or owners of stakes in businesses – were able to make significant gains in earnings, and still leave scope for benefits and services to be distributed to those excluded from the formal economy by these systems.

Welfare state development was possible because of the *closed national economies* of the postwar period. As a result of wartime constraints, following the inter-war depression, trade in goods and services was very low, and there were strict controls of capital movements. Governments could control their national economic boundaries; behind protective barriers on trade and mobility of capital they built social protection, on the basis of agreements between 'captive capitalists' and organized labour, passing on the costs of restrained competition and state regulation mainly to 'captive consumers' (Scharpf, 1999), and gaining also from 'unequal exchange' with less developed countries (Standing, 1999). Hence the 'embedded liberalism' of welfare states (Ruggie, 1983) allowed market correction systems and redistributive schemes for full employment and social security, even though the organizational means by which this was achieved varied between the advanced capitalist countries (Esping-Andersen, 1990).

These systems were eroded or collapsed in the 1970s and 1980s because trade was gradually liberalized through the General Agreement on Tariffs and Trade and the World Trade Organization; because international firms found new ways to break out of capital and exchange controls; because of the oil price shocks; because the newly industralizing economies, especially in South-East Asia, began to expand and accelerate, leading to a new international division of labour in manufacturing; and because, through all these developments, welfare states were forced to compete with each other for investment and jobs (Scharpf, 1999). Above all, *tax competition* meant that smaller countries were able to offer attractive locations especially for international companies and individuals to declare their profits or interest payments, which limited the extent to which national governments could tax capital or personal savings. This meant that governments were forced to borrow, to tax earnings, or to increase social insurance contributions, and most did all three (Genschell, 1999). Rises in social insurance contributions, such as those that occurred in Germany, were particularly damaging to employment in low-skilled occupations, and help explain the failure of the German economy to reduce unemployment (Scharpf, 1999).

Another consequence of this was the erosion of the *tax base*, because people with clear entitlement to social security benefits who were excluded from the formal economy during the 'shake-out' of less skilled labour were able to adapt by doing undeclared work for cash, which was advantageous both for them and for those who paid them, because it escaped the tax net. The growth of the shadow economy was an international phenomenon, but in the UK it took a particular form. First, large numbers of formerly excluded married women took formal employment throughout the Thatcher–Major years, as part of a main-stream household strategy for maximization through one secure 'insider's' job (usually for the man) with an occupational pension, perks and welfare benefits and part-time secondary earnings by the partner (normally a 'supportive' wife, who invested in the man's career as her main source of security and advantage) (Jordan et al., 1994). Second, as we have seen (pp. 31–3), in households with no such 'insider' in employment, often no other member had an incentive to take formal jobs, though one or more would do some undeclared work to supple-ment their benefits (Jordan et al., 1992; Evason and Woods, 1995; Rowlingson et al., 1997).

Hence the significance of the informal economy changed. As well as consist-ing of unpaid household activities and self-provisioning, including do-it-yourself home improvements – part of the mainstream strategy which expanded in the 1980s (Gershuny, 1983; Pahl, 1984) – it included both self-help and community groups (usually underfunded, and run mainly by women, especially lone parents), *and* the shadowy world of undeclared work for cash. The latter merged into criminality, including drug dealing, prostitution and hustling, all of which grew to fill the economic vacuum of very deprived districts, with neither employment opportunities nor market outlets (Jordan, 1996a). It was the erosion of the tax base, the leakage in public expenditure through benefits 'fraud', and the links with crime, that New Labour sought to challenge through its welfare-to-work New Deals (DSS, 1998); but this has also had effects on the rest of the informal economy, of caring, volunteering, self-help and mutual support.

All this affects social work in a number of ways. Much of the work of social control, investigation and enforcement, focused on families with children and on young people, has brought social workers into conflict with service users over the cultural practices of poor people, especially undeclared work, serial partnership, drug use, prostitution and criminality – all of which represent adaptation to or resistance against economic disadvantage and exclusion, but which have bad con-sequences for children, more vulnerable members of the community, and the quality of life of these districts. Yet the same economic conditions have generated mutual support groups, survivor organizations, community associations and action committees, all of which sustain the bonds of these communities, and build up social capital (Jack and Jordan, 1999). To be effective, social work needs such social capital (network-generated norms of trust, co-operation, reciprocity and mutuality); there is massive evidence that the presence of groups, associations and organizations of all kinds is positively correlated with reliable child protec-tion and child care (Garbarino and Sherman, 1980; Garbarino and Kostelny, 1992). In so far as recent developments in the formalization of practice and the reliance on arm's-length methods isolates social workers from these cultures of support and assistance, they have reduced its effectiveness. However, new groups, projects and units have sprung up, mainly in the voluntary and community bridge the gap between over-formal practice and the everyday, guts world of small local informal organizations.

Social work's position is therefore in the shadow of the market economy in two senses (Jordan, 1999d). First, all activities connected with community, co-operation, caring and sharing are overshadowed by activities that produce goods and services for markets, for personal gain (paid employment) and through processes of competition. By the same token, activities that build or sustain social capital are overshadowed by activities that build or sustain financial and physical capital (money, plant, machinery, etc.). Hence activities in the shadow of the market economy must always be accountable to that economy in terms of efficiency, cost-effectiveness, value for money, and a contribution to productivity or growth. They must always uphold the values and priorities of the market, including the commodification of labour power – so there is pressure, including official pressure, on people doing unpaid caring or community work in the informal economy to take paid work, contribute through such paid employment, and see this as fulfilling their citizenship obligations. This may deplete the social capital on which social work practice depends for its ethical validity and practical effectiveness.

The second sense is the whole shadow economy of work that is not declared for tax and benefit purposes, and is done by unauthorized workers (including undocumented immigrants), merging into crime itself. This shadow economic activity is important, in that it indicates a possibility for exchanges outside the formal, regulated economy which are advantageous for the participants. It may also indicate potential for economic and social regeneration that cannot be realized through the present programme of the Third Way. While there are some strong arguments for limiting the scope of the shadow economy (see pp. 32–4), to broaden the tax base and ensure that 'hypercasualisation' (Jordan, 1996a) and unrestricted competition (Jordan and Travers, 1998) do not lead to a 'race to the bottom' in terms of undercutting of wages and conditions, there is also a part of this activity that can generate new skills, new enterprises and new formal employment, if it is channelled as a link to the formal economy (Jordan, 1998a, Chapter 5).

Box 18   Poverty and inequality under New Labour

Despite New Labour's success in expanding employment, there is as yet little evidence that its programme has reduced poverty or inequality among the millions who continue to depend on benefits.

During the previous twenty years there was a widening of the gap between rich and poor greater than in any country except New Zealand. The decision to continue to tie benefits to prices rather than incomes leaves large numbers of people – those with long-term disabilities and illnesses, and the long-term unemployed in depressed regions – falling further behind those in work (whose real earnings have risen 50 per cent in twenty years). David Piachaud (*Guardian*, 1 September 1999) showed that although New Labour's policies on child benefit and tax credits had lifted 800,000 children's incomes above the poverty line, another

3.7 million remained on or below it. And even among those in work, Gordon Brown has acknowledged, 230,000 still face a poverty trap through withdrawal rates of more than 70 per cent for each extra £1 earned (*Guardian* letters, 9 September 1999).

In an era of rapid economic and social change, those on low incomes are also more vulnerable than under old, collectivist regimes with employment and income protection. People in the lowest 20 per cent of earners are twice as likely to suffer poverty if they become unemployed or lone parents (Peter Taylor-Gooby, *Guardian*, 28 September 1999). They are also the most vulnerable to the economic insecurities that have accompanied globalization. They have the worst opportunities, the highest risks, and the least scope for private provision.

Other losers from change are peripheral regions, like Cornwall (with a mean household income of £17,400 a year and GDP of £7,511 per capita, the lowest in the country) and Tyne and Wear. With the decline in manufacturing employment, large cities are suffering economic decline, and smaller towns prospering as sites for service expansion (*Guardian*, 7 December 1999). Inequalities in health provide further evidence of these trends. Infant mortality rates are twice as high in Glasgow as in the Home Counties (*Guardian*, 4 December 1999), and there is a difference of 9.5 years between the life expectancy of professional men and their unskilled manual contemporaries (*Guardian*, 3 December 1999); both gaps have widened under New Labour.

In this chapter, we will look at the origins and consequences of the separation of social work from economic activity, both formal and informal, and at how this might be remedied to the advantage of both practitioners and service users. We will also analyse the likely longer-term consequences of New Labour's bias against the informal economy (of care as well as informal, undocumented or deregulated production and exchange) and some of the unintended outcomes of the Third Way's approach. In particular, we will show how the emphasis on formal employment over other activities relevant to the regeneration of deprived areas can have undesirable social consequences, and give perverse incentives. For the sake of its broader values and longer-term prospects, social work cannot afford to ignore these issues, or to become marginalized in these policy debates. The growth of new official agents and organizations concerned with employment counselling and semi-compulsory guidance, using quasi-social-work methods, along with the growth of project, street-level and support work concerned with economic activity (see pp. 125–7) highlights these dangers, and these possibilities for change.

Community Development and Social Work

Some of these divisions and rigid distinctions can be traced to the history of social work, rather than that of the welfare state. In the earliest days of the profession, charitable workers were involved in economic activities of many kinds as they strove to help 'deserving' poor people earn their livings, and some 'undeserving' ones (in prisons, reformatories or psychiatric hospitals) learn to work and improve their skills. Furthermore, the Settlement Movement pioneered by Canon Barnet in the late nineteenth century focused on the economic plight of poor areas in industrial cities, and how poor people could take collective action to improve their situation (Woodruffe, 1962). It was only with the advent of psychosocial and psychodynamic approaches from the USA that British social workers, especially in psychiatric hospitals and child guidance clinics, concentrated on the intrapersonal and therapeutic aspects of their tasks, to the neglect of the economic ones (Jordan, 1983, Chapter 3); and the postwar local authority services subsequently concentrated on the family or substitute care, leaving the major national ministries to deal with economic issues.

Community work, as a distinct occupation, moved in and out of the social work mainstream during the second half of the twentieth century. It became a distinguishable method or approach in the 1950s (Leaper, 1968), and was most closely identified as a major element in social work in the early 1970s. In the early postwar years, the idea of work with a collective focus in deprived areas, organizing self-help and networks of mutuality, owed as much to the Settlements and the socialism of Clement Attlee (1920) as to the British colonial tradition of community development – attempts to mobilize local communal ties and social systems, and reconcile them with processes of education and political democratization (Batten, 1957). But by the 1970s, when the Labour government had set up community development projects to tackle inner-city problems of housing decay, racism and deprivation, these were resolutely orientated towards the state, activating citizens for political claims for redistribution, and shunning both self-help and economic enterprise (Benington, 1972). Thus although these developments gave a strongly left-wing, collectivist, radical push to social work's methods, and provided a tough critique of the traditional individual or family focus of casework, along with the uncritical acceptance of racist and sexist social structures, they acted in many ways to reinforce the established exclusion of economic practice (as opposed to economic theory about the origins of social problems) from social work's canon.

However, the consolidation of poverty, homelessness and unemployment in the UK social landscape provoked the grassroots emergence of all kinds of projects, especially in the early 1980s, which combined elements of social support with attempts at small-scale local economic regeneration, through co-operatives and community businesses as well as informal community groups (Deakin, 1987). In cities such as Sheffield (Blunkett, 1983), and through the Greater London Council, local governments promoted these initiatives during the early Thatcher years, as bastions against the impact of the global market forces her policies embraced. A 'community sector', distinct from either the public sector or the voluntary sector (of larger charities, many of which became engaged in service provision under contract to local authorities), and involved in informal economic activity as well as social support, became an institutionalized, long-term feature of UK society.

A few leading writers about social work have made the connections between these changes in First World societies and the social relations of the Third World. In particular, James Midgley has consistently emphasized the relevance of economic globalization and its consequences for those on the margins of society, concluding that 'Social workers in the industrial countries are able to benefit from the extensive experience of their Third World colleagues with developmental forms of social work' (Midgley, 1997, p. 65). These approaches stress both the improvement of individuals' capacities and collective, communal strategies, all used to enable people to act in pursuit of their social and economic development (Midgley, 1995). Mayo writes of a 'radical' or 'transformational' tradition in British community work, which underlines the promotion of approaches 'which empower communities to develop strategies to tackle deprivation and disadvantage' (Mayo, 1998, p. 169). This implies a whole sector of activities through which local people come together to work out their needs, and then join in taking action to meet those needs – including those for economic development.

The activities of the community sector echoed the British colonial tradition of community development as well as broadening the forms of community work that evolved in the postwar era. That earlier tradition shaped many of the ideas of Gandhi, whose thinking about communal production and mutuality in rural India was influenced by his early years in South Africa; it contributed strongly to policies of community development in post-Independence Indian economic policy in the 1950s (Gwynn, personal communication, 1999); and, of course, it moulded Nelson Mandela, a product of the educationalist and democracy-promoting tendencies in that tradition, through his boarding-school background in the Transkei (Mandela, 1996, Chapter 6). Community development sought to strengthen the informal economy as an alternative, *moral* system (Scott, 1970), based on communal ownership, co-operation, sharing and redistribution, collective production and consumption, and the conservation of the commons (Ostrom, 1990). It was, as economists have pointed out (Popkin, 1975), rational and efficient for peasants to pool their resources in certain circumstances, especially where partitioning of land was costly and difficult to enforce, where such divisions would lead to an under-supply of public goods like water and storage space, and when a short harvest season required collective labour. Furthermore, such practices were not necessarily inconsistent with private property and markets; peasants could divide their time and energy between communal activity and production for sale outside the immediate local economy. Hence values like reciprocity, sharing and redistribution (present in all the great world religions) could flourish alongside a developing market and even eventually capitalist production.

However, there have always been issues about the balance of these two spheres of economic activity, in the developing world of Africa and Asia as much as in the advanced industralized economies. The informal sector is always vulnerable from two directions. First, the formal, commercial and capitalist sector may simply devastate it by the introduction of new technologies and organization of production. New kinds of planting, weeding and harvesting machinery can lead to new patterns of larger-scale landholding, new divisions of labour, consumption patterns, family lifestyles and economic preferences, to the point where communal values and systems survive only as resistance practices (Scott, 1985, 1990). Second, unsympathetic government policies can shift the balance of advantage from common ownership and co-operative methods towards commercialization and capitalism, for instance by poll taxes, land taxes, or other levies on local resources, or positive incentives for 'modernization' and 'development'. The informal economy then becomes little more than a collective memory, or a residual, impoverished ghetto. In the industralized countries of the West, the communal traditions of the medieval guilds and corporations live on in various mutual aid societies and foundations, but since the nineteenth century, when they still had a key welfare function (Hirst, 1994; Green, 1993), they have had mainly a symbolic social significance and little relevance for the economy itself. Attempts to revive these forms of associationalism sound somewhat backward-looking or utopian.

The re-emergence of the community sector of informal economic activity in the UK does not signal the rebirth of traditional self-help and working-class mutuality, as writers like Green (1993) would recommend, nor yet of associative democratic principles, as Hirst (1994) hopes. Rather it indicates the need for a bridge between the residues of communal organization and resistance, and the formal public world of the economy and local polity. The community sector draws on older notions of self-help and organizes itself in a bottom-up democratic way, but it also draws on many ideas from the emancipatory political agendas of the 1970s (especially feminism, anti-racism, anti-ableism and empowerment), and from the practices of resistance and mutual support in disadvantaged communities. It reflects the growth of survivor groups in fields like child sexual abuse, mental illness and domestic violence, as well as ideas of socialist co-operation, environmentalism and sustainability. All the projects and movements used in Chapter 6 as case studies in alternative approaches to social provision are also examples of the community sector in action – for informal production, advocacy and campaigning, often in the same organization.

But in addition to this the community sector reflects the growth of new ideas on social reproduction and grassroots production of goods and services, which are critical of the goals of market-making, commodification and the great transformation of the richness of social life into market exchanges and market values (Polanyi, 1944). At one end of this continuum of new ideas are radical greens, who choose to live communally, simply, and by practices of low energy use and recycling of waste from the industrial and commercial process. At the other are co-operatives, trying to find niches in the market and simply to use alternative organizational structures for production and alternative principles for distribution and earnings, rather than challenging the processes of exchange within which their products find ultimate users. The obvious criticism of all these groups and organizations is that they are so small and marginal that they trap participants in economic ghettos, where the absence of the division of labour, capital equipment, new technology and marketing sophistication denies them proper access to the benefits of the wider (global) economy (6, 1998; Buchanan, 1994): in other words, participation, choice, resistance to alienation and the values of opportunity, fulfilment of potential and choice. So the latter set of Third Way principles are deployed against the informal economy, as relatively unproductive and inefficient, a mistaken and even dangerous way to try to empower disadvantaged people, as well as a threat to the tax base and the rule of law (Jordan, 1998a, Chapters 3 and 5). The New Labour government is not against the community sector as such; but it is against the informalization of work, and for increasing formal economic participation. Hence the community sector suffers – indirectly – from Third Way policies.

There are some interesting parallels here with economic developments in the Second (post-communist) World, and also some interesting comparisons in relation to social work's position in this debate and these changes. In that part of Europe, the drastic de-industrialization that followed from the change of 1989 has resulted in a 'forced informalization' of parts of the economy. Whereas state socialism drove a whole generation of peasants off the land and into the city and the factory, the advent of global market forces is driving the next generation back into subsistence informal production, often of foodstuffs and fuel. In parts of the former Soviet Union and Ukraine, the whole of the middle and working classes have been driven down to the income levels of the poorest tenth under state socialism (Revenko, 1997); informal production of fruit and vegetables has become the main output of cities like Kiev (ibid.). In Central Europe, this has been less dominant as an economic trend, but in Slovakia especially it has been an important survival strategy since what some ordinary people still call 'the coup' of 1989 gave priority to profits, cost-effectiveness and productivity (Kusá, 1997). In other parts of Bulgaria, east Slovakia and northern Hungary, where formerly rural areas with iron mining were turned into specialist steel-producing districts, entire communities have been devastated by the 'new great transformation' of markets and the commercial imperative (Bryant and Mokrycki, 1994). The following case study illustrates how a local example of an informal economic initiative can alter the social as well as the economic prospects of a depressed community.

CASE STUDY: SZENTROLÁD COMMUNITY ASSOCIATION, HUNGARY

The village of Szentrolád is in a fairly remote, mountainous area, since the Middle Ages known for iron mining, in northern Hungary, close to the border with Slovakia, where many large steel mills were built in the communist era. The population of the area is some 40 per cent Roma (gypsy), a distinctive ethnic minority that has suffered racial discrimination throughout Central Europe and is now the focus of concern because of 'mass' applications for asylum from the Czech Republic and Slovakia. Roma people are generally housed together, in accommodation that is separated from ethnic Hungarians, in the towns and villages of this region. Whereas the unemployment rate for ethnic Hungarians is somewhere between 30 and 50 per cent, that for Roma is almost 100 per cent; the birth rate for ethnic Hungarians is virtually zero; that for Romas is still quite high. In many of the villages there is almost no indigenous economic activity, the shops are very sparsely stocked, and little but decline has occurred since 1989. Local authorities lack ideas and initiatives, and most inhabitants either seek family survival strategies, or migrate towards Budapest.

In Szentrolád, a local association was started five years ago. The driving force for its foundation was a Hungarian steel-factory worker, who has since been made redundant and is now unemployed. He had a normal factory worker's education and training, and described his motive for starting the association as 'local patriotism'. He saw that in the transition to a market economy the whole basis for formal economic activity in the area had collapsed. The association, which comprises some 70 per cent of the village, both ethnic Hungarian and Roma, decided to try to rent *all* of the surrounding land from the local co-operative (collective farm), which had ceased to function. They needed to have a monopoly of the land to create conditions for equal co-operation, and to eliminate speculation, exploitation and defection. They divided the land into halves, one for large subsistence-orientated family vegetable plots, the other to produce for markets. With the help of a grant from the Autonomia Foundation in Budapest, they bought a lot of machinery, most of it pretty useless (gigantic socialist tractors, suitable for ploughing the Great Hungarian Plain but not their steep hills), and some seeds, and began to produce. Mistakes have been made (everyone in the village was a miner, a factory worker or a service worker, no one a farmer), and little profit has resulted but the association has kept going and the family plots are flourishing. Once again there is a local economy, and people are active in shaping their own destiny.

The leading members of the village association explain that their original idea was that the plots and farming should be a temporary measure, to tide them over an economic crisis. Now they see that there will be no central or regional government 'solution' to their plight. As they say, they are now learning to be peasants; eventually there will have to be a market in land, and some will become owners, others waged workers. Till then, they have resorted to a system of primitive communism, which is the best they can manage in the circumstances. The benefits authorities have allowed them to continue to draw social assistance payments while working for the association, as they have done for other such projects – and especially for indigenous Roma agricultural co-operatives – all over Hungary, and elsewhere in Central Europe.

Discussion

This project has echoes of many rural co-operatives of the nineteenth and twentieth centuries (Jordan, 1973), but its setting is an unlikely one. In the beautiful yet economically devastated landscape of northern Hungary, a post-industrial, post-communist community is required to start again a process which began hundreds of years ago, when iron was first mined in their area. The monopoly of the land has enabled them to start with equal shares, as in some counterfactual thought experiment on distributive justice (Rawls, 1971; Dworkin, 1981), where humanoids meet behind a veil of ignorance of their genetic endowment, luck or property holdings, or survivors of a shipwreck consult about their future interactions on a desert island. Giving each family the autonomy of benefits plus a piece of land for subsistence, and then creating the beginnings of a market economy, they set off gingerly down a 'capitalist road from communism', to reverse a famous question about justice (Van Parijs and Van der Veen, 1987), and to discover what, if anything, is wrong with the former, given such a basis (Van Parijs, 1995).

What is both interesting and sad about this story is the absence of social work from it. If this is not social work, then it certainly achieves social work's goals by other methods. Hungarians and Roma co-operate on a non-discriminatory basis, overcoming centuries of resentment and injustice. All are empowered for independence and given a choice about how to develop and enhance their shares of the commons, as well as responsibility for sustaining themselves through their own efforts. All have voice and influence in the governance of the association's affairs. Yet the leaders are not social workers, they are not even educated or trained people; and they have no support from the local authority or from any local professional person.

A few hundred miles away in Budapest, and all over Hungary, sophisticated university courses are training young people for social work to Master's degree standard. Indeed Anna Csongor, Director of the Autonomia Foundation that helps fund the association, teaches on such a course, at the prestigious Eötvös Loránd University, Budapest. Many of these graduates work in agencies involved in crisis intervention, statutory child abuse investigations, youth justice projects, or social assistance programmes. Some of the biggest employers are shelters for homeless people, where social workers ration places, dispense rations of food and care.

Before 1989, social work in Budapest had begun with local authority community development projects that addressed local issues of social and economic co-ordination and exclusion by means of radical collective action and political initiatives (Gosztonyi, 1993). Some of the leaders of that early movement were inspired by British community social workers (Sabel, 1983). Yet the introduction of the market economy has led to a withdrawal of social work from many of these issues, and to a focus on the consequences of inequality, polarization and marginality – as in the West.

This story can be used to symbolize the plight of social work in Europe as a whole but also to inspire the approach that we are recommending in the final part of this book. Many lessons can be learned from Szentrolád. First we can learn from the energy, initiative, enterprise, expertise and determination of the local people. Not only did they see that they could do something, but they saw that they needed to act together, Hungarians and Roma, white and black, to overcome their powerlessness and poverty. Second, they had to rely on informal economic activity, based on self-help and mutuality, rather than formal employment, to achieve social inclusion and cohesion. Obviously, in one way the dilemmas of such situations in the UK were absent, because there was no alternative – no Employment Zone, or Single Gateway, or training agencies, or New Deal counsellors, and no employers looking for subsidized workers either. So there was no danger of unnecessarily creating an informal economic ghetto, or actually disadvantaging members, by holding them back from leaving more specialized, better-paid work roles or delaying their transition into the formal economy. Third, the *collective* basis of their action is important. In many other villages, citizens had combated despair and exclusion by reverting to subsistence activities, but individually, and hence with different and restricted opportunities. Here every member had access to land, seeds and implements, as well as to a tractor and plough to prepare the soil of their plots. Fourth, economic co-operation addressed the causes of their common plight in market failure. In mainstream social work, poverty's consequences, not its causes, are tackled; interventions are mainly directed at women and children, and the deleterious results of exclusion for family life. Here men, women and children all worked together on family plots, and men and women in the market-orientated activities.

Finally, the role of the benefits authorities should not be underestimated. Because of the depth of poverty and unemployment in this part of Hungary, they generally allow people to pursue informal economic activities (including production for markets) without giving up entitlements to social assistance. This allows them to use benefits as a kind of unofficial basic income (Fitzpatrick, 1999), or as a 'social and economic participation income' (Atkinson, 1995; Jordan et al., 2000, Chapters 2 and 3). In the UK this would not yet be possible. As we show in Chapter 8 (pp. 195–8), New Labour's dogmatic insistence on formal employment and earnings, and the use of tax credits to supplement low wages, rules out many of the options that are available in the former communist countries of Central Europe – but this may change over time.

Tackling Social Exclusion: Empowering People to Help Themselves

So far, we have not given any convincing reasons why a community development approach to poverty, social exclusion and the deteriorated quality of life in deprived communities might be more successful than the Third Way's programme, either as an alternative to it, or as a supplement to it. Such communities do have underused resources and potentialities but, we will argue, these can best be tapped by community development methods, and not by New Labour's policies, or by traditional social work approaches.

Many people are not reached by policies for increased labour-market participation. Even after New Labour's success in widening the workforce to 27 million in some kind of employment, this still falls well short of the participation rate of the early 1960s, when only 24 per cent of people of working age were not economically active. Furthermore, it is in deprived neighbourhoods that the proportion of those outside formal employment is the largest. Much of the new growth in employment is part-time in nature, and clearly the attempt to increase participation in deprived areas is likely also to increase this proportion, since many potential workers are single parents or people with disabilities and incapacities. In the economy as a whole, by 1995, 58.2 per cent of total work time was accounted for by unpaid work, compared with 48.1 in 1985–86 (Murgatroyd and Neuburger, 1997; Gershuny and Jones, 1987), reflecting as much the greater participation of married women, mainly in part-time jobs, as the increase in non-employed beneficiaries.

This section is mainly based on two research projects. The first was carried out by Professor Norman Ginsburg, Dr Stephen Thake and colleagues from the University of North London, as part of the ESRC Cities Programme on Competitiveness and Cohesion (Ginsburg et al., 1999). This studied the socio-economic assets in poor communities in north London (Islington, Tower

Hamlets, Haringey and Hackney) – the so-called 'hidden' aspects of deprived neighbourhoods, though they were obvious enough to anyone looking from the community outwards, rather than from a government office downwards. The second project, by Dr Colin C. Williams and Dr Jan Windebank, studied self-help activities in deprived neighbourhoods of Southampton and Sheffield (Williams and Windebank, 1999). What the two sets of findings have in common is the revelation that such communities are rather generously endowed with socio-economic assets and self-help activities, but that these suffer from underfunding from outside the districts, and lack of recognition and support from official agencies, either in local or in national government. Of course, there is a real danger that once such official agencies start to interact with these groups and activities, they actually destroy them (Ostrom, 1990; Dryzek, 1994). In particular, the Third Way's implementation approach would probably have fatal effects. One purpose in this section is simply to point to the existence of these assets and activities; in the next chapter we will show the opportunities and constraints of developing them as an engine of social and economic regeneration.

Ginsburg et al., found that there was a distinct black community sector in north-east London made up of a wide range of organizations servicing and advocating the needs of communities of identity and interest, committed to a black perspective and to the empowerment of service users, and constrained by lack of funding and barriers to involvement with partnership and regeneration bodies (Ginsburg et al., 1999, p. 1). They were set up, mainly in the 1980s, in response to the failure of the traditional voluntary sector and mainstream public sector organizations to meet the needs of minority ethnic people. They draw on workers from these communities, understand their languages and cultures, and are accountable to them; but demand for their services outstrips supply. They draw eclectically on a range of ideas, from black perspectives, feminist theory, community work, rights-based approaches, empowerment principles and consciousness raising. Although valued by local authorities, their training and logistical support needs were not being met; and their relationships with regeneration agencies were distant or disappointing (ibid., pp. 2–3).

In addition to these community organizations, there is a sizeable base of larger, independent, community-based organizations, operating in many poor neighbourhoods, all engaged in making multiple links and building the capacity of interest groups, local associations and identity communities. Ginsburg and his colleagues call these community-based regeneration organizations, and they found that they made contact with isolated individuals, gave practical entry activities, built trust and improved people's self-confidence. Their networks channelled social capital and human resources, which could be used to link such individuals with wider society, and to support smaller community groups. They also provided benefits advice and advocacy, and enabled individuals to build up expertise to act as volunteers. These in turn allowed community sector agencies to provide good value for money in delivering services and making use of local knowledge (ibid., pp. 5–6).

The researchers investigated minority ethnic businesses and local cultural producers. In the former, informal, family and co-ethnic ties were of greater importance than contracts with public and private business support agencies, in which they had little representation (pp. 3–4). This is significant, since other research has found that such businesses are often semi-informalized, relying on unpaid family labour power (Lasch, 1994) or undocumented work by immigrants without proper status (Düvell and Jordan, 1999). Cultural producers represented a bridge between local creative activity and markets – self-employed artists and designer-makers, micro-businesses delivering cultural services, promotions and events management, web design, etc. There was a high rate of business failure and/or low return in this high-risk area, intensified by rising rents for workshops and houses (Ginsburg et al., 1999, pp. 4–5).

In their research project, Williams and Windebank interviewed over 400 households in deprived neighbourhoods of Southampton and Sheffield, to discover the extent of self-help and motives for undertaking such activities. They concluded that the promotion of self-help was a policy principle that had hitherto been neglected, and was complementary to, not a substitute for, formal employment and welfare provision. Far from being a last resort, self-help was a *choice* of how to get work done, and over half of all self-provisioning was undertaken out of choice rather than necessity – 18 per cent of respondents said it was easier to do it oneself rather than rely on others, 16 per cent considered the end product of a higher quality, 5 per cent felt that in this way one could individualize the end product, and 14 per cent found intrinsic pleasure in doing the work in this way (Williams and Windebank, 1999, p. 6). These findings are crucial when we consider the alternative means of accomplishing the tasks of social reproduction with which New Labour's policies are increasingly concerned (see pp. 172–5). However, this study also found that poor households were disadvantaged when it came to self-help (particularly in the South of England) because they lacked money for equipment, materials, a network of people to assist, skills and physical capacities, and feared being reported for breaking the rules of benefits (Williams and Windebank, 1999, p. 6).

The authors conclude that, to empower people to help themselves, complementary social inclusion policies aimed at promoting informal economic activities should be implemented alongside conventional employment-creation measures. This requires the development and support of grassroots initiatives (such as Local Exchange and Trading Schemes (LETS) and mutual aid contracts), which tackle some of the barriers to participation in self-help. They argue that the 'voluntary and community' sections of the New Deals (at present completely subservient to the formal employment principle) should be modified so as to allow a 'social contribution' that counts for the various budgets, targets and tax credits. This might make the Third Way's programme far more acceptable, both in terms of liberal values, and in allowing communities to engage in productive and meaningful work they might not otherwise have been able to undertake. Alternatively, the authors recommend transforming the Working Families Tax Credit into a guaranteed minimum income paid for active citizenship, through creating something called Community Enterprise Employment, for caring, volunteering, etc. – thus both activating many at present blocked from participation, and recognizing the value of much unpaid informal work that is already happening (Williams and Windebank, 1999, pp. 7–8; see also pp. 194–8).

CASE STUDY: RATIONALES FOR PAID INFORMAL EXCHANGE

This case study draws on Williams and Windebank's (1999) research report of the results from their Southampton and Sheffield surveys. The paid informal economy is often thought of as consisting of unauthorized cash exchanges that are undertaken covertly, mainly to evade tax payments and benefit rules. It is an important aim of the Third Way's policy programme to clamp down on such activities (DSS, 1998, Chapter 9; Jordan and Travers, 1998), by better intelligence on fraud, by encouraging citizens to report neighbours' activities, and by extensive benefits fraud investigation and enforcement services. However, this research shows that paid informal exchange, when taken to include gifts as well as money, encompasses wide range of activities and motivations. Less than one-third of the work involved formal firms or the self-employed not declaring their earnings or transactions, and this mostly concerned house maintenance (e.g. outdoor painting), home improvement (e.g. plumbing), hairdressing, window cleaning and car repair (Williams and Windebank, 1999, p. 35).

The other two-thirds (70.8 per cent) of paid informal exchange is more often a transaction between a customer and a provider who have close social relations – a friend or neighbour is either paid cash-in-hand (24.6 per cent of all paid informal services) or given a gift in lieu of payment (8.9 per cent) – or work is done by relatives who are paid cash-in-hand (16.2 per cent) or given a gift (3.2 per cent) (ibid.). These exchanges are regulated by a blood-and-guts code of proprieties and equivalencies, though other social relations of exchange – for instance between workmates doing off-the-book tasks together, sharing information, materials and tools – are more often governed by generalized than by balanced reciprocity (Jordan et al., 1992, Chapter 7). Children, brothers or sisters, and parents who live in the household may also be paid or given a gift for housework, car or home maintenance (Williams and Windebank, 1999, p. 36).

Only 18.1 per cent of all paid informal work is motivated primarily by saving money, as an alternative to formal employment or formal purchase of a service. For the rest of paid informal exchange, the rationale given was 'community building' and/or 'redistributive' motives – to maintain or initiate connections with someone, or to provide an opportunity to transfer resources to someone in a manner that does not demean them. Similarly, only half of those who supply paid services say that they do so for financial motives (50.9 per cent), and even then often with a secondary motive of helping out, or 'getting out of the house' (Williams and Windebank, 1999, p. 36). In the other half of activities, the rationale was assisting the customer (36 per cent) because the work was enjoyable (7.5 per cent) and to develop new skills (5.6 per cent) (see also pp. 198–201).

Discussion

These findings complement others which show that paid informal work is justified by participants in deprived neighbourhoods as compensating themselves for lost rights to social benefits (especially exceptional needs payments), for lost employment opportunities, for declining wage levels, for the insecurity, irregularity and unpredictablity of available work, or for the boredom and passivity of unemployment (Jordan et al., 1992; Dean and Melrose, 1998; Rowlingson et al., 1997;

MacNichol and Smith, 1999). They are also borne out by research that found poor people's official income levels to have fallen quite sharply between 1979 and the early 1990s, but their expenditure to have remained puzzlingly constant (Goodman and Webb, 1995). The value of Williams and Windebank's work is in locating these phenomena in the social as well as the economic relations of poor communities. These transactions help maintain or restore the social fabric of neighbourhoods, as well as filling the gap left by failure of markets in goods and services.

Far from feeling embarrassed or defensive about self-provisioning, people in these districts would do more – both paid and unpaid – informal work, if it were not for shortages of material resources, skills, network links, time and physical energies. Furthermore, they were inhibited by fear of being reported to the benefits authorities – one-third said they would participate more if there were not a risk of losing their entitlements. Others held back because of fears about the dangerousness of their neighbourhoods (Williams and Windebank, 1999, pp. 37–41). All this led the authors to argue for changes in the benefits and in-kind welfare state systems to support a 'full engagement' society that would take a more holistic view of citizenship and social inclusion, recognize self-help and informal activity, and give citizens more choices between formal and informal work, and over how to combine them (Williams and Windebank, 1999, pp. 42–3). Such a policy programme would include 'bottom up' initiatives such as community exchange and mutual aid contracts, and changes to the rules on in-work and out-of-work benefits, so as to promote the informal, community sector and other unpaid activities. Notions of social and economic participation or citizens' service (Briscoe, 1995; McCormick, 1994) would activate people according to different principles, regenerating the social as well as the formal economy (Ginsburg, 1999; Macfarlane, 1996; Mayo et al., 1998; Rifkin, 1995). The New Labour government pays some heed to such ideas (Social Exclusion Unit, 1998), especially in its guidance on the Single Regeneration Grant, but this has not yet influenced its main policy programmes on employment and welfare reform.

Local authority social services departments in general, and the social work profession in particular, have become separated from these debates. Although social workers are extremely intensively involved with residents in such districts, over a range of child and social care issues, it is rare for them to be directly concerned with economic issues, either in promoting self-help initiatives, or in dealing with problems concerning the legality of informal work strategies. There is something odd about such a rigid division of labour, since the welfare of poor people is quite clearly tied up with how they are able to get work done and increase their incomes, and since economic activity has an impact on relationships (for instance, in relation to child care). This will be more fully discussed in Chapter 8 (see pp. 195–8).

Exploitation and Exclusion in the Formal and Informal Economies

All these arguments for recognizing and valuing the informal economy would be invalid if it could be shown that particular groups of citizens – for instance women, or minority ethnic people – were being exploited or excluded by being confined to informal activities, and that such goals as equal opportunities and the maximization of human potentialities could be better served by providing paid employment. But in the present UK context, such issues are inseparable from questions about the most efficient and equitable way in which the task of social reproduction can be done in society. What is at stake for New Labour's policy programme and for social work is the best way to organize and regulate the official systems through which people nurture, socialize, sustain and service each other – feeding, grooming, protecting, caring, correcting, tending, recreating, curing, cosseting and finally laying to rest. New employment in manufacturing, extracting, constructing and financing may be possible, and new developments in imagining, simulating, creating and marketing will certainly bring more jobs; but the main source of increased formal work has for some time been (both here and in other advanced industralized economies) in the tasks of looking after people's everyday needs outside such workplaces (Esping-Andersen, 1996, 1999; Iversen and Wren, 1998).

From an economic point of view, two iron laws meet around social reproduction work, and the outcome of this clash is contested. On the one hand, Adam Smith's law of the division of labour says that prosperity is intimately linked to the constant refinement and specialization of work tasks, and this is achieved only through labour *markets*, which allow productivity to be maximized (Buchanan, 1994). On the other, Engel's law says that the more prosperous a society, the greater its need for paid services; but the tasks of social reproduction are not susceptible to productivity increases (it takes as long to cut someone's hair or nails now as it did in 1820). As prosperity grows, some new well-paid service jobs will be created; but the majority of new employment will be in these basic tasks. So *either* the incomes of the growing proportion of people engaged in such work must remain very low relative to those of people in high-productivity manufacturing; *or* increasing transfers will be necessary (Gershuny, 1983; Iversen and Wren, 1998).

The Third Way addresses this problem through its welfare reforms, which encourage paid work in social reproduction to expand, but transfer substantial sums to support this growth in low-paid employment through tax credits. It also explicitly aims to expand employment in social care by its programme for the social services (DoH, 1998a). The conscious aim is to make it more attractive for benefits claimants to go and work in a restaurant, child care centre, leisure complex, shop or old people's home than to cook, clean, shop, garden, decorate, care or wash for their families on an unpaid basis, at least during working hours. Whether this kind of work is done formally (through employment) or informally (through networks of exchange in communities), much the same people will be doing it; and the outcome will always be some balance between the two systems. This will be more fully discussed in Chapter 8 (see pp. 195–8).

The question therefore arises: who is more exploited and excluded, a citizen (usually a woman) who stays at home and does these things on an unpaid basis for her family (and perhaps also her neighbours), or one who goes to work and does them for very low pay, without prospect of escaping the poverty trap? The question poses itself because tax credits provide a strong incentive for *taking* work, but a very weak one for increasing earnings; people who work long hours get very little extra reward, because of withdrawal of credits and the impact of taxes; and the worker may then have to go home and do the unpaid tasks anyway (especially if he or she is a lone parent).

The pragmatic answer to the question is that it depends whether the first job taken by someone previously outside the labour market is a dead end or the first step on a ladder to higher earnings, with better qualifications leading to wider employment options. Some research suggests that, in relatively buoyant labour markets, the rule of optimism holds (6, 1999b). But the logic of Engel's law suggests otherwise. If our increasing proportion of paid work is in low-paid social reproduction services (because of technological improvements in other branches), more and more jobs will be dead ends. Otherwise why has it become necessary to introduce in-work benefits like tax credits now, for the first time since the Speenhamland system (1795–1834), and how can we explain the enormous increase in expenditure on such benefits since they were (re)started in the late 1960s (Jordan, 1973)? Engel's law would predict that the net of in-work benefits must go on widening as employment in low-productivity social reproduction grows, so that people who receive the same (poverty) levels of income no matter how hard they work will become more and more numerous over time (Jordan, 1998a, Chapter 3; Iversen and Wren, 1998). That is what has happened for the past thirty years.

On the other side of the argument, it is forcefully maintained that the informal economy, and especially the domestic economy, turns its participants (especially women) into oppressed and exploited serfs who are ruled by duty and altruism and denied access to the wider world. The case stated above can all too easily become a justification for trapping women, and oppressed minority groups, in situations of exploitation and exclusion, based on patriarchal or racist relations. Above all, such roles deny informal participants opportunities and choices. The Third Way is founded on the repeated assertion that claimants *want to work* (focus groups must echo to such pleas). By what paternalistic edicts should they be denied that chance?

Again pragmatically, those who argue the opposite case maintain that *real* choice lies in the opportunity to choose between formal and informal work, and to combine them in ways that suit the citizen, not the system. Although certain groups are always at greater risk of exclusion than others, and women are especially vulnerable to patriarchal forms of exploitation, these groups will only begin to be free to assert their claims when they have the same choices as mainstream citizens, who can and do balance the demands of earning and caring. Research suggests that most mainstream women do not choose to follow male-style incremental careers, with pensions, perks and promotion, but compensate for this by interesting and challenging combinations of paid and unpaid work (Jordan et al., 1994, Chapters 2 and 5). All that the demand for a social and economic participation income approach to a 'full engagement society' implies is that these choices should be extended to the whole population, including low earners.

Box 19   Women, work and the family

Research commissioned by BBC TV *Panorama* programme (24 January 2000) shows the proportion of women who withdraw from full-time work, even when they have returned to their former job after having a baby. A third of the 560 mothers in the survey, who returned after having their first child, left for part-time positions or quit work altogether within two years, according to an analysis carried out by Bristol University researchers.

A follow-up study of 73 mothers by Susan Harkness of Sussex University found that these women tended to be working very long hours before their children were born, and that employers were unwilling to make allowances for the other demands on their time when they returned. Hence the women interviewed experienced stress and conflict, because they were unable to negotiate flexibility in their working arrangements.

This evidence can be interpreted in two ways. Some women argue that their preference is to continue in full-time work, and that law, policy and practice should facilitate this. Others claim that the government should legislate to give them rights to claim their former job back on a part-time basis, to enable them to spend more time with their child.

This debate is fuelled by controversial research findings about educational achievement levels of children whose mothers work full-time. Professor Heather Joshi of the Institute of Education analysed 9,000 young adults' records, and found that girls were 10 per cent less likely to advance from GCSE to A level, and boys 12 per cent less likely, if their mothers were employed in their pre-school years (*Guardian*, 24 January 2000).

The larger shift from full-time to part-time work among mothers comes with the birth of the second child. Both better-off women with professional qualifications (Jordan et al., 1994) and women from low-income households who had done low-skilled manual work (Jordan et al., 1992) said that they chose to work part-time or not at all at this stage.

Social work is tied into these questions in two ways. In itself, the social care sector constitutes a big part of the social reproduction workforce (over one million jobs' worth of it). Most of these jobs are low-paid, and many people work under exploitative conditions in the commercial sector. Hence social care work embodies the problem. In addition social work's clientele are the main targets of compulsory activation, which often clashes with their preferences and responsibilities in the informal economy. This will be more fully analysed in the next chapter.

Conclusions

Social work's separation from economic issues in the welfare state period has led to many of the paradoxes of the present situation. First, officials using quasi-social-work methods are now being imported into the public sector as employment advisers, counsellors, trainers and so on. Second, street-level, project and support workers are becoming involved in economic issues, especially over informal economic alternatives to paid work. Third, social work is intensively involved in the lives of the claimants under most pressure to shift from informal to formal activities – but not over this issue. Fourth, social care itself is the site of many of the contested developments in the expansion of social reproduction work, but social work is not concerned with the policy debates about these issues.

We have put forward general arguments for greater involvement by social workers and local authority social service departments in economic issues, and especially in informal economic activities concerned with improving the quality of residents' lives in deprived districts. In the next chapter we will look at the possibilities of such approaches, and barriers to their development. In particular, we will consider how Third Way policies on tax-benefit reform, to improve labour-market incentives, have some unintended and paradoxical consequences, and argue that these may contain the seeds of new relationships between formal and informal work, and a transformed role for social work in the informal economy.

8

The Public Authority:
Social Work and the State

Although the Third Way makes large claims about its radical redefinition of the contract between the citizen and the state, there is a big hole at its centre. Nowhere does it satisfactorily define the role and responsibility of the public authority in the democratic governance of society. For all the detailed prescriptions of top-down supervisory boards, regional authorities and regulatory committees, there are no clear principles in accordance with which a complex, plural, multi-racial, open system can practise self-rule, by and on behalf of citizens.

Instead, what is outlined in its various policy documents is a set of institutions through which one part of that system (the public sector and its various clienteles) can be very strongly directed and made accountable in terms of budgetary efficiency and a stern work ethic, while the rest can regulate itself according to the laws of the market and the logic of the collective actions these generate (see pp. 108–10). The only links between these two are the unconvincing conception of 'community' (a traditional system of social discipline, funded on blood-and-guts bigotry) and the narrow interpretation of 'social responsibility' that is built into this. New Labour hopes to foster these, both through 'partnerships' with its cowed and compliant public services, and through the local leadership of 'community champions' – Third Way councillors who are unable to get seats on the local authority's executive or scrutiny committees (see pp. 68–71).

Yet this lopsided vision is not merely incomplete, it is dangerously skewed, because of the new kinds of power it creates, and because of the peculiar kinds of accountability to which they are subject. Because New Labour is so hostile to the forces of Old Labour, which it sees as ensconced within the local authorities, the public service professions and the public sector trade unions, it not only seeks to regulate these from the centre, but also to create a panoply of new public service occupations, all highly specialized and focused on specific social problems, all in smaller and more narrowly instrumental agencies, and more under the control of its ministries. These will exercise very direct power over citizens, have enormous discretion over the distribution of resources and the rules by which individuals will be required to live, and yet not be accountable to local democracy. Furthermore, they will be only loosely tied in with the machinery of local governance, since the funds they will hold and the powers they will exercise will often be greater then those of their supposed NHS and local authority 'partners' in the policy domains in which they operate.

This model prescribes a variant of the dangerous developments for present-day society recognized by such theorists as Habermas (1987) and Dryzek (1994). In their analyses, the 'lifeworld' of civil society is in increasing peril of invasion by the 'systems world' of state regulation (Habermas), and the discursive, democratic governance of public issues of collective interest – such as environmental sustainability – is jeopardized by the intrusive managerial monopolism of the central power (Dryzek). This undermines the spontaneous or longstanding capability of populations to conserve and develop their own collective resources in democratic ways (Ostrom, 1990), as well as squandering the social capital that such democratic associations generate (Putnam, 1993). In their analyses, civil society's democratic institutions for the common good must flourish and provide the bedrock for democratic practice, if the polity is to function efficiently and responsively in the name of its citizen-electors.

In this chapter, we will go beyond such theories to argue that there must be a more consistent and systematic link between local associations and their practices and the institutions of public authority, if democracy is to work. A strong civil society, with a diversity of formal and informal groups and associations, is the first requirement of a democratic society. But the public authority has two main contributions to make that complement this. On the one hand, local government is required to play a role in co-ordinating the various ways in which community groups and voluntary organizations manage local resources and resolve local issues. On the other, central government should not shrink from tasks of social engineering: its duty to harmonize conflicting interests and reduce costly conflicts for the sake of desirable collective outcomes is inescapable. But this requires an overall strategic intelligence, and a respect for citizens' autonomy and enterprise, that has hitherto been lacking in New Labour. Instead of seeking ever more direct (but fragmented) control of aspects of citizens' behaviour, what good governance requires is a more detached, overall vision of the direction of social development, and a more subtle strategic perception of how to reconcile individual initiatives with collective purposes.

Nowadays every child knows, from computer games which simulate complex interactions, that it is counterproductive to try to accomplish changes in one part of a system without compensating changes in all other parts. Above all, it is always a mistake to try to produce large changes in one part of the system, because this causes unintended and largely unpredictable shifts in other parts; and an even bigger mistake to try to make large changes in all parts simultaneously (Krempel, personal communication). Unfortunately, New Labour ministers have never played games like SIMcity, and the civil servants who try to anticipate the effects of policy cannot avail themselves of models which are as sophisticated as present-day children's games (Jordan et al., 2000).

The New Labour government is explicitly ambitious in its reform goals (DSS, 1998, p. 27 and title). It aims to change the behaviour patterns of public sector staff, service users and claimants in all the major services, and to transform the social security system from a generalized safety net into a set of customized trampolines (launching individual citizens into independence). Policies to 'make work pay' are the key to many other aspects of the programme. But – despite claims about joined-up government and coherence between programmes – there are serious issues about the interactions of tax-benefit reforms with other policies, and how changes in economic behaviour will work themselves out in other policy domains. Many indications already point towards unintended consequences and moral hazards, with implementation of the main programme (for increased labour-market participation) acting as a fetter on other policies and on the promotion of Third Way values and goals more generally. Our case studies in this chapter are chosen to illustrate these issues and to show ways in which the problems identified might be resolved.

We will argue for tax-benefit reforms that allow individuals to choose how to combine paid and unpaid work. Although this approach is apparently anathema to New Labour, its programme for 'making work pay' paradoxically leads in this direction. A new principle for tax-benefit integration would constitute a far more effective way to realize Third Way values, and to find a balance between state authority and individual autonomy (Jordan, 1985). As a general principle, democratic, self-governing associations pursuing their goals by their own chosen means, including informal economic activity, are the best hope for progress on these issues, including campaigning for the above reform. However, both local authorities and the public service professions have an important role to play in co-ordinating their efforts, reconciling their strategies, and empowering their members.

Benevolence and Abundance:
the Roots of Community and Co-operation

To set the scene for these arguments, it is useful to trace the origins of the debate in present-day political thought about the possibility of co-operation over collective goods – those aspects of public life that involve sharing, accepting joint responsibility, and making collectively binding decisions through dialogue and consensus-building. These origins lie in the thinking of the British Enlightenment philosophers, and especially Adam Smith and David Hume, whose work was so influential on the liberal tradition that came to dominate nineteenth-century British political theory. Like Jeremy Bentham's, their ideas are highly relevant for today's policy debates, and for the detailed implementation of New Labour's programme. It may seem a far and fanciful cry from Third Way Employment Zones and the New Deal for Communities to Hume's ideas on benevolence and abundance, but we hope to show that these notions are directly relevant to social work practice in the present context.

The questions which the eighteenth-century philosophers addressed were pressing at that time because of the establishment of nation states and the spread of commercial (market and capitalist) economic relations. The formal regulation of the state was replacing the old order of traditional authority and face-to-face blood-and-guts codes, and commercial exchanges were eroding the communal relations of the village and kinship network. Smith, Hume and their colleagues justified these encroachments in two ways. First, old-style feudal obligations and moral bonds relied on small-scale communities and personal ties for their effectiveness; this limited the scope of societies, and prevented the larger mobilization of mass forces that was necessary for nations to defend themselves and hold their own in competition with other great powers. The rational-legal authority of the state was therefore a political necessity in the modern age. Second, communal production and exchange was too cumbersome and insufficiently specialized to promote economic growth based on improved productivity and long-distance trade, because of this same reliance on face-to-face relationships and personal trust, as well as an archaic division of labour between participants. Only markets, including labour markets, could allow the specialization and contract-based trust in strangers that alone could produce prosperity (or 'abundance', as they called it).

Both of these arguments rested on the idea of 'limited benevolence' – that people are capable of co-operation and trust only with the finite number of others with whom they can have fairly frequent, direct interactions, can discuss and communicate over problems, and hence develop common solutions to shared issues. In particular, Hume argued, this was possible only where goods were held in common, as collective property of the group, so that mutual interests in conserving and improving them were obvious to all. Since nation states and long-distance trade created large societies and anonymous, impersonal exchanges, this implied that such relations must diminish and be replaced by ones that were more reliable under modern conditions – for revenue collection, military mobilization and market relationships; in short, more proof against free-riding and the 'tragedy of the commons' (Hardin, 1968), strategies for exploiting others and the shared environment, which result in the erosion of social capital and the common heritage of resources. Hume argued that, in large-scale modern societies, rules and norms must rely on instrumental motivation and self-interest: 'every man must be presumed a knave' (Hume, 1742, p. 342).

These arguments justified the relentless extension of bureaucratic governance and commerce. But of course they equally showed that *common ownership, shared resources and democratic governance were both viable and desirable under certain circumstances*. These circumstances held when partition into exclusively owned goods is too costly, when sharing is seen as a benefit rather than a cost (as in social clubs and cultural facilities), and when institutions and traditions of democratic management of resources exist, or can evolve spontaneously. Ostrom's researches have shown that such niches of common property and democratic governance have survived the spread of rational-legal state authority and markets world-wide (Ostrom, 1990), and that states and markets constantly threaten to undermine them. Dryzek has given examples (mainly relating to water supply) of new systems for 'governing the commons' that are evolving, even in very advanced societies and economies, such as California (Dryzek, 1994, Chapters 3 and 4). Taylor (1987) has developed a general model of co-operative relations which is entirely consistent with these historical and recent examples (Singleton and Taylor, 1992).

All these can be seen as instances of Axelrod's research on the 'evolution of co-operation' (Axelrod, 1984), where he showed that reciprocity and non-defection is a rational response in many environments, and the only way to overcome the kinds of pervasive prisoners' dilemmas that would otherwise turn serial life into a Hobbesian war of all against all (Hobbes, 1651, Chapter 13). In all these ways, the other side of Hume's arguments – that community, co-operation and communism (in the sense of common ownership) can and do flourish, and *create* benevolence, through the practice of democratic governance over shared resources – has been reasserted, against the relentless tide of bureaucracy and markets.

Of course, every social worker, and above all every street-level, project and support worker, knows this. The art and science of group work, day care and residential work is to foster co-operation and sharing, through developing the sense of a common stake in the resources of the group, unit or project; and hence to encourage participation in the responsible management of these for the common good. The case studies in Chapters 5 and 7 (the Emmaus Community, the Clubhouse Movement and the Szentrolád Community Association) are examples of exactly these aspects of social relations – that individuals, however isolated, oppressed, problem-ridden, preoccupied, deprived or even deluded, can quickly learn to work together and to manage jointly owned or collectively shared resources, given a democratic voice. The fact that most present-day mainstream social work does exactly the opposite – individualizes provision, and bureaucratically allocates a specific share of welfare to be consumed in privatized or commercialized facilities (such as a lonely room in a small residential home) – is a waste of the potential of both staff and service users, and a squandering of the social capital that would be generated by more imaginative methods.

The wider point about all this is that a community development approach to social work, especially in more disadvantaged neighbourhoods, could aim to develop exactly this potential for co-operation in the improvement of the facilities and the quality of life of the residents. This would not require leadership by local authority workers, more a reorientation towards the existing community sector and the kinds of projects which are at present seen as marginal or eccentric. It would also mean recognizing street-level, project and unit workers as colleagues, with much to teach as well as to learn about these approaches.

From a political perspective, however, it would require a reversal of the priorities of the Third Way – changing from an attempt to make all individuals accountable to officials or supervisory boards, and all organizations into compliant partners in top-down policy development, to making officials and organizations accountable to citizens, members and service users. This bottom-up democratization would be a necessary condition for the implementation of otherwise frothy aspirations and empty promises of empowerment: it would give people a real voice in determining the actions needed to raise standards and improve facilities in their neighbourhoods.

It would also require a reversal of a far longer process of change, through which associations and community groups have gradually lost control of resources, either because of their expropriation by the state, or their engrossment by commercial companies. Even in the nineteenth century, local communities and working-class co-operatives, friendly societies and sickness clubs controlled substantial assets, and were therefore economic actors to be reckoned with. Over time they have shrunk to a symbolic role, or one concerned exclusively with cultural issues. Part of this process was accomplished in the creation of the welfare state, as associations lost the right to provide exclusively for their members' benefits, and this function was taken over by the state; other organizations, like co-operatives, were bought out, or adopted the commercial logic of their economic environment. The idea of restoring the associational basis for welfare provision has been canvassed in recent years (Hirst, 1994; Green, 1993; Field, 1997), but more as an alternative system of collective responsibility than as a measure for empowering deprived or excluded citizens. In our argument, one of the advantages of this approach to democratization is that it would start by giving a new voice to those at the bottom of society, who most need empowerment. Instead of breaking up the state's services and distributing them amongst mainstream associations, it would aim to give real power to just those members of the community who are at present on the receiving end, as the subjects of the new conditionality and compulsion under bureaucratic rules, and as price-takers in various markets.

CASE STUDY: THE 'DEPRIVED COMMUNITY' EXERCISE
The following exercise has been used in social work education classes on numerous occasions, usually with almost identical outcomes, in the UK, Western and Central Europe.

The Situation to be Role-Played
The members of the class are all residents of, or workers in, a very deprived neighbourhood of a city somewhere in Europe. *The good news* is that the district has been granted a sum of 5 million euro by the European Commission for social and economic regeneration. *The bad news* is that none of this will be paid unless *all* are agreed on how the money will be spent. The exercise starts in a dilapidated local school, in which groups of residents and workers meet together (but separately) to frame their claims, with one eye to their group's needs, and the other to achieving consensus. Under the chairmanship of M. Jourdain from Brussels they then bid for how they consider the money should be spent. Depending on the size of the group as a whole, these subgroups may consist of the following:

- parents of young children
- older and disabled residents
- young people – adolescents and young adults
- members of minority ethnic groups
- local professionals in health and social care, planning, education, police, etc.
- local voluntary and community organizations.

At the end of this first round of bidding, groups can then negotiate with others to reach compromise solutions, eventually leading to a joint bid (which, if agreed, would automatically succeed). In the absence of agreement, the money goes back to Brussels.

Outcomes
In all but two of the many times this game has been played, agreement has been reached. In the great majority of cases, *all groups* suggest building (or

reconstructing) a community centre, in which a variety of activities can be held, and services provided, all under the control of residents. The professionals sometimes try to nuance the latter form of accountability, to give themselves more influence and control over resources, but seldom push this. It should be emphasized that this 'prominent solution' is reached by all parties *without any consultation*. In the majority of versions played, no second round of negotiations is needed.

The two exceptional plays, where no agreement was reached, were in Huddersfield and Bratislava. In both cases, agreement on the concept of a community centre was immediate, but there was no compromise on how resources should be deployed within it. In the Huddersfield play the young people insisted on a disproportionate amount being spent on an ice rink, and nothing could convince them of the unfairness of this allocation. It seemed that this reflected past disillusion over being marginalized and excluded. In the Bratislava instance, the Slovak residents adamantly refused to share the centre with a Roma association, even though the latter were almost absurdly reasonable about the terms for this. In a fairly accurate representation of Slovak obduracy, they preferred to see the money go back to Brussels rather than compromise over this.

Discussion

The point of this exercise is to illustrate that, once the condition of agreement by the residents is asserted, public social services take an entirely different form. Whereas under present regimes most new resources going into a district like this would be spent on child protection investigations or residential care for old people, under these rules it goes on the kind of facilities that are seldom seen as a priority, and with terms of accountability that are equally rare.

The other striking thing is that the diverse groups of residents and the professionals seem able to see a common interest in these arrangements once the democratic (or consensus) condition is made. Only in the two instances quoted (out of some twenty plays) was there stalemate. Residents are willing to share facilities and pool resources, and professionals to make themselves accountable for the way they use their expertise and allocate services, but there must first be a common facility or resource in which they all have a stake, and can recognize a mutual interest. This is what community means in Hume's analysis of benevolence – the experience of 'sympathy' or fellow feeling, because people identify as sharing certain interests and experiences. It is more difficult in a plural society than a monoculture, but still possible.

Local Government Co-ordination

The obvious criticism of this approach to policy development and implementation is that it would be incoherent. Various groups of citizens would assert various claims and needs, there would be some overspecialization and some duplication, and above all no reliable coverage to meet very general needs, or the specific claims of less visible minorities. Services would fragment, and localities would defend their resources against encroachment from outside. Territorial justice would be inconceivable.

The Third Way makes large claims of coherence and consistency in its approach to social policy. Its programme aims at 'holistic government', with 'joined-up' thinking and working between agencies. At the top level there is to be policy integration, but co-ordinating the planning and implementation of New Labour's programme. Yet this also involves greater devolution to regional and local government, mainly of implementation tasks, and accountability and evaluation mechanisms. Finally, there should be 'joined-up, front-end consumer interfaces' – one-stop shops, integrated consumer information systems, and so on. 'Holistic government is a distinctive and radical agenda ... both in its execution and in familiarising the public with a new understanding of how public services work' (6 et al., 1999, p. 10).

There are risks in this approach. For example, if delivery of benefits and services is focused on a single outlet, those who fail to make this connection, or who are disqualified from one benefit or service, are likely to lose out in other ways, and hence be more excluded. But our focus here is on the invisible barriers to co-operation between agencies or co-ordination of programmes.

Many examples could be given here of initiatives that are fettered by the apparent intransigence of public services, either over the setting up and working of joint committees or action groups, or in referring suitable work to new projects or units, or in transferring relevant funding to the appropriate bodies. But these do not stem so much from resistance, or from the pull of other interests and accountabilities, as from the sheer weight of their overall responsibilities, and the underfunding of the public sector for its core tasks. Since resources for health and social services are now closely tied to targets and indicators, it is not surprising that the central focus of their work is the achievement of these, to secure their core funding; other initiatives, whatever the possible incentives and advantages, cannot be given the same priority, especially when the partner organizations will be the lead players in implementation, and get the bulk of the finance that is at stake. Hence what looks from the top like a well co-ordinated and coherent programme turns out on the ground to be beset by delays and frustrations.

Some of the rules and conditions of New Labour's flagship programme – the reform of the tax-benefit system and the promotion of labour-market participation – actually hinder the implementation of other aspects of the programme. The unintended consequence of tax credits and the New Deals may be a *deterioration* in the quality of life of poor neighbourhoods, because they obstruct the development of these other initiatives. The government has brought forward numerous measures for economic and social regeneration of poor districts, through the Single Regeneration Grants, the New Deal for Communities, the Social Exclusion Unit and the Employment Zones. The first two of these, and aspects of the third, are as concerned with social as with economic regeneration. For instance, the new terms of the Single Regeneration Grants indicate that community groups should be consulted about plans, and may even play a lead role in their implementation (Ginsburg, 1999). So these initiatives would seek to link social with economic action, through projects that spring from grassroots organizations. But the

Employment Zones are strictly concerned with getting claimants off benefits and into employment; other private sector agencies are 'parachuted' into these areas, to claim a bounty on maximizing such placements. But this emphasis on formal work and private sector employment may actually cause social deterioration, even if it does achieve some economic growth; and it frustrates the purposes of other actors concerned with regeneration more broadly.

CASE STUDY: EMPLOYMENT ZONES

One of the cornerstones of New Labour's version of The Third Way is its commitment to 'joined up solutions'. Given the proliferation of measures for social and economic regeneration in deprived districts the test is: how do the many different zones, schemes and programmes 'join up' top-down policy with bottom-up initiatives? The Employment Zone (EZ) is a government measure initially piloted in three areas of the country and subsequently rolled out to a further twelve zones, allocated to urban areas experiencing a high concentration of long-term unemployed people. The EZ is designed to address the individual needs of 48,000 unemployed people over the age of 25. The key new elements of EZ are as follows:

- A Personal Job Account (PJA) has been introduced. This rolls up all existing benefits into a flexible fund to be jointly spent by the participant (zoner) and the personal adviser (EZ operator employee) on whatever measures they agree are appropriate.
- Each EZ will be subject to tender: bidders may be private, public or voluntary organizations.
- Payment to the EZ operator will be by results: the scheme pays the EZ operator a small initial per capita fee, the PJA (most of which must be paid to the zoner but which may be match-funded) and a premium of £3,000 for each successful 'zoners into jobs' output (a higher-rate premium is paid for the very long-term unemployed): all zoners will be required to participate in the scheme for a period of 26 weeks on pain of sanctions.

The fifteen zones were to be spread across the whole of the country and ranged in size from relatively small zones which projected only 900 zoners over the two-year period of the scheme to very large schemes which would aim for a throughput of over 10,000 zoners. The Smortham zone (pseudonym) anticipated 2,000 long-term unemployed people coming on to the zone during the two years of the contract.

The bid guidance states clearly:

> We are interested in seeing innovative and varied approaches to the Personal Job Account. We hope that bids will reflect flexibility and choice in the approach to the Personal Job Account itself as the level of detail or choice which suits one participant may not suit others. We expect a commitment to provide information, including financial information, to participants in order to help them choose the right course of action to meet their goals. This should be linked to real opportunities in the labour market.

If flexibility is the name of the game so far as the Personal Job Account is concerned, it is certainly not the case as far as the rules of the scheme are concerned. They are extremely tightly drawn, in such a way as to ensure that the Treasury's desired outcome of moving people into paid employment and off benefits is achieved. Bidders require considerable working capital to cover negative cash flow during the initial period of the scheme before premiums start to roll in. Considerable risks are entailed in being an EZ operator. The government makes it quite clear in the bid guidance that the purpose of the scheme is to 'test whether existing spending can be used more effectively'. The guidance states: 'We believe that adequate resources are currently devoted to getting (long-term unemployed people) back to work, but the rules governing how it is spent may not always lead to the right results. We want therefore to see if we can bring much of the existing funding together to use it more flexibly. We also want to make it easier for job seekers to understand and influence how the money is spent.'

Compare these concerns with those expressed at a meeting to promote social entrepreneurs in one of the areas designated as an EZ. While the government was drafting the bid guidance for the Employment Zones, a group of services managers from the public sector and street-level workers from voluntary and community organizations were meeting to discuss ways of improving local networks and their ability to promote social entrepreneurialism. All were agreed from their various perspectives that the benefits trap excluded a large number of people from the process of developing a strong and healthy voluntary and community sector, especially in the most excluded neighbourhoods and communities of interest. Some of those present were community workers concerned with the recruitment of community leaders and activists to take responsibility for organizing community groups. Some were managers attempting to recruit people to become involved in 'community governance'. Some were social entrepreneurs looking for people to join them in trying out innovative ideas for social change. All recognized the major stumbling block of the benefits trap.

The idea that emerged from this group was a 'Passport to Participation'. This was the name given to an alternative benefit payment, which would entitle claimants to sign off the normal qualification requirements for their benefit. It would pay them a weekly amount, not less than what they were currently receiving, and enable them to participate in a range of socially beneficial activities, from which they would personally benefit, without any additional conditions. Participation would, of course, be voluntary.

For several weeks after this discussion the idea continued to reverberate around discussions in the voluntary and public sectors concerned with community development and social enterprise. It was rumoured that representations were being made to government by passing Treasury officials, who happened to overhear conversations about it. Mention was made of the requirement for legislative change. Murmurings were heard that the government was considering including such legislative changes in a forthcoming Bill. When the bid guidance on EZ was published, it became apparent that enabling legislation would be required to remove the normal conditions applying to Job Seeker's Allowance and income support for the unemployed. Could this offer a glimmer of hope on the horizon for those who were advocating a 'Passport to Participation'? Was it possible that there would be scope for at least some of these 2,000 zoners to be allowed to use EZ as a form of 'Passport to Participation'?

A flurry of activity on the part of all those involved in the proposal immediately ensued. Contacts were made with people operating in other pilot EZ areas to find out what ideas they were pursuing. Consultation with other local interested parties took place. The views of national experts and think-tanks specializing in economic strategies and employment initiatives were sought. Local politicians and trade unionists were lobbied. An attempt was made to prepare a series of questions to put to the Minister responsible.

The result of the local consultations revealed some interesting information. First, amongst those people who worked with the long-term unemployed there was virtually universal cynicism about the likely outcome of the Employment Zone in Smortham. It was clear from the statistical data that the highest concentrations of long-term unemployed people lived in high-rented private sector accommodation in the town centre. They would require relatively well-paid employment to continue to subsist in their present accommodation and would be likely to resist attempts to push them into low-paid menial work in fast food joints and supermarkets. The cynicism deepened when it became apparent that included in both consortium bids for the Smortham EZ were private sector employment agencies. Without a clear lead from government indicating that it wished to see the voluntary sector actively included in the provision of unconditional placements, the expectation was that there would be insufficient benefit to private sector zone operators to include this option amongst the range offered to zoners.

The reaction from local Labour politicians was equally indicative. All were cautious about the possibility of influencing government as to how the Employment Zone might be adapted to local circumstances. Privately they all welcomed any initiative which genuinely increased the flexibility and choices available to people who were long-term unemployed, but considered that it would be most unlikely that the government would concede even 10 per cent of the EZ places to a 'Passport to Participation' option.

Consultation with people planning Employment Zones in other areas of the country was equally gloomy. The experience of the Liverpool prototype EZ was as follows. The government had invited comments from all three prototype EZs. Each had made representations requesting that the EZ be made longer than twenty-six weeks and that there should be greater flexibility, to allow participants to be involved in intermediate labour markets (ILMs). After all, ILMs had been the inspiration for the EZ scheme. The government had rejected outright any attempts to modify the redrawn scheme, which was considerably more restrictive and inflexible than the original prototype EZs.

Only one experience offered any hope and this came, surprisingly, from a regeneration project without any aspirations to operate an Employment Zone. Canning Town Community Links had embarked on a course of declaring their own zone irrespective of how this met any government-defined zones in Newham. They called their zone a 'Social Enterprise Zone' and made it the basis of a Single Regeneration Budget Round 5 bid for a ten-year development programme. Their bid was based on the notion that public sector spending in Newham accounted for approximately 70 per cent of the local GDP for the borough. Of this 98 per cent was spent on mainstream public services, benefits, etc. Their aim was to use the

2 per cent of regeneration money to free up as much of the mainstream public sector spend as possible to create real opportunities for local citizens. Benefits were a significant target. The group had consulted with local trade unionists, politicians, civil servants and ministers to create a programme of discussions involving local people aimed at achieving a relaxation of the benefits rules within their Social Enterprise Zone. The success of their application gave them encouragement to believe that their proposals met with approval, if only from the London Regional Development Agency. It was, however, recognized by the advocates of the 'Passport to Participation' in Smortham that this model, which had been designed over a considerable period, could not be adapted to fit the bid timetable for EZ. It was therefore decided that there was no point in pursuing any attempt to influence ministers and the objective of the group shifted to trying to find a sympathetic EZ bidder.

With help from the Centre for Social Inclusion a draft plan was drawn up for how the scheme might be operated by a local voluntary organization. It quickly became apparent that the cash flow and general financial risks were too great for any voluntary organization to take on, on its own. An organization with the potential to attempt the bid came forward but decided that it needed a commercial partner. Approaches were made to one of the major bidders but were flatly dropped after one initial meeting. Given the way that the rules of the zone were structured, from the point of view of an investor in a profit-making enterprise it is entirely understandable that no commercial enterprise should want to handicap itself by entering into a partnership with a voluntary organization with a broader agenda.

Discussion
We have seen that self-help and self-provision are widespread in poor areas of the UK, and would be even more extensive if residents had the materials, skills, physical energies and networks to do more tasks in this way (see pp. 165–72). Most self-help and self-provisioning, including paid informal work, is done *by choice*, partly because the process and product are preferred to formal exchange, partly to strengthen community or kinship ties (Williams and Windebank, 1999). Research also shows that poor districts have extensive community groups, supportive groups and voluntary agencies, all of which reach residents far better than official social services (especially where minority ethic communities are concerned). Volunteers are crucial in linking isolated individuals with local support systems (Ginsburg et al., 1999). In other words, grassroots local groups and volunteers – the informal community sector – constitute significant social capital in such districts, and require conservation, funding and support.

Instead, these groups and networks are threatened by approaches to economic regeneration (like the Employment Zones) that rely on crude incentives or compulsion to take paid employment, often outside the district or in an activity which makes no use of the human capital accumulated in informal work. This threatens to weaken networks and destroy social capital and increases the need for official services, which cannot be as efficient.

Agencies that know the districts chosen as Employment Zones, and that would want to involve residents in collective projects to improve their quality of life, or as individuals to build on their existing skills and networks, both social and economic, are frustrated by the rules of benefits generally, and the structures and incentives of Employment Zones in particular. But efforts to persuade the government to relax these rules or vary these incentives have fallen on deaf ears.

There are many voluntary and community sector organizations, and some staff in social services departments, who would support the movement to shift towards a more inclusive, less conditional approach to participation. Those that rely heavily on volunteers are especially frustrated by pressures on some of these to enter unsuitable employment. Arguments for change from such organizations will focus on the need to conserve and build on social capital, which is essential for the regeneration of these neighbourhoods, rather than waste it.

The strategy of using the informal sector as a bridge between poor and excluded people and the formal economy has been successful in other countries, notably South Africa (Mazibuko, 1996). It should at least be tried, by allowing pilot Employment Zones to experiment with this approach, using the community sector as lead agency. There is little point in setting up a number of pilot projects, all doing almost exactly the same thing, as the government has done with Employment Zones. This typifies its blind spot over implementation – New Labour has clear, *a priori* models of how to put its programmes into practice, all top-down in structure, and is never ready to learn from local practitioners, seldom from local activists. Both these groups form potential constituencies for a campaign for a 'full engagement' rather than a 'full employment' approach to economic and social regeneration (see below, pp. 194–203), and could help to change the rules of benefits to enable this.

To return to the topic of *co-ordination*, it is plain from these examples that the top-down 'coherence' of 'joined-up solutions' at ministerial level is no guarantee of co-operation and effective partnerships at the local level, or of consistency of the parts of the overall programme – especially in issues of social and economic regeneration. The Canning Town example shows that local initiatives – that engage the co-operation of a number of leading actors and agencies across a policy domain, all knowledgeable and committed to a co-ordinated approach to local issues – may be much more effective, when not fettered by a central government programme's rules and incentives.

Our bottom-up approach to questions of accountability, flexibility and responsiveness needs to be matched by a willingness of a 'large actor' – the local authority being the most obvious candidate – to act as a centre for co-ordinating grassroots initiatives. There needs to be some kind of 'civic forum' in which groups, projects and units can come together and discuss their efforts and their difficulties, share resources and ideas. The co-ordinator would mainly be acting as an information exchange centre, but could also have the responsibility to monitor coverage, to draw attention to duplication as well as gaps, and to address the overall coherence of initiatives. If some new meta-project or form of supportive service was required, it would be the role of the co-ordinator to identify, to initiate, or in some cases even to provide it. The function of local authority staff would be much more to support and respond to grassroots groups' activities, rather than try to control or steer them – as in the 'Deprived Community' exercise.

Obviously these organizations and groups could not replace local authority services, but would complement them. Their leading role in local communities should gradually transform the work of many local authority, health service and other state agency staff from individualized surveillance and persuasion to collective support and empowerment. This approach would bring together professional staff with street-level support and project workers across a number of fields, and gradually lead to a similarity of method and outlook, within a locally-co-ordinated system of measures.

Especially in deprived districts, the common theme of many initiatives would be regeneration through informal economic and social support activities, building up physical and social capital, and improving the physical and social environments. There is massive experience of these methods, especially in Scotland (Donnison, 1998; Holman, 1998) and in Northern Ireland.

Finally, from the standpoint of democratic theory, the co-ordinating role of the local authority should ensure a link between the 'direct democracy' of community initiatives, and the representative democracy of the public authority (Jordan, 1990, Chapter 6). It would be important for local councillors and senior officers to be involved in the co-ordination role, and to understand the methods and principles of the community development approach.

CASE STUDY: TRAINING FOR SOCIAL AND ECONOMIC REGENERATION

The need for training that will embrace politicians, public and voluntary sector workers and local activists, and equip them to work together for social and economic regeneration, has led to new consortia being formed. Here is an example of the kind of programme now being pioneered.

The Community Capacity Development and Training Network for South East England

The network has been formed to draw together teachers and researchers from higher education and community work trainers from the field in a new partnership to respond to the skill shortage in this sphere of operation.

The network aims to build on good practice in community work training across the region by sharing information, skills, trainers, experience of what works, curricula, learning materials, course accreditation and validation. In the first instance it will focus on those key areas targeted for major regeneration expenditure but it will then build outwards to work with others in pockets of social exclusion in the South-East.

In particular, it will apply experience from community development to the training needs of managers and policy makers, from first-line managers and 'community champion councillors' to senior managers and leading local politicians, giving them practical opportunities to work alongside residents from disadvantaged communities. It will draw on know-how from trainers concerned with managing change and partnership building. It will approach training from both a bottom-up and a top-down perspective, creating opportunities for joined-up learning.

It will address training needs in relation to four key government agendas:

- social inclusion
- promotion of local democracy
- partnerships for local regeneration, health improvement, lifelong learning, community safety, etc.
- development of regional training resources

At its first meeting it adopted the following general principle which should underlie any initiative promoted by the network:

> Wherever possible, the aim of the Network will be to bring together policy-makers, managers, activists and community workers, beneficiaries, diverse professionals and users.

Some measures were agreed which were intended to lead to the formalization of the network:

> Two pilot projects are to be attempted, which will involve a mix of members in their planning and delivery. Each pilot project will involve the organization of an event or series of events which bring together people from all levels concerned with community development in their locality to engage in:
>
> - joint training at all levels to meet locally defined needs arising from current partnership working between voluntary and public sector;
> - identification of future needs for training at all levels;
> - helping all levels to plan together for the benefit of socially excluded groups.

Discussion

This kind of new initiative should alert social workers and social work educators to the changing context of practice. It should show that in future training for the role of professional practitioner in child protection and adult social care will be one part of a broadening range of opportunities for the development of skills and work opportunities that include social and economic regeneration. This is part of an already transforming role of state social work in relation to people experiencing poverty and social exclusion.

The Social Engineering Role of the State

The second role of the state is in engineering solutions to issues where individual or household strategies that are rational from these standpoints, but result in collective outcomes which are less than optimal, can be mitigated by the use of public power. The New Labour programme for welfare reform, and especially its attempt to improve labour-market incentives and increase formal economic participation, is very much in this tradition. However, the Third Way is, as we have argued (see pp. 109–10 and 158–9), at best an interim solution to the collective action problem of insiders and outsiders bequeathed to it by the Conservatives. It will be required to adapt and change its policies to avoid creating a new set of opportunities for strategies with socially undesirable consequences.

But how can such exercises in public power be justified in terms of the standards of democratic accountability employed in the first parts of this chapter? And which particular solutions could overcome the new problems that will emerge?

An answer to the first of these questions can easily be assembled from the Third Way's present political resources. Democracy is the collective construction of political authority, and entails the transformation of individual choices into collective actions (Jordan, 1996b, p. 76): Citizens' diverse views and interests are transformed into a collective will for the common good (Rousseau, 1762, Chapters 3 and 6). Successful social engineering overcomes collective action problems by designing, maintaining and updating democratic institutions, through which in turn citizens' common interests become apparent, and the undesirable consequences of individual and group choices are mitigated or resolved. Government is necessary because citizens have conflicting interests; it is possible because they have common interests (Ryan, 1983, p. 54). The territory of common interest can be enlarged by social engineering, thus increasing the scope for democratic community of the kind explored in the previous section.

Thus both the active, participatory democracy of associations based on shared resources, reciprocity and co-operation, and the more technical, instrumental approach to government of the Third Way, are indispensable elements in the democratization of society; but they are in some tension with each other. Community in the former sense is a public good like any other; it has to be constructed through the resolution of conflicts of interest. But solutions to collective action problems that are imposed by external authority undermine participation and limit choice. Hence there has to be constant communication between the two levels of governance, involving informal as well as formal exchanges (Jordan, 1996b, pp. 78–9 and 92–5).

Democratic community can arise either in the absence of scarcity or because relevant actors trust and co-operate freely (Hume, 1745, pp. 494–5). Whereas the increased involvement of citizens in associations and groups educates and equips them for self-government through the creation of shared interests and resources, social engineering tends to aim at economic growth (and hence 'abundance', as Hume called it) as the source of consensus and cohesion. New Labour emphasizes that institutional reform can refine citizens' preferences to create 'new' social actors who reorientate their choices to the common good, recognizing interdependence and demonstrating mutual responsibility. But this is achieved by appealing to their self-interest in the first instance, by redesigning welfare systems so as to make such socially responsible choices consistent with maximizing individual utility in transactions with the tax-benefit system. Reforms should make the system self-enforcing (Elster, 1986) in the sense that it will pay citizens to behave in socially desirable ways.

This task is by no means straightforward. The history of top-down social engineering is full of examples of reforms which 'solve' existing or inherited problems, only to create new ones – either immediately, or because citizens later discover strategies that defeat their intentions. We will see that the Third Way's reforms are full of such instances, already visible; and these stem mainly from the attempt to improve incentives to participate in the labour market, in paid employment.

We have acknowledged that New Labour had to address the impasse under which over 5 million households of working age were excluded from formal employment (no member was in paid work) because of lack of opportunities and incentives (see pp. 158–9). However, the route to reform chosen – strict conditionality, through tests of willingness to work or train – is at best only a short-term, interim solution to this problem. Tax credits and negative income tax schemes (see pp. 35–6) have built-in perverse incentives and 'moral hazards', because of poverty traps. These issues link directly with the question of allocation of paid and unpaid work, formal and informal activity, but they do so in a rather different way from the one illustrated in the last two sections.

It seems obvious at first sight that the incentives of the Working Families Tax Credit (WFTC) and the other tax credits, both already in place and promised, should encourage greater labour supply. In one sense they do – more people have reasons to participate in paid work, and more do so. But this does not necessarily mean that these individuals work harder, for longer hours, or have incentives to improve their skills and competences. Indeed, as we argued in Chapter 1, pp. 34–7, recipients of WFTC and other tax credits may have incentives to work less, not more. Consider the following case study.

CASE STUDY: JIM AND BRENDA SHAW

Jim and Brenda Shaw, in their early thirties, are both model New Labour citizens (and voters). They have two sons, aged seven and three, and live in a house that they are buying on a mortgage. Jim works nights in a food-processing factory, earning around £200 a week, Brenda does three day jobs, at a supermarket checkout, as a cleaner, and at a child care centre. Together they work about seventy hours per week, with Jim looking after the children when Brenda is working.

The couple have never previously claimed (or been eligible for) in-work benefits, but with the advent of WFTC, the high-profile publicity on TV drew their attention to this possibility. On further investigation, they discovered (to their surprise) that they were eligible for a small amount, given the fact that for the next five weeks Jim will be working slightly short-time in the factory, because of slack demand at this time of year.

On further reflection, they found that the benefit opened up new options for them. With the prospect of the two boys being at school, Brenda is considering doing an education or training course, perhaps in bookkeeping. Jim is fed up with his routine, and would like to reduce his working time. They calculate that they will be only about £20 a week worse off if they reduce their joint working hours to 16 per week (i.e. by about 54 hours). Either Jim could go part-time, or Brenda could give up her jobs to study; or both.

Implications

Usually when a new benefit is introduced, it takes some time for claimants to work out strategies for maximizing claims. No system is strategy-proof, but the moral hazard (in terms of the work ethic) of WFTC is transparent. Despite their lack of previous claiming experience, Jim and Brenda have already seen the opportunities for reducing their labour supply it affords. The authors know other couples who have spotted the same openings.

WFTC functions as a kind of (otherwise unconditional) basic income for households with children, where one parent has the chance to do sixteen hours a week of paid work; after that, they are free to combine paid and unpaid work as they wish. In Jim and Brenda's case, this means they can (at last) spend more time with each other, and with their sons. It is a liberating opportunity for them, and also (of course) a good chance for lone parents to gain access to labour markets. But we doubt whether a reduction in work effort of this order was quite what the legislators intended.

To counter this the government might vary the stipulated hours for various categories of claimants, or categories of tax credits, leading eventually to differentiated conditions for eligibility. But it is doubtful whether moral hazards of all kinds can be eliminated altogether. The trouble is that a form of tax transfer that favours paid over unpaid work is vulnerable to another strategy, when the tasks involved are identical and can be done by either work process. Child care, washing, gardening and home improvements are all obvious examples. Under tax credit and negative income tax systems with work tests, it always pays for claimants to do these tasks for each other (on some kind of exchange basis) for cash, rather than doing them informally for themselves. It is hard to avoid the conclusion that lone parents (for instance) will pay each other to look after each other's children, or pay others in their district to do their gardens, in return for being paid for some reciprocal service. This will, unlike the case study, certainly promote the paid work ethic, but not economic efficiency.

Alternative Approaches

In the previous section we indicated some of the internal tensions and contradictions in implementing the tax credit and negative income tax approaches to tax-benefit reform. These problems are not incidental or technical ones – they are inherent to this whole approach (Redmond and Sutherland, 1995). The trouble is that in order to give people outside the labour market better incentives to *take* work (i.e. to mitigate the 'unemployment trap' by ensuring that 'work pays' better than benefits), these measures extend the poverty trap. People like Jim and Brenda Shaw find that they have little or no incentive to work long hours, so they reduce these; people who join the labour market are likely to prefer to take part-time work; and employers are likely to offer employment at around the points (sixteen and thirty hours per week) where people get tax credits, or tax credit 'bonuses'. This makes some sense for parents with young children, like Jim and Brenda; but not for childless households, who are now also promised tax credits (Treasury, 1999). Overall, econometricians calculate that work effort will be *reduced* as a result of the Working Families Tax Credit (Blundell et al., 1999). This is an intrinsic problem for the whole UK (Third Way) approach, based on selective means-tested benefits for those outside and inside employment; it can be ameliorated but not solved by these approaches (Jordan et al., 2000).

Even in an improved version of tax credits, which irons out the perverse incentives to work part-time, there would be an injustice between those doing *paid* social reproduction, social care and community work for family or neighbours, as carers, volunteers or activists. Suppose that, as a result of revenue buoyancy, and in order to pursue his goals for greater social inclusion, Gordon Brown was minded to push forward the New Labour programme for tax-benefit reform and improved incentives. The most efficient way to achieve his goals would be to increase personal tax allowances to just over £6,000 a year, and to allow those on income support to keep about 50 per cent of each £1 they earn by way of declared, part-time earnings. Public finance experts have calculated that this combination would redistribute most to people in the bottom three deciles of income receivers, but give some gains to all income groups, and therefore be poltically feasible (Jordan et al., 2000, Chapter 2). It would also make feasible a fuller integration of the tax-benefit system, into a negative income tax scheme, thus saving some administrative costs.

However, there would still be many who would receive neither an on-wage tax credit nor a cash benefit under such a system. All those outside the labour market but unable to show they were actively seeking employment, or totally incapable of work, would receive nothing. Political pressures would then build up for including carers, volunteers and activists under something like a 'participation passport' of the kind discussed in the case study above (pp. 186–91). Since these groups would have some political clout, they might well destabilize the Third Way 'new contract for welfare', leading to pressures from students and others to include them also. In the post-Blair period, New Labour would face the need to find a new moral and political settlement.

At this point, there would be an opportunity for advocates of the Basic Income (BI) or Citizens Income (CI) principle to push for the adoption of their approach to tax-benefit integration. For many years, they have argued that this would be the only long-term way to reconcile equality and freedom, social inclusion and social justice (Jordan, 1973, 1976, 1987, 1989, 1996a, 1998a; Van der Veen and Van Parijs, 1987; Van Parijs, 1995; Fitzpatrick, 1999). The main difference from the negative income tax scheme that would spring logically from tax credits is that eligibility would be *automatic* for all citizens, and *unconditional* – no tests of willingness to work, or disqualification of partners doing unpaid household or caring work. It would save the very costly casework and enforcement duties of the 'participation passports', and enable individuals to negotiate on how to combine paid and unpaid activities (see Box 20).

Box 20   The Basic Income (BI) principle otherwise known as Citizens Income (CI)

The Basic Income principle for tax-benefit integration argues that tax allowances and social security benefits of all kinds should gradually be replaced by a single tax-free sum, guaranteed for every individual, irrespective of labour-market or household status. It would vary only with age and ability/disability, and be unconditional, paid on the basis of either residence or citizenship (the latter giving rise to the term CI). It would operate much like a child benefit for adults.

The origins of the idea have been traced to Tom Paine, Saint-Simon, Bertrand and Dora Russell, Major C.H. Douglas and others (Van Trier, 1995). It is now advocated by several eminent economists, such as Professor A.B. Atkinson (1969, 1995) and Lord Desai, and political philosophers, such as Philippe Van Parijs, Brian Barry and Carole Pateman. Among leading UK politicians, only Paddy Ashdown (1988) has given it support, and his party went into the 1992 general election with BI in its manifesto. But research shows that it is now supported by many backbench MPs in all parties at Westminster, as well as being on the mainstream policy agenda in Ireland (Jordan et al., 2000, Chapter 1).

Among the main advantages claimed for BI/CI are:

- *It is neutral between paid and unpaid work*, giving better incentives for low-paid employment than tax credits, but allowing choice over how to combine the two.
- *It treats men and women as equals*, allowing them to negotiate how to share unpaid work in households.
- *It combats exploitation*, by allowing individuals to survive without relying on dangerous or demeaning work.
- *It promotes economic efficiency*, by ensuring that low-paid work is not given a special subsidy (as in tax credits), and hence labour power is not wastefully deployed.
- *It promotes social justice*, by treating all individuals alike, and giving extra income only to those with special care needs.

But it might be argued that we have not yet shown how this could be reconciled with one of New Labour's goals – that rights and responsibilities should be balanced. There may be some weaknesses in the New Labour programme, but its insistence on this balance has been crucial in correcting the residual impasse of the economic individualism of the Thatcher–Major reforms – the insider–outsider problem identified on pp. 158–9. By instigating a transparent 'contract for welfare', New Labour has convinced mainstream citizens that money allocated to welfare is well spent, and it has required claimants to give up their (illegal) self-compensatory strategies of informal earnings.

However, this solution is at best a temporary one. The problem is that 'reciprocity' (something for something) and 'responsibility' cannot be imposed from above, as civic obligations, except as an interim part of a crash programme of reform. This is because – at least in liberal democracies – work must be motivated by some gains, if not material then psychological. Employment taken under the threat of loss of benefits must yield other advantages, or it will not be efficiently done, or perhaps not done at all. This is where the impact of Engel's law on work in social reproduction is crucial (see pp. 173–5). If such employment turns out to be a 'dead end' in income terms, and larger and longer proportions of employees find themselves in poverty traps, then it will only be a matter of time before this is reflected in work effort reduction, falling productivity, absenteeism, and all the other typical symptoms of forced labour systems.

A BI or CI scheme, *would increase incentives for citizens to participate in paid labour-market activities*. The kinds of people excluded under negative income tax regimes would have inducements to take such work and – above all – those in poverty traps under such regimes would have the incentive to work longer hours and earn more. The net benefit of participation in paid work would be higher for low earners. So New Labour's value of responsibility and its goals of empowerment and inclusion would be better served.

But if CI is wholly unconditional, how can it provide any elements of reciprocity or responsibility? Here again it is important to distinguish between top-down versions of accountability, and bottom-up communal ones. New Labour relies on obligations imposed by officials, albeit often individual, personal advisers. These are conceived in terms of responsibility to the state, not to fellow citizens. We have shown how these can be difficult or even counterproductive to implement. The alternative is to draw on, support and strengthen the obligations that citizens actually feel to fellow members of kinship and friendship groups, associations, clubs, community groups, organizations and communities. Such activities and movements rely on reciprocity and responsibility, because it is the very stuff of co-operation and collectivity (Jordan, 1998a, Chapters 2 and 3). Thus it is in informal activities that individuals actually *experience* the requirement to reciprocate and take responsibility, not in relation to officials. This increases *engagement* in society and social cohesion.

For these reasons, it makes sense for policy to move in the direction of an unconditional CI. The organizations and groups that can move their members towards voluntary participation and willing contribution are small-scale, face-to-face ones, doing informal work that improves the quality of life and replenishes the social and physical capital of their communities. We have seen from our case studies and in the work of Williams and Windebank (1999) and Ginsburg et al. (1999) that self-help, mutual assistance, volunteering and community work are already strong, though largely invisible, aspects of deprived areas. Informal economic activity flourishes, and many skills that have been developed in this might be harnessed to more orthodox purposes. The goal of policy should be to build bridges between the formal and informal economies, by gradually linking the community sector of social support networks and the informal sector of undocumented production and exchange with the formal systems of social care and the economy.

Political theorists and researchers have in recent years explored the relevance of informally generated reciprocity, trust, co-operation and the conservation of common resources, for prosperity and good governance. Writers like Taylor (1987) have shown that voluntary co-operation is possible with frequent interaction, building trust through mutual adjustments in shared tasks. Ostrom (1990) has shown that democratic processes of management evolve so that groups of stakeholders can conserve and improve common property co-operatively, and Dryzek (1994) gives up-to-date examples of these forms of 'discursive democracy' in solving disputes and conflicts of interest over resources in developed economies. Finally Putnam (1993) has drawn attention to the correlations between associational experience that builds reciprocity, trust and social capital, and both economic growth and efficient democratic institutions. All these point in the direction of local, spontaneously evolving and informal groupings, responding to their shared conditions and issues as far more reliable sources of responsibility and community than state-led, imposed obligations.

Under a CI system there would of course be some individuals who reneged on their responsibilities to others, as there are under any system. But research suggests that policies for promoting and supporting local activism in all spheres, through democratic and self-governing groups, would be more likely to succeed than top-down, official measures. Furthermore, by breaking the impasse of the Thatcher–Major era, and giving far more citizens the experience of economic participation (while denying them illegal alternatives) New Labour will have created a better platform for this approach. For all these reasons, a CI would be a suitable instrument for the implementation of the final stage of the reform programme, because it allows all citizens to participate through chosen combinations of paid and unpaid work, under divisions of labour and shares of the burdens and benefits of co-operation that are negotiated between them – in groups, associations and households.

To summarize, a movement for a CI is likely to be generated by criticism of the tax credit approach, and would have as its natural constituents carers, volunteers, the community sector, and many others who recognize the shortcomings of the Third Way's version of distributive justice. It would emphasize that a CI would be a more effective means of combating any remaining elements of

- social exclusion – new kinds of 'outsiders';
- inequality of opportunity – of chance, access and share;
- disempowerment – including educational, health and cultural factors.

At the same time, it would be a more effective means for promoting the growth of

- social capital – responsibility through trust and co-operation;
- democratic voice – self-governing associations and groups;
- lifelong learning – flexibility that allows time for study and training;
- social cohesion – links between all members of society.

Will Communities Work? The Evidence

It seems highly speculative and risky to base a set of policy proposals on hypotheses about changed motivation and behaviour under socially engineered conditions. What evidence is there that communities could provide the basis for work of the kind outlined in this chapter? The relevant research comes, surprisingly, from a kind of social laboratory usually seen as suitable only for the study of neo-Hobbesian social relations – the deprived Catholic neighbourhoods of Northern Irish cities.

What is most distinctive about these communities, in comparison with similar ones in Great Britain, is that they have hitherto been policed by indigenous paramilitary units rather than the agencies of the state. Although the paramilitaries have been violent and ruthless in the suppression of certain kinds of activity (especially drug-related crime), and political solidarity has been brutally enforced, obedience to the rules of the UK tax-benefit rules has certainly not. As a result, residents have been largely free to develop their own economy and their own community collective action, unencumbered by the restrictions of bureaucratic authority, but within the framework of a strongly sanctioned local order.

We have already noted that fear of exposure, and particularly fear of being reported to the authorities by neighbours, is a major factor limiting activity by claimants. This has been a finding in studies from Pahl's (1984) to Williams and Windebank's (1999). But Leonard's research in West Belfast (Leonard, 1994, 1998a, 1998b, 1999) investigated a community with unemployment rates among the worst in Northern Ireland (Boal et al., 1974; Doherty, 1977) but rates of informal economic activity far higher than those recorded by researchers in Great Britain (Sheenan and Tomlinson, 1996). Leonard's study was carried out in 1988–90, and in her survey of 103 males and 114 females living in 150 households, only 25 per cent of male and 22 per cent of female respondents had access to formal labour markets. By contrast, 36 per cent of male and 21 per cent of female respondents held paid occupations in the informal economy, mostly gender-specific, such as construction work for men, and sub-contract cleaning for women. In addition to this paid work, higher rates of self-provisioning than in comparable surveys in Great Britain were reported, again gender-specific, such as home and car repairs for men, and baking, knitting and sewing for women (a quarter baked weekly, and one in three knitted clothes). Leonard found that 86 per cent of households relied on neighbours for help, including loans of money and clothes; they commonly carried out work for each other (such as decorating or repairs) in a paid or unpaid capacity, or knitted and made clothes for each other, many preferring to build up favours which could be recalled at some future date, rather than accept cash (Leonard, 1999, p. 6).

Leonard concluded that informal activity contributed to self-worth, upholding the values of family life and self-reliant economic behaviour in a community that was very poor, in terms of formal economic measurement. This is not an essentially different finding from those derived from studies of deprived neighbourhoods in Great Britain (Jordan et al., 1992; MacDonald, 1994); what is distinctive is the sheer extent of informal work, its overt nature, and the strong preference for this kind of activity stated by the respondents. Rather than the shame and retreatism reported by Williams and Windebank, especially in their southern England survey among workless households, Leonard found that these respondents blamed the UK government for their economic marginalization, and felt perfectly justified in what they were doing. In this respect, because of their lack of loyalty to the state and its rules, their behaviour could be compared with those of informal actors in transforming post-communist societies in East Central Europe (see pp. 165–8 and Kolankiewicz, 1996; Piirainen, 1997), where state policies had over a long period 'rather than displacing the need for informal networks, ... sustained and enlarged the space for their operation' (Weiss, 1987, p. 231).

Leonard's research turns on its head the whole case for formalizing work urged by the Third Way. Drawing on the research of Sassen (1996), she argues that informal economic enterprises in the community she studied were successful precisely because they were informal; in such districts there was a demand for low-cost goods and services, and the consumption needs of low-income households were met by small-scale producers and retailers who relied on family or informal labour and operated outside the health and safety regulations (Leonard, 1999, p. 15). In a globalized economy such businesses occupy a protected niche, as amongst immigrant and other marginalized communities in many large cities world-wide they can provide cheap goods because they evade state controls, save transport costs of all kinds, and meet local preferences (Sassen, 1996).

Her respondents positively chose informal economic activities for two main reasons. The first concerned the labour market, where screening based on educational qualifications (Jordan et al., 1994, Chapter 7) has excluded job applicants from this kind of community. This sort of credentialism favours the middle classes, and allows them to benefit even from state job-creation schemes, like the Community Programme in the 1980s, which were supposed to combat unemployment in this kind of district. One community activist in Belfast said:

> 'We prefer the autonomy of doing our own thing without any formality or regularity. We're in control here and we like to keep it that way. If we started to formalise, you might say that that would be a good thing, it could lead to a few jobs being created. But who would those jobs go to? Certainly not any of us. We've no fancy qualifications. In fact, to be quite honest, we've no qualifications. So how would any of us have a chance? Who would employ us? The only way we can do community work is to do it voluntary.' (Leonard, 1999, p. 17)

The second reason was that, the more informal the exchange of services, the more those involved in exchanging them were tied into reciprocal relationships. As Leonard puts it, 'Reciprocity is most effective when individuals are uncertain whether or not favours have been fully repaid. It is this ambiguity that locks individuals into long-standing relationships with each other' (ibid., p. 19). Those who did favours in her study were unwilling to accept payment, because they wanted to build up a stable network of mutual help, based on habitual exchanges, with ambiguity about who owed what to whom. One respondent said, when asked about being paid for favours:

> 'You're missing the whole point. If you take money, that's it. The debt's repaid. But if you get nothing then the person's indebted to you for his whole life.' (Leonard, 1999, p. 19)

Another aspect of this reasoning was that such networks often involved exchanges between women. Women's activities are often difficult to commodify or quantify, and women who offered less tangible services to each other (e.g. emotional support) often failed to mention these in research interviews, whereas men who did more material favours could enumerate them. Hence women's exchanges were inherently ambiguous and incommensurable, which in this part of the informal economy is a strength, not a weakness of a network (Leonard, 1999, p. 17).

These values and systems, elaborated into a whole culture of informal exchanges in this West Belfast estate, were developed under conditions of extreme economic adversity and political conflict. Nonetheless, they show that reciprocity and mutuality are sustainable ways of getting things done, and that people are more likely to use them when there are no third-party state enforcers to stop them. Research studies like these in the 1990s cast doubt on the general-izabilty of those of the 1980s, such as Pahl's (1984) and Smith's (1986), which found less self-provisioning among claimant households. They suggest that this is specific to a context of poverty *plus* surveillance and stigma.

It seems likely, from studies in other countries and cultures, that the real problem for public policy is not that community, reciprocity and informal activ-ity are in danger of being lost altogether, or that those who get unconditional benefits become passive and dependent, but that the interface between formal and informal economies is problematic. This is where the public authority can play a more constructive role. Social work and community work have a lot to offer, both in helping to build bridges between the two sets of activities and systems of regulation, and in helping individuals use human and social capital accumulated in the one to their advantage in the other.

The community surveyed in Leonard's study was hardly a model for future social relations. In terms of its gender relations and the violently exclusive blood-and-guts order it sustained, it was in many ways the antithesis of a caring, sharing social system. Many of its economic features had the hallmarks of the ghetto. Its lessons are more about the viability of community as a set of social interactions than the desirability of this particular collection of cultural practices. The purpose of social work in such a situation might be to soften the harshness of the informal code, to uphold the rights of the oppressed within all social units, and to develop more constructive links with the world outside. This would be a more positive role for social workers than the one envisaged in the programmes of the Third Way.

Conclusions

Many of the criticisms of local authority social work developed in the policy documents reviewed in Part II of this book, and those elaborated by ourselves, prompt the question: should social work as a profession become detached – disestablished in a sense – from the structures of local government, from the tasks of social control and enforcement, and from the provision of state social services? Aspects of this question are clearly under debate in government circles at the time of writing. Press reports indicate that Hackney council has become the first local authority to be issued with a formal, official warning about the standard of its services for children in care, thus risking having its social services depart-ment taken over under new powers which take effect in April 2000 (*Guardian*, 21 December 1999). The Social Services Inspectorate had found that arrange-ments for dealing with children coming into care in one part of the borough were 'unsafe', that almost one in four children had no care plan, that half were not being visited as often as required, and that 19 per cent of children had missed one of two statutory inspections. The Minister, John Hutton, said that in Hackney immediate measures were needed to secure 'an appropriate environment in which these services can be delivered', through addressing 'political and corporate issues' (ibid.).

However, New Labour's approach to such issues has by now been indicated in the implementation of its education programme. Hackney has already had two parts of its education services parcelled out to external consultants, as a result of similar criticisms. The problems are seen as ones of management and the enforcement of standards, not the suitability of an organizational environment for the professional task. Because of the limited role of social work in the Third Way's vision of welfare reform, the more fundamental questions raised in this chapter are not on the agenda.

Indeed New Labour's reasons for taking social work out of local government would be quite different from the ones that might inspire professional arguments for a similar organizational change. The latter could be in part motivated by an attempt to reduce the already narrow focus of enforcement, investigation, assessment and rationing work done in local government departments, and escape the negative effects of central government's emphasis on surveillance, measurement, standards and targets, and top-down implementation of policy. New Labour would introduce changes to strengthen all these aspects.

More generally, a professional argument for separation would advocate a greater distance between professional practice and the overall enforcement of government measures of social discipline and control. But this is where our analysis parts company with such an approach. It is precisely because of New Labour's authoritarian tendencies that much social work should remain within the state, and as part of the local and central authority. New agencies set up to implement the Third Way programme spread the net of intervention into the lives of citizens, and use quasi-social-work methods to try to influence their behaviour and decisions. New Labour extends the role of the public authority in civil society, and introduces new forms of individualized care-and-control through its implementation. If professional principles, and the accumulated experience of fifty years of practice, are not deployed in these fields, it will be like trying to reinvent the wheel on many different public policy sites. Professional social work has a responsibility to try to influence these developments, if only by drawing attention to the limitations of this approach, to which its own history attests.

The second argument we have developed in this chapter stems from the role of the state in planning services and co-ordinating the voluntary and spontaneous responses of communities and groups to change. Ideas like 'partnership' and 'holistic governance' are empty without a confident and competent public authority, which can take a broader view of society's development but be accountable and sensitive to the voice of democratically run associations. This social-engineering role has traditionally been in tension with the freedoms and accountabilities of a healthy civil society; and this has never been more the case than now, with New Labour's tendency to try to control all alternative power centres. But here again, this does not constitute a convincing long-term argument for weakening local authorities, or removing professional work from their ambit. Once the first phase of New Labour reforms has run its course, these will be more necessary than ever, to balance Third Way megalomania and Benthamite bureaucracy.

Our analysis rests on an understanding of the overall direction of welfare reform that emphasizes the limitations of the attempt to improve labour-market incentives and broaden formal participation. Instead, we have drawn attention to the continued importance of informal interactions as a sphere of economic activity, and to the potential of social and community work for developing and promoting it, and empowering actors within it. This argument does not rest on an uncritical acceptance of the current practices and cultures of such activities. Instead, we recognize the very negative features of the blood-and-guts codes of deprived districts, and the need to soften them and to build bridges for individuals trapped in 'communities of fate' (Marske, 1991) into mainstream society. We have shown how a Basic Income (or Citizens Income) is the long-run welfare reform most likely to combine neutrality between formal and informal economic activity with social justice for men and women, and inclusion and empowerment for all citizens. It is both a technical solution to the problems of incentives that would persist after New Labour's present round of reforms is completed, and a measure for improving social cohesion.

Social work would have one vital role to play in Basic Income society. But this role would be less about enforcing individual conformity to government rules and standards, and more about improving social relations through relationships of trust and mutual accountability. It is to the practice methods appropriate for these tasks that we now turn.

9

Front-Line Practice

This has not been primarily a book about social work practice, in the sense of a detailed account of how to assist and influence service users in face-to-face encounters. It has been more about the current dilemmas of an occupation which is half marginalized in a process of implementing a programme that is only semi-successful, but might evolve into one that is genuinely radical and pathbreaking. If the Third Way is to work, it needs something of what social work can offer; and if it succeeds, social work definitely needs to be part of it.

We have argued in some detail that social work should take a broader view of its remit, to include economic activity, social regeneration, community work and many projects and units that do not at present think of themselves in its terms. It will also need to consider its position in relation to the new agencies set up by New Labour, especially those concerned with education and training for public service work. But many of its central tasks are likely to remain the same – concerned with human suffering that is linked to the life cycle, to illness or disability, or with conflicts of interest between people tied by bonds of family and kinship, or with the iniquities, cruelties, betrayals, misunderstandings, mistakes and accidents that go to make up everyday life. In this sense, it will still be about work with individuals and families, even if it does take the broader perspective recommended in the previous two chapters.

Between them, the authors have had about thirty years' experience of this type of practice. We will draw on this to suggest developments in the profession that would make it better suited to the challenges identified in the book. We will cite a number of sources of inspiration for such developments, mainly from other English-speaking countries (notably Australia and New Zealand), which are becoming available for students and trainees in this country (Parton and O'Byrne, 2000). Building on the wealth of experience in the UK, in community work and related projects as well as in the public and voluntary sectors, there are reasons to be optimistic about the prospects for social work in a modified 'tough love' regime.

However, we will argue that the biggest threat to such optimism lies in a mind-set about practice that is currently fashionable in social work (and related occupations). Unfortunately, this orthodoxy fits all too well with New Labour's; it is hand in glove with top-down policy prescription and accountability, with the *ad hoc* development of 'solutions' to particular problems, with targets and standards, and with the obsession with effectiveness and value for money that the government inherited from its predecessors.

Yet this orthodoxy is in some tension with the requirements of tough love, because it prescribes very technical methods and measures for addressing particular needs and objectives. Tough love (if it is to be convincing) means the capacity to communicate optimism and energy for the solution of problems, and the confidence that service users can rise to new heights, reach new milestones, and fulfil unrealized potential. Such practice requires charisma, flexibility, and above all the capacity to improvise and innovate – to think on one's feet, respond to the unexpected with the even less expected, and to build small triumphs into the midst of serious adversities. What it does not need is the dreary, mechanistic, systematic, technocratic approach that puts clients into categories, and produces a ready-made package according to a pseudo-scientific classification of their deficits.

In this chapter, we will criticize the positivist pursuit of 'what works' in social work research – the attempt to detach practice both from the context of social relations in which it is located, and from the person of the practitioner. Much that passes for an evidence-based approach is derived from narrowly conceived studies of particular settings, which see social work activity as the delivery of a set of pre-packaged responses to need that can be broken down into minutely specified elements and then recombined in many different forms, like a kind of chemical potion. This is presented in largely impersonal terms, as requiring technical understanding and some quantitative research sophistication (to match the remedy for the assessed needs), but little in the way of empathy or communication, and nothing resembling intuition or flair. Practice is therefore reduced to the implementation of detailed guidelines and instructions from government-sponsored researchers.

Of course, practice is in reality never like this. Practitioners continue to use judgement and accumulated experience in their decisions, and to offer support and challenge in ways that draw on their own feelings and fantasies. The requirements of survival alone demand humour and adaptability of a kind largely unknown to the hegemonic view. However, practitioners are nowadays encouraged to see these as incidental, or as sugaring the pill, or as office counterculture rather than as bona fide elements in practice skills. We will show that there are now good theoretical and research grounds for reversing this perception – for seeing these latter qualities as the essential elements in good practice, while the more technical ones are important background features that apply only to certain settings or contexts.

Furthermore, social work research is coming increasingly to deal in these elements of communication, meaning, identity and fantasy, as new studies in the narrative, discursive and allegorical aspects of practice come to the fore. In a strange way, these may fit tough love better than the technical means at present espoused by the Third Way. There is something to be rescued from New Labour's approach to implementation, but the analysis and the style of practice this calls for is very different from the currently fashionable one.

Evidence-Based Social Care

Although the hegemonic view is broader than the new social work orthodoxy, we will deal here mainly with the intellectual origins of the movement for evidence-based approaches to social care, and why such approaches are unsuitable for the implementation of New Labour's programme. The movement is relatively new, but its antecedents are longstanding, and some of its advocates have been urging its cause for many years (Sheldon, 1978). The recent flowering of prescriptions for practice in probation (MacDonald, 1994) and child care (MacDonald, 1998) springs from more general models of the role of research in informing practice (MacDonald and Sheldon, 1992), and on the substantial literature on effectiveness and evaluation (Lisham, 1984; Bloom, 1993; McGuire, 1995; Cheetham et al., 1992; Kazi, 1998). The movement combines elements of behaviourist analysis, medical and health care studies, positivist and empirical science and managerialist policy implementation to prescribe specific interventions (Webb, 1999). In essence it argues:

1 that practice is about accomplishing measurable changes in behaviour or outcome ('what works'), based on clear objectives;
2 that there exist a great number of well-constructed empirical research studies that can inform practice directly, so long as social workers have the necessary critical appraisal skills to assess these, and select the ones relevant for the case or cases in hand;
3 that the methodology most appropriate for such studies is derived from quantitative social science, or (indirectly) from medical and health science, and rests on framing clear and testable hypotheses, and measuring concrete changes attributable to specific interventions;
4 that social workers should be encouraged or required to build evaluation of the effectiveness of their work into their practice, to implement agency plans and policies, and to contribute to the dissemination and application of research outcomes.

Criticism of this set of principles has focused on each of these elements, and on their combined application. Not all social work is concerned with short-run behavioural change; much manages adversity or decline. Objectives are inevitably complex, reflecting the political, moral and social context of human problems; hence social work involves uncertainty, confusion and doubt, often shared between practitioners and service users (Jordan, 1978). Practice methods are seldom clearcut, and cannot be imposed; they need to be *negotiated*, paying attention to service users' understandings of their needs and goals (Jordan, 1987). If it is to empower and enable service users, social work must co-operate with them in research as well as in practice, and qualitative methods are often more appropriate to such aims (Heron, 1996; Gould and Taylor, 1996; Greene, 1994; Fuller and Petch, 1995). Hence behavioural change and measurable outcome are often neither feasible nor desirable, and quantitative methods may be inappropriate.

The goal of analysing problems and deciding on interventions in line with the best available research evidence may in many instances be impracticable. The 'best evidence' of what works in medical and health care (Sackett et al., 1996) is usually taken to be based on randomized control trials, which are conspicuously lacking for the whole field of social care – partly for ethical reasons, and partly because the conditions for such experimental research are seldom present. The strict standards of scientific method (Miller, 1974) require that predictions can be made about measurable phenomena, with tests of the reliability and validity of research design. These methods have been extensively criticized in the social sciences (Keat and Urry, 1975; Held, 1980), and medical studies under clinical conditions rely on professional power and prestige for their investigative processes, as well as a scientific ideology for their influence on practice. In social care, government guidance and managerial policy substitute for these, prescribing an approach to practice which focuses on the evaluation of the details of service users' behaviour but seldom asks questions about power or choice.

On their own, none of these arguments constructs a knock-down case against evidence-based methods, which appeal to a shared consensus among politicians, managers and service professionals about the need to demonstrate effectiveness and value for taxpayers' money. However, as an approach to implementing New Labour's programme there is a far stronger set of criticisms that can be brought to bear. In spite of the apparently snug fit between the empirical scientific basis of evidence-based care and Third Way prescriptions, the two are ultimately incompatible because of New Labour's ambitions for institutional transformation, cultural change and moral rearmament. The kinds of small behaviour modification required by the practice, the controlled and constant conditions needed for the research method, the scientific assumptions built into the evaluation, and the managerial style of dissemination and implementation, are all destabilized or made redundant by the wider goals of the Third Way's reform programme.

This becomes clear if we list the assumptions on which that programme is based, as follows:

(a) Claimants and service users behave in ways that are conditioned by the institutional rules of welfare systems, the structure of payoffs and opportunities in the labour market and the tax systems and the cultures of resistance that developed under Thatcherism–Majorism. Institutional rules, incentives and opportunities must change to alter behaviour, and practice must reinforce these changes.

(b) Empirical studies conducted under previous social conditions are unreliable guides to practice, since the goal of policy is to change service users' responses by changing the context for choices. New studies must be conducted under new rules; but in the meanwhile, practice must promote change, not consolidate previous behaviours and strategies. Practice theory must therefore be derived from the ethical and social aspirations of policy, not from older studies.

(c) Cultural and moral considerations are an essential element in the changes to be promoted. Large shifts in behaviour, not small modifications, are required; hence practice methods must appeal to such moral ideas as responsibility, community and co-operation, not just instrumental factors. The whole programme aims at social inclusion and social justice, not just gains in prosperity and security. Welfare services should increase self-worth, autonomy, responsibility and community; practice must aspire to emancipatory and transformative aims, and confront dishonest cultural practices.

(d) The management of change should aspire to large shifts in organizational behaviour and professional expectations. Public sector agencies are required to transform themselves, through partnerships with voluntary and community sector associations, and by the co-ordination of a 'holistic governance' approach. Local politics is to be overhauled and redirected, under the supervision of new regional authorities. Policy is directed towards the dissemination of new attitudes and practices, as much as to the achievement of standards, goals and targets.

Tough love in the Third Way revives the vision of social work (and the welfare occupations more generally) as a moral enterprise, concerned with changing society rather than suppressing disorder or enforcing conformity. The ethical justification for New Labour's toughness is the recreation of a sense of justice, inclusion and cohesion, not the imposition of a rigid discipline. It is a dynamic process, concerned with democratization, the building of new institutions and the strengthening of interpersonal bonds and loyalties. Although this book has been highly critical of New Labour's limited conception of the implementation of these ideas (through top-down, Benthamite methods), the fact remains that the Third Way contains many powerful reformative concepts and energies, and has begun an important process of social change. Evidence-based approaches are inadequate vehicles for this programme; they correspond to the pseudo-scientific elements in Benthamism, rather than the more generous ideals and values of the Third Way, or its more lofty ambitions. As Weick and Saleeby (1998) have suggested, 'the early moral and social orientations of the [social work] profession run deep in memory but they have become part of an increasingly silent language as the weight of the scientific world view suppressed these appreciations' (p. 22). New Labour provides an opportunity for their renewal and redirection.

What changes of these kinds reveal is that the evidence-based approach is not so much wrong as terribly limited and blinkered. Despite the grandiose claims of scientific probity and methodological soundness, most of the studies undertaken are context-specific: they examine the effects of interventions undertaken in a very specific set of cultural, environmental and administrative circumstances, such as a particular residential or day care regime, or battery of investigative procedures. This is necessarily so, because in social care what corresponds to a dose of chemotherapy or the provision of an artificial joint is such an environmental regime or investigative procedure, since these are the measurable, quantifiable and controllable elements in practice. It is important to keep evaluating the impact of such regimes and procedures; but to get a broader, more reliable picture of the overall effectiveness of policies, such as occurred in child care in the mid-1980s (Packman et al., 1986; Millham et al., 1986; Rowe, 1989) takes time. In the conditions of rapid change promoted by New Labour, this kind of in-depth, synthetic investigation is unlikely to be feasible for a while yet.

Of course, none of these criticisms is well made if the social work profession is willing to accept the very limited role assigned to it in the Third Way, and if local authority social services are to become a residual, last-resort provision for the poor, and the enforcement-orientated assessors of needs and risks that policy documents envisage. Evidence-based social care would be a very good way to tie the profession and the agency into a conception of their tasks that effectively deskilled and shackled them, while seeming to raise their status to that of scientific researchers. But we are assuming here that neither academics who study social work nor practitioners who do it want this to happen. Furthermore, our argument and analysis in this book are aimed at demonstrating that tough love will be a central aspect of the implementation of a revised and enhanced New Labour programme, and that social work has much to offer this moral enterprise. Evidence-based approaches should be relegated to an important support role, rather than promoted to the front line in the development of practice knowledge.

This line of argument assumes that practice is taken to include all the activities reviewed and illustrated in this book – the broader view of social work that we have advocated. Once it is understood in this way, then it is clear that every project unit and team should indeed have an orientation towards research and learning, but that this will not consist of critical appraisal of studies of similar interventions (since often none will exist), but a reflective perspective on their own work.

Research, Knowledge and Learning in Social Work

While evidence-based social care has been establishing itself as an official orthodoxy in the UK, another tradition of research, knowledge and practice has been developing in other countries, and in pockets of unorthodoxy at home. It is based on practitioners researching their own interventions by reflecting on their actions with colleagues and service users (Schön, 1983; Fook, 1996). This approach stems from the recognition that the *process* of social work, as well as the outcome, requires analysis and evaluation for learning to occur, and that the research methods used should be suitable for an interactive profession, concerned with issues of personal change and social justice (Denscombe, 1998; Sheppard, 1998; Hinks, 2000). This involves detailed, rich and accurate descriptions of what actually happens in practice; reflection on the language and conceptualization used in this, and the kind of account given by the practitioner (and others); and questioning of the methods, purposes and results of the intervention (Fook, 1996). It should also include reflection on the values and principles at stake, and how these are linked with the actions taken.

It is interesting to note that in some countries these developments have been explicitly seen as the emergence of a new kind of welfare regime and as a kind of knowledge suited to 'work in a complex, contingent and pluralistic world' (Karvinen et al., 1999, p. 9). In Finland, where the collapse of the neighbouring Soviet Union in 1989 coincided with major structural changes in the economy and the public sector, a stable system with generous provision of social care as an aspect of welfare citizenship was replaced by rapid change, variability and mobility, and the need to reflect on what was previously taken for granted (Eväsaari, 1995). Research methods and practitioner evaluations therefore set themselves new tasks.

> When practice increasingly takes place under mobile circumstances and conditions of life, it is unlikely that there exist policies or theories that can cover all cases. In actual practice, the practitioner is continuously faced with situations that can only be handled by constructing both the objectives of action and its necessary knowledge base in the working process case by case. There are neither ready-made packages of theories nor ethical truth-telling principles; rather it is the practitioner who negotiates case by case how to manage in complex situations.... This puts a great deal of emphasis on the practitioner's personal ability both to practice ethical reflection and to make relevant choices between theoretical concepts and methods of handling situations. (Satka, 1999, p. 21)

It is this combination of value-based research, developing knowledge in partnership with service users, and recognizing issues of power and justice, that has been pursued in Australia, New Zealand and in some agencies in the UK. Issues can be identified with other colleagues, agencies and service users; an investigation initiated, with a research team; research methods agreed, and necessary training undertaken; analysis can be presented in forms relevant for all stakeholder groups; future action can be jointly planned. This approach emphasizes what research and practice have in common: 'we need to get on with the collective job of exploring a creative way forward which allows and preserves social work's capacity, and, on the other hand, to be able to respond in a clear, enthusiastic and imaginative way to unlock the potential of the people with whom social workers work' (Peile and McCouat, 1997, p. 356).

In these schools of thought, the ideas of reflective practice and critical reflection (Schön, 1983; Jones and Jordan, 1996) are central, and encourage practitioners to become more aware of how they think, communicate and decide, what they know and how they learn (Fook et al., 1997; Fook, 1996; Gould and Taylor, 1996). This kind of research, and the practice knowledge it generates, is appropriate for a profession in which solutions to people's problems have to be *negotiated*, using largely informal methods, and paying close attention to how service users define their needs and to the informal processes by which they get by together. Because work takes place mainly in people's 'natural' settings, and because decisions can only be imposed as a last resort, by using formal, legal procedures, social workers are required to be 'more sensitive to the significance attached to words and actions by clients and others, and to the subtleties of the processes by which people co-exist and co-operate in communities' (Jordan, 1987, p. 143).

We can summarize the alternative view of research and knowledge for practice that fits with our broader and more discursive view of social work as:

(a) concerned with moral and political issues in, and understanding of, practice, and with practice-as-policy, as much as with the technical aspects of professional interventions;

(b) including service users and their organizations in the design and conduct of investigations, rather than as passive or non-participant research subjects, thus enabling them to influence the language and ethics of research;

(c) negotiated between academics, practitioners and service users, and its meanings and findings interpreted, not imposed on those constituencies as prescriptions or expert scientific knowledge;

(d) paying close attention to the details of language (narratives and interactions), the face-to-face exchanges of meaning, the identities, the relationships (of power and of support) and the processes of change that occur in practice, and hence more likely to use qualitative methods than qualitative ones.

Social Work Face to Face

It may be useful at this point to recapitulate the central arguments of the book about social work practice. While we have been highly critical of the Third Way's ideas about implementing its programme, we endorse the idea that something like tough love (as we have defined and illustrated it, comprising far more generous and expansive practice) is an essential element in the alternative version of this. In particular, a directly negotiated style of implementation, using face-to-face encounters between public sector officials (or their partners in joint public–voluntary or public–private initiatives) is crucial because:

1 it can provide an important link between the formal and the informal economies, and promote the informal (social) economy as an efficiency and dynamism (Chapters 7 and 8);

2 it can make a bridge between the formal code of rules for social justice, social inclusion and social cohesion, and the informal ('blood-and-guts') codes of everyday life in local communities (Chapters 4, 5 and 6);

3 it can be a means of negotiating the ways in which formal rules apply to the myriad circumstances of service users' lives, the meanings they attach to these, and the identities they construct, helping them to make sense of the social world, and to be full citizens (members of society);

4 it can be a channel for criticisms and protests about the rules of the polity and the economy and their consequences, and the practices of the mainstream culture, by service users and their organizations, and hence can create possibilities for dialogue between the latter and both formal organizations and mainstream citizens.

Although the theories and research studies that might inform such practice have not been prominent in the 1990s, there are longstanding traditions that can provide useful starting points for such practice. We have already referred to the community work and community development traditions (Chapters 7 and 8); here we will focus on the above list, and show which ideas, studies and methods are relevant for these tasks.

The first of these is the interactionist tradition in sociology (Goffman, 1968, 1972; Garfinkel, 1967; Rawls, 1989; Hilbert, 1992; Travers, 1999). The work of Goffman was initially inspiring for social workers, but has since fallen into disuse. It provides an extremely valuable resource for understanding how the process of communicating meaning simultaneously constructs an informal order of its own between the partners in any interaction, and gives the participants the sense that a moral bond encompasses them, to which they make themselves accountable. This is why processes which may seem casual, *ad hoc*, provisional and unstructured are often far more lasting and effective than ones which, though apparently leading to formal agreement or even a written contract, have only superficial consent, and do not create a sense of shared purpose or mutual obligation. If interventions are really to 'stick', and be translated into lasting changes in behaviour or relationships, it is vital to understand how this can occur in such unlikely ways.

Interactionists were interested in how people who conversed with each other accomplished meaningful communication, since language was imprecise and meaning fluctuated with context (Garfinkel, 1967). Goffman's analysis showed that this was done through reciprocal claims and concessions of *social value*, which he called 'face'. Communication ('face work') involved making, giving and saving 'face'; in this process, interactants construct an everyday order of social identities and mutual trust. Social work's professional ethics have always insisted that the *value of each individual* is the fundamental basis of all practice (see for instance Biestek, 1961). Goffman showed that this was not only an ethical but also a practical requirement; by negotiating and discussing in a manner that involved ritual exchanges of value, social workers and service users created the conditions in which co-operation and support were possible, and change achievable. This was only partly a consequence of rational deliberation and consensus-building (Habermas, 1987; Dryzek, 1994); in substance it stemmed from the unintended consequences of communication itself (Rawls, 1989). Because one of the participants in such interactions is the direct or indirect representative of the public power, a bridge is thus constructed – by means of this *ad hoc*, provisional, informal order, created through face-to-face exchanges – between the everyday world of service users' lives, and the official world of formal regulation.

Furthermore, professional judgement and expertise rely on interpretation of the shared codes, and application of the common standards, by which members of the community of practitioners sustain the 'normal appearances' of practice in the distressing, chaotic and sometimes bizarre worlds of their everyday work (Garfinkel, 1967). Since rules can never unambiguously prescribe behaviour, because the norms that supposedly stabilize actions are themselves imprecise and have to be interpreted, practitioners are constantly constructing and reconstructing order from this jumble of events and emotions. Research into all kinds of expert practice reveals that this often involves departures from the literal prescriptions of laws and procedures, and acting in line with the contingencies of identity and context (Sudnow, 1967; Bittner, 1965). Social work is no exception to this; professional concepts are quite differently interpreted within the cultures and practices of particular teams (Jones, 1990). The orderly and normative nature of 'good standards' consists of members' interpretations and common commitment to their shared tasks, rather than the stipulation of precise principles and rules (Garfinkel, 1967, pp. 7–11). Reasoning and deciding draw on members' cultural resources, and the accounts that practitioners give each other in meetings and reviews create the sense of stability, predictability and obligation to good standards on which professionalism relies. In conditions of rapid change and frequent crisis, such discussions become improvisations that try to restore the fabric of normal appearances, in order to reconstitute the moral framework for the participants' activities, and indeed the sense of an external and constraining reality itself (Durkheim, 1933; 1983, pp. 14–46; Hilbert, 1992).

The second element in the analysis of these tasks is the anthropological and sociological study of how inequality of power is handled in such encounters. Social work theory has always been uncomfortable with this topic, often juxtaposing emancipatory values with justifications of authority without any indication of how these might be reconciled (Jordan, 1990). As educated professionals with secure jobs and official status, social workers seem to have the kinds of power that make a dialogue of equality and partnership problematic, even when the will to conduct this is strong. New Labour's programme encourages professionals not to shirk tasks of enforcement and control. How can these requirements be made compatible with each other?

Important clues to the answer are found in the work of James C. Scott (1985, 1990) on how subordinates resist the attempted domination of those with power over them. Through anthropological and historical examples, Scott shows that – even under quite ruthless forms of oppression – apparently powerless groups are able to resist the regimes imposed upon them, by mobilizing the rhetoric and cultural resources of their oppressors against them. They deploy the discourses to which those in authority subscribe (such as Christianity in the case of slave owners, or human rights with communist rulers in Central Europe) to claim a certain room for manoeuvre within these regimes, which they then use for covert practices of autonomy and subversion – absenteeism, go-slows, malingering, petty theft and sabotage, slander, and so on. These practices greatly add to the costs of authoritarian regimes, making them inefficient and wasteful to the point where they are finally no longer viable. We have argued (pp. 148–9) that it was the transaction and enforcement costs associated with Margaret Thatcher's policies (such as the poll tax and benefit cuts) that eventually made them unsustainable. There is a risk that the Third Way could fall victim to the same arts of resistance if it does not sustain its momentum of reform, and recognize its vulnerability to strategic action (Chapter 8).

But these ideas also show how officials can best handle issues of power and resistance. Authority has natural limits, because of the very nature of the face-to-face processes by which it must eventually be implemented; but these same limitations can be turned to the advantage of those seeking change within a framework of social justice. Dialogue between social workers and service users, for example, often involves disputes and conflicts of interest. But the process of dialogue and negotiation itself can considerably soften these, as has been demonstrated by recent political events in the Middle East and Northern Ireland. Ritual reciprocity of respect in such dialogue is at least as important as persuasive argument in building trust and creating a sense of common interest. But the evolution of a shared language in which to discuss differences is also vital. Scott (1990) shows that where provisional agreements are reached, the terms of these may be given radically different interpretations by the parties, according to their cultural practices and interests. What is agreed is sufficiently imprecise to allow this divergence of interpretation. Far from precluding co-operation, such ambiguities allow autonomy and flexibility within roles and relationships that are necessarily asymmetrical in terms of resources and power, given current economic and political structures. Research shows that this happens between partners in households, for example (Jordan et al., 1994, Chapter 7).

Community groups and social movements in dialogue with official agencies and their partners on the boundary between the state and civil society help establish new connections between the public and the private. Despite the power inequalities in such relationships, and the fragility of co-operation and trust, these interactions extend the scope for democratic practices and inclusive policies. Within public sector agencies, including social services departments, such dialogues can empower service users and gradually extend their influence on official actions (Leonardis, 1993).

Such exchanges allows the development of a new discourse which combines elements of the official formal code of welfare provision with the blood-and-guts code of everyday life. This is not the kind of wholesale adoption of supposed principles from the latter into the former that was criticized in Part I of this book (see pp. 52–4). Rather it is the gradual evolution of a medium for the communication of shared meanings and purposes, reflecting many reciprocal exchanges and the building up of trust, so that professionals and service users come to have a real sense of community, as members in a common enterprise to improve the quality of life in their neighbourhoods.

Constructive Social Work

These ideas provide the background for methods of practice that recognize it as a reciprocal construction of meaning, identity and change. Instead of a legal and procedural means of categorizing service users according to scales of risk and vulnerability, using manuals, guidelines and checklists (Howe, 1992, 1996), this emphasizes creativity and imagination in making sense of experience, self and relationships. Parton and O'Byrne (2000) trace many of the principles of their updated version of this approach to the sociological and psychological interactionism of the 1960s and 1970s, and the attempt to use these to enhance and modify the insights of the psychodynamic schools (Mattinson, 1975; Mattinson and Sinclair, 1979; Jordan, 1970, 1972). Parton and O'Byrne stress the role of talking and language in making sense and gaining control of their lives through conversation. As Howe puts it, 'clients seek to control the meaning of their own experience and the meaning that others give to that experience. Control helps clients to cope, and it empowers' (Howe, 1993, p. 195). Social work practice is a specialized version of the processes by which people define themselves, participate in their social worlds, and co-operatively construct social realities. That is why their term 'constructive' is chosen, to underline both the shared building of identity and meaning that is the basis of effective practice, and the positive results for service users that stem from this approach.

The common theme of the many techniques and practices that Parton and O'Bryne review (from Australia, New Zealand and the USA, and from counselling and therapy as well as social work) is that constructive work should be concerned with narratives of solutions to problems, and with change. Instead of providing the practitioner with information about the causes of problems, so that he or she can make an expert assessment and prescribe a 'scientific' solution, the service user is encouraged to tell the story of the problem in a way that externalizes it, giving more control and agency and creating a new perspective on how to manage or overcome it. These narratives construct the future and anticipate change; questions encourage the service user to identify exceptions to the apparently overwhelming and disabling nature of problems – situations where she or he has done something that made a difference. This leads to talk about how aspects of the service user's life could be seen differently, or lived differently, or both; in other words, it leads to constructing solutions. Service users are encouraged to discuss when the problem diminishes, when it is absent, less of a worry or less of a barrier to goals; exceptions to the problem are discussed in great detail, to clarify how there could be more of these, and how actions, talk and feelings could extend control and change.

The authors make extensive use of the work of Shazer (1985, 1988, 1991, 1994), whose training and background was not in practice but in research, and who studied counselling and therapeutic methods with a view to identifying the essential elements in effective practice. His approach has been rigorously tested over many years, and is focused on what service users say and how to help their talking become less problem-ridden and more empowering.

Shazer and his colleagues aim to identify instances where service users experience changes for the better, and to help them recognize how they have achieved these improvements. This encourages the sense of self-agency and regaining control, and opens up the possibility of new meanings, behaviours and solutions (Shazer, 1993, pp. 116–19). Questions elicit clear goals, what the service user wants, in their own words, and that involves him or her in doing something in the immediate future, making an effort, to launch a new beginning (Berg and Miller, 1992). It is easy to see how these ideas fit well with the Third Way's emphasis on achievement and change rather than passivity and provision. What is ironic is that the methods suggested by these researchers and practitioners are very much at odds with those of 'scientific' assessment and prescription. The practitioner's mode of address is one of 'curiosity and respectful puzzlement' (Parton and O'Byrne, 2000, p. 137) at the service user's unique way of making things better, rather than expertise in fitting an intervention to a need. Service users are encouraged to repeat successes, to identify solutions as theirs and right for them, and as steps to the achievement of their own goals.

Much writing about social interventions fails to take account of the stigma attached to social work, counselling and therapy, and the fact that many contacts with official agencies which see themselves as helpful and supportive are deeply resented by those who are required to experience them. This is particularly relevant for the Third Way's tough love regime, because it involves the imposition of requirements and demand on claimants, applicants and service users, and the shift from a long-term maintenance to a change-orientated approach. Constructive methods must take account of the fact that those who receive services may be suspicious or hostile to practitioners, and reluctant to risk embarking on a programme of change in which they have to sacrifice the security of well-tried strategies in favour of an untested reliance on new systems, agencies and counsellors.

In particular, service users react negatively to what they perceive as attempts to blame them for their problems, and to attribute causation to their character, personality, attitudes or motivation, pathologizing their behaviour and locating all their difficulties in themselves (White, 1996). Many government programmes and technologies of intervention have this flavour about them, and politicians' speeches often reinforce the impression of judgmentalism, blame and scorn. Among New Labour ministers, Jack Straw and Paul Boateng are unfortunate examples of this tendency, reserving their compassion for the likes of General Pinochet and Mike Tyson.

Claimants, applicants and service users are expert in rejecting these discourses of stigma and dysfunction and in developing their own narratives of injustice, oppression and exclusion, identifying the external forces in the economy and polity which disadvantage and trap them (Jordan et al., 1992, Chapters 4 and 5; Dean and Taylor-Gooby, 1992, pp. 69–74). Instead of trying to discredit and replace such accounts, constructive practice can develop them by encouraging stories which illustrate 'preferred identity claims and alternative preferred practices of self and relationship' (White, 1996). Survival strategies are identified and valued; problems are seen as problems, and not part of the person; protest at subjugation and oppression is encouraged; people's struggle to use local and personal experience to regain control over their lives is supported. Service users are invited to tell their stories using the cultural resources of their communities – local language and interpretation of the problem and the origins of oppression – because 'people's lives are shaped by the meanings that they ascribe to their experiences, by their situation in social structures and by the language practices and cultural practices of self and of relationships that they are recruited into' (White, 1993, p. 38). Parton and O'Byrne write: 'We use the language of oppression, domination, subjugation, enslavement and recruitment, finding the specifics of how the problem is dominating the person' (2000, p. 114). The service user is encouraged to distance him or herself from the problem, to give it their own unpleasant name, using their own metaphors. It can then be 'politicized' in terms of the powerful forces operating against empowerment and achievement in society – style, appearance, gender, race and family relationships, consumerism, or whatever.

All this both defeats the stereotypes of the blaming official agency, and offers the service user new ways of starting to give an account of their situation in which their agency becomes central, and they begin to gain control over it. In White's work, this reduces conflict between the practitioner and the service user, and between the latter and significant others, preparing the ground for co-operation in fighting against or reducing the influence of the problem, empowering and offering more possibilities (White, 1993). It undermines the sense of failure and allows a new narrative of solutions and achievements to be begun. None of this is supposed to reduce accountability for mistakes, offences or abuse of others, though it may challenge beliefs about more fundamental issues of self-worth and potential for change. According to O'Hanlon (1995), accountability is distinguishable from blame, because it promotes self-agency and responsibility.

A key aspect of this approach is that it encourages service users to retell their stories in terms of courageous opposition to their disadvantages and heroic resistance to their problems (O'Hanlon, 1995). Service users are invited to say how they try to overcome difficulties and adversities, and to recount their triumphs. As Parton and O'Byrne put it,

> Inviting people into a hero/heroine identity, in which there is personal agency, courage and self-value, is a major step towards change and empowerment. Actions that do not serve the person well, stories that blame or invalidate, or close down possibilities, need to be externalized.... Particular attention is paid to those occasions when the hero/heroine stood up to the problem, made it wait or exercised some power over it. (2000, pp. 122–3)

Like O'Hanlon, they use stories 'to co-construct change, to open up options and to leave the person free, to decide whether, and how, to act in new ways' (p. 123).

All this is very different from the kinds of methods associated with New Labour's regulation and guidance of social services, and the prescriptions of the evidence-based approach – but it is far better suited to the Third Way values of equal worth, opportunity, empowerment and choice. It sees the practitioner as an imaginative, enabling and creative influence, using humour, tricks, allegories and quirky questions to stimulate optimism and innovation in the service user's thinking and talking. It is constructive in encouraging co-operative exploration of a positive attitude towards change and uncertainty, risk and doubt.

CASE EXAMPLE (FROM PARTON AND O'BYRNE, 2000, PP. 125–7)

A teacher asked a social worker to talk with a child who was crying a lot at school. The girl seemed very distressed, especially approaching weekends. It transpired that her parents had recently separated and she was being forced to have 'contact' with her unloving and uncaring father with whom she never had a good relationship. Her main memory of him was of his abusive shouting at her mother and his coming home drunk. As she told her story of helplessness, it became clear that most people were afraid of her father; her mother wanted her to see him 'for peace's sake' and the child felt she had to do this or everyone in the family would 'get it'. After exploring several options, the worker could find no one who could help the child: the court had ordered weekly contact. The child felt her father was seeing her only to get even with her mother. The visits were miserable for the child and her father was always cross with her. But there seemed to be no way out.

The worker was reminded of a common Western movie tale of a quiet little town being bullied by a tyrannical gang, of whom even the sheriff was in fear. It was only when one unarmed citizen decided to take a stand, because no one else would, that the tables began to be turned on the oppressors. He mentioned this story to the child and said, 'Sometimes people just have to do it themselves – it looks like you might be the only one who can start to change things, but think carefully about your own safety.'

After some time wondering together about what she could do, how she could trick him or undermine his power, the child came up with the idea of sabotaging the contacts by 'giving him a rotten visit'. Her eyes lit up as she pondered on subtle ways of making the time with her miserable for her father. With very little encouragement she was able to plan pains and aches, coughing fits, spilling her drinks and so on. She laughed with glee at the thought of spewing out a well chewed mixture of hot dog and Coke over his shoelaces. She loved the idea of secret power, so much so that she was almost looking forward to the next meeting. This empowerment however took a different turn. While she felt better about the next contact, she decided to hold back her 'big guns' and 'play along' with being given treats. Her father seemed more friendly and they talked better than ever before. During several more visits she never needed to use her weapons. All she had needed was someone who believed in her, who valued her and validated her story and who believed she had the imaginative resources to handle the problem. It was the cowboy story that first helped her to experience the possibility of devising actions that could turn her story around.

Social Work and the Third Way

The reform programme initiated by the New Labour government is both a great opportunity for social work, and also a potential cul-de-sac. The opportunity arises from the new cultural and social context created by Tony Blair's rhetoric and the reform process. While much of the talk of beacons and moral renewal is empty, it does break out of the narrow economic individualism and blinkered vision of the Conservative period, and create a climate of change and excitement. The achievements of the programme are still questionable, and government ministers are wise to emphasize that only a 'beginning' has been made. But the atmosphere is different, and new things are now possible.

Set against this is the very restricted view of social work's role in this in New Labour's policy documents, its suspicion of the public sector, and its top-down notion of implementation. All these could easily box social work into a style of practice that serves neither its own nor the government's best interests. There are professional and managerial forces that would prefer this option, for the sake of security and comfort; there are also academic and research interests that would benefit from it in the short run. The danger is that this narrow view will prevail, because the relevant leading actors lack the vision to resist it, and the vast number of practitioners are too busy and dispirited to do anything proactive.

Tough love as a slogan for the implementation of the programme has itself an ambiguous connotation. We have used the phrase to try to capture the Third Way's emphasis on a more demanding, active, achievement-orientated style of welfare state, stressing responsibility and work, as well as support. This is positive, as long as it is linked to a flexible, adaptable and sustainable version of the labour market and the wider economy, and an imaginative approach to social welfare practice. We have criticized New Labour's assumptions about the former, but there is still plenty of time for those to be altered as events unfold and some of the hidden pitfalls of their reforms are revealed. In relation to the latter, indications have been less favourable; hence the attempt to deal in detail with issues of implementation throughout this book.

We have paid particular attention to the parts of New Labour's programme concerned with economic and social regeneration of deprived districts, such as the Employment Zones, Single Regeneration Grants and Social Exclusion Unit. It is in these programmes and schemes that there will be a huge expansion in personnel and expenditure, and that public sector initiatives will link most closely with the voluntary and community sectors. At present, social work – as conceived by both its professional practitioners and the government – is on the margins of these developments and unlikely to influence them a great deal, or be a significant aspect of their implementation.

This is a mistake. All those who will be centrally involved in these initiatives, whether as new-style government enforcement agents, professionals in existing welfare state services, voluntary or community sector staff, politicians, activists or service users, will be engaged in exactly those issues that our analysis identifies as the defining ones for New Labour's programme. The success or failure of this whole nexus of implementation will be decisive for the government, as Tony Blair's millennium message to the nation recognized. Whether or not it is called social work, and whether or not professional social workers take part in it, the policies, approach and style that we have set out seems to have the best chance of producing the results that New Labour is looking for, and that is consistent with Third Way values and goals.

In that message, Tony Blair said that he wanted to see 'a Britain that is defined to the world as a beacon of tolerance, liberty and enterprise'. He continued:

> nations that succeed will be tolerant, respectful of diversity, multi-racial, multicultural societies. Faith is important for people and will remain so. But faith is at its best when allied to reason and tolerance. (Blair, 1999b, p. 9)

This aspiration to cosmopolitanism and openness is not matched by all New Labour's policies (see Chapter 6), and it remains to be seen whether liberty and respect for diversity will be hallmarks of the Third Way. While we have tried to make allowances for the problems inherited by the Blair administration, its authoritarian tendencies have been evident in much of the social welfare programme, and this means that those who implement it must find ways to negotiate with citizens and engage their motivation. Cultural resources for these tasks exist within social work (broadly conceived to include counselling and therapy as well as social care). To make the most of these, the profession (and its kindred occupations) must reject pretensions to science on the medical model, and embrace a more fluid, creative and imaginative version of practice.

Above all, to be appropriate for the new political climate, the social welfare services need to recapture their sense of moral purpose, as transformative agencies that thrive on change and uncertainty, rather than structural features in a system of regulation and control. Tough love is a concept that expresses the Third Way's ambivalence about the process of change, emphasizing the requirements of obligation, responsibility, restraint and control, but desiring achievement, opportunity, learning and inclusion. All the evidence of policy statements, White Papers and guidelines suggests that New Labour really doesn't know how to achieve the balance between these elements in the implementation process, and wants to keep a firm central government steer on the whole programme, not trusting the public sector, and local government in particular, with its tasks.

Successful implementation of a programme for equal worth, opportunity, responsibility, community and justice cannot take the forms that the government prescribes. This is partly a matter of the rules governing benefits and services, as we saw in Chapter 8, pp. 183–98; and partly a question of practice methods. In this chapter we have tried to deal in some detail with the latter, and to present a clear model of how practitioners might reason and negotiate with service users, and challenge them when necessary. There is nothing esoteric or mystical about these methods – they stem from the ordinary rules of communication and co-operation between members of a community, respecting each others' identities and values and trying to make sense of their shared social world. Social work has no need to be ashamed of the fact that its expertise consists in the systematic and disciplined application of principles of decency and respect to all its interactions with service users who are also fellow citizens.

Social work must remain a human and creative activity, that uses imagination, empathy and commitment as well as reason and evidence, and engages with people's emotions and vulnerabilities as well as their rights and obligations. In a culture of rapid change and uncertainty, what social work would have to be ashamed of is if it came to represent rigidity, resistance and stagnation, or stigma, blame and exclusion. It should also be ashamed if it is boring and oppressive, rather than energizing and liberating.

Weber (1922) wrote of *charismatic* authority as a requirement of that type of leadership appropriate for situations where order and organization is at a discount, and more informal, less structured relations prevail. Social work should seek these situations, and forge links with other like-minded workers who thrive under these conditions. Charisma does not mean wild prophetic visions or demagogic ranting, merely the capacity to surprise, to say and do the unexpected. If social workers cannot manage to stimulate, amuse and engage their fellow citizens, as well as support and sustain them, then it will not have much to contribute to the Third Way project.

Bibliography

Adelman, H. (1991) 'Canadian Refugee Policy in the Post-war Period: An Analysis', in H. Adelman (Ed.), *Refugee Policy: Canada and the United States*, Toronto: York Lanes Press.

Aldgate, J. and Hill, M. (1996) *Child Welfare Services: Developments in Law, Practice, Policy and Research*, London: Jessica Kingsley.

Aries, P. (1983) *Centuries of Childhood: A Social History of Family Life*, New York: Knopf.

Arnold, J. and Jordan, B. (1995) 'Beyond Befriending or Past Caring? Probation Values, Training and Social Justice', in B. Williams (Ed.), *Probation Values*, Birmingham: Venture Press, pp. 75–92.

Ashdown, P. (1988) *Citizens' Britain*, London: Fourth Estate.

Atkinson, A.B. (1969) *Poverty in Britain and the Reform of Social Security*, Cambridge: Cambridge University Press.

Atkinson, A.B. (1995) *Public Economics in Action: the Basic Income/Flat Tax Proposal*, Oxford: Oxford University Press.

Attlee, C. (1920) *The Social Worker*, London: Bell.

Audi, R. (1997) *Moral Knowledge and Ethical Character*, New York: Oxford University Press.

Audit Commission (1994) *Seen but not Heard: Co-ordinating Community Health and Social Services for Children in Need*, London: HMSO.

Audit Commission (1997) *The Coming of Age: Improving Care Services for Elderly People*, London: HMSO.

Auletta, K. (1980) *The Underclass*, New York: Vintage.

Axelrod, R. (1984) *The Evolution of Co-operation*, New York: Basic Books.

Axline, V. (1964) *Dibs: In Search of Self*, London: Gollancz.

Badelt, C. (1990) 'Institutional Choice and the Non-profit Sector', in H. Anheier and W. Seibel (Eds), *The Third Sector: Comparative Studies in Non-profit Organizations*, Berlin: de Gruyter, pp. 53–64.

Bailey, R. and Brake, M. (Eds) (1975) *Radical Social Work*, London: Edward Arnold.

Barnes, C. (1991) *Disabled People in Britain and Discrimination*, London: Hurst and Co.

Batten, T.R. (1957) *Communities and their Development: An Introductory Study with Special Reference to the Tropics*, Oxford: Oxford University Press.

Beck, U. (1992) *Risk Society: Towards a New Modernity*, London: Sage.

Becker, H. (1963) *Outsiders: Studies in the Sociology of Deviance*, New York: Free Press.

Behan, B. (1956) *Borstal Boy*, London: Hutchinson.

Benington, J. (1972) 'Community Work as an Instrument of Institutional Change', in *Lessons from Experience*, London: ACW.

Bentham, J. (1780) 'An Introduction to the Principles of Morals and Legislation', in J. Bowring (Ed.), *The Works of Jeremy Bentham*, Edinburgh: Tait, vol. 1.

Bentham, J. (1791) 'Panopticon, or the Inspection House', in *Works*, vol. 4.

Bentham, J. (1798) 'Pauper Management Improved', in *Works*, vol. 8.

Bentham, J. (1843) 'Constitutional Code', in *Works*, vol. 9.

Beresford, P. (1997) 'The Last Social Division? Revisiting the Relationship between Social Policy, its Producers and Consumers', in M. May, E. Brunsdon and G. Craig (Eds), *Social Policy Review*, 9, pp. 203–26.

Beresford, P. and Croft, S. (1993) *Citizen Involvement: A Practical Guide for Change*, London: Macmillan.

Beresford, P. and Croft, S. (1995) 'It's Our Problem Too: Challenging the Exclusion of Poor People from Poverty Discourse', *Critical Social Policy*, 44/15, pp. 75–95.

Berg, I.K. and Miller, S.D. (1992) *Working with the Problem Drinkers: a Solution-Focused Approach*, New York: Norton.

Beveridge, W. (1942) *Social Insurance and Allied Services*. Cmd. 6404, London: HMSO.

Biestek, F. (1961) *The Casework Relationship*, London: Allen and Unwin.

Bittner, E. (1965) 'The Police on Skid Row: A Study in Peace Keeping', *Sociological Review*, 32, pp. 699–715.

Blair, T. (1996) Speech to Labour Party Conference.

Blair, T. (1997) Interview in *The Big Issue*, 6–12 January.

Blair, T. (1998a) *The Third Way: New Politics for the New Century*, Fabian Pamphlet 588, London: The Fabian Society.

Blair, T. (1998b) Preface to *A New Contract for Welfare* (DSS), Cm. 3805, pp. iii–v.

Blair, T. (1999a) Speech on moral standards, *Guardian*, 6 September.

Blair, T. (1999b) Speech to Labour Party Conference, *Guardian*, 29 September.

Bloom, M. (Ed.) (1993) *Single-System Designs in the Social Services: Issues and Options for the Social Services*, New York: Haworth.

Blundell, R., Duncan, A., McCrae, G. and Meghir, C. (1999) *The Labour-Market Impact of the Working Families Tax Credit*, London: Institute for Fiscal Studies.

Blunkett, D. (1983) 'Towards a Social Policy; Service "Delivery" or "Community Participation"?', in B. Jordan and N. Parton (Eds), *The Political Dimensions of Social Work*, Oxford: Blackwell.

Boal, F.W., Doherty, P. and Pringle, G.D. (1974) *The Spatial Distribution of Some Social Problems in the Belfast Area*, Belfast: Northern Ireland Community Relations Council.

Bowlby, J. (1951) *Child Care and the Growth of Love*, Geneva: World Health Organization.

Breuer, M., Faist, T. and Jordan, B. (1996) 'Collective Action, Migration and Welfare States', *International Sociology*, 10 (4), pp. 369–86.

Briscoe, I. (1995) *In Whose Service? Making Community Services Work for the Unemployed*, London: Demos.

Brown, G. (1997) 'Why Labour Is Still Loyal to the Poor', *Guardian*, 2 August.

Brown, G. (1999) Interview, *Guardian*, 31 May.

Brown, G.W. and Harris, T. (1978) *Social Origins of Depression*, London: Tavistock.

Brown, H. and Smith, H. (Eds) (1992) *Normalisation: A Reader for the Nineties*, London: Tavistock/Routledge.

Bryant, C.G.A. and Mokrycki, E. (Eds) (1994) *The New Great Transformation? Change and Continuity in East-Central Europe*, London: Routledge.

Buchanan, J.M. (1965) 'An Economic Theory of Clubs', *Economica*, 32, pp. 1–14.

Buchanan, J.M. (1994) *Ethics and Economic Progress*, Norman: University of Oklahoma Press.

Butterworth, E., Lees, R. and Arnold, P. (1981) *The Challenge of Community Work*, Papers in Community Studies, 24, York: Department of Social Administration and Social Work.

Campbell, B. (1993) *Goliath: Britain's Dangerous Places*, London: Methuen.

Campbell, P. (1996) 'The History of User Movements in the UK', in T. Heller, J. Reynolds, R. Gonun, R. Muston and S. Pattison (Eds), *Mental Health Matters*, Basingstoke: Macmillan.

Campbell, S. and Oliver, M. (1996) *Disability Politics: Understanding our Past, Changing our Future*, London: Routledge.

Carling, A. (1999) 'New Labour's Polity: Tony Giddens and the "Third Way"', *Imprints: Journal of Analytical Socialism*, 3 (3), pp. 214–42.

Castles, F.G. (1996) 'Needs-Based Strategies of Social Protection in Australia and New Zealand', in G. Esping-Andersen (Ed.), *Welfare States in Transition: National Adaptations in Global Economies*, London: Sage, pp. 88–115.

Cawson, A. (1982) *Corporatism and Welfare*, London: Heinemann.

CCETSW (Central Council for the Education and Training of Social Workers) (1990) *Statement of Requirements for the Diploma in Social Work*, Paper 30, London: CCETSW.

Challis, D. and Davies, B. (1985) 'Long-Term Care of the Elderly: The Community Care Scheme', Discussion Paper 386, Canterbury: Personal Social Services Research Unit, University of Kent.

Cheetham, J., Fuller, R., Petch, A. and McIvor, G. (1992) *Evaluating Social Work Effectiveness*, Buckingham: Open University Press.

Clarke, J., Cochrane, A. and McLoughlin, E. (1994) *Managing Social Policy*, London: Sage.

Coleman, J.S., Katz, E. and Menzel, H. (1957) 'The Diffusion of Innovation among Physicians', *Sociometry*, 20, pp. 253–70.

Cormack, U. (1945) 'Developments in Case-work', in A.F.C. Bourdillon (Ed.), *Voluntary Social Services: Their Place in the Modern State*, London, Methuen, pp. 111–27.

Corrigan, P. and Leonard, P. (1978) *Social Work Practice under Capitalism: A Marxist Approach*, London, Macmillan.

Cox, R.H. (1998) 'From Safety Nets to Trampolines: Labour Market Activation in the Netherlands and Denmark', *Governance: An International Journal of Politics and Administration*, 11 (4), pp. 397–414.

Cox, R.H. (1999) 'The Consequences of Welfare Reform: How Conceptions of Social Rights are Changing', Norman: Department of Political Science, University of Oklahoma.

CRE (Commission for Racial Equality) (1997) *Race, Culture and Community Care: An Agenda for Action*, London: Commission for Racial Equality.

Darling, A. (1999) Speech on reducing child poverty, *Guardian*, 19 July.

Davis, H. and Bourhill, M. (1997) 'Crisis: the Demonisation of Children and Young People', in P. Scratton (Ed.), *Childhood in Crisis*, London: UCL Press.

Deakin, N. (1987) *The Politics of Welfare*, London: Methuen.

Dean, H. and Melrose, M. (1998) *Poverty, Riches and Social Citizenship*, Basingstoke: Macmillan.

Dean, H. and Taylor-Gooby, P. (1992) *Dependency Culture: The Explosion of a Myth*, Hemel Hempstead: Harvester.

Denscombe, M. (1998) *The Good Research Guide for Small-Scale Research Projects*, Buckingham: Open University Press.

DETR (Department of the Environment, Trade and the Regions) (1998) *Modernising Britain*, London: Stationery Office.

DETR (Department of the Environment, Transport and the Regions) (1999) *New Deal for Communities. Learning Lessons: Pathfinders Experiences of NDC Phase I*, London: Stationery Office.

Diani, M. (1997) 'Social Movements and Social Capital: A Network Perspective on Movement Outcomes', *Mobilisation*, 2 (2), pp. 129–47.

Dobson, F. (1998) 'Frank Dobson Outlines the Third Way for Mental Health', Department of Health press release 311, 29 July.

DoH (Department of Health) (1997) *Review of the Safeguards for Children Living Away from Home*, London: Stationery Office.

DoH (Department of Health) (1998a) *Modernising Social Services: Promoting Independence, Improving Protection, Raising Standards*. Cm. 4169, London: Stationery Office.

DoH (Department of Health) (1998b) *Modernising Mental Health Services: Safe, Sound and Supportive*, London: Stationery Office.

DoH (Department of Health) (1998c) *Working Together to Safeguard Children* (Consultative Paper), London: Stationery Office.

DoH (Department of Health) (1998d) *Quality Protects: Framework for Action and Objectives for Social Services for Children*, London: Stationery Office.

DoH (Department of Health) (1999a) *Modernising Social Services: Implementation Diary*, London: Stationery Office.

DoH (Department of Health) (1999b) Press release, *Guardian*, 21 July.

Doherty, P. (1977) 'A Geography of Unemployment in the Belfast Urban Area', Unpublished PhD thesis, Queen's University, Belfast.

Dominelli, L. (1988) *Anti-Racist Social Work*, London: Macmillan.

Dominelli, L. (1989) *Feminist Social Work*, London: Macmillan.

Donnison, D. (1998) *Policies for a Just Society*, Basingstoke: Macmillan.

Douglas, M. (1996) *Thought Styles*, London: Sage.

Driver, S. and Martell, L. (1997) 'New Labour's Communitarianisms', *Critical Social Policy*, 17 (52), pp. 27–46.

Dryzek, J. (1994) *Discursive Democracy*, Cambridge: Cambridge University Press.

DSS (Department of Social Security) (1998) *A New Contract for Welfare*, Cm. 3805, London: Stationery Office.

Dudek, K.J. and Stein, R. (1999) 'Organising for Clubhouses: The Massachusetts Success Story', New York: ICCD.

Durkheim, E. (1933) *The Division of Labour in Society*, New York: Free Press.

Durkheim, E. (1983) *The Rules of Sociological Method*, New York: Free Press.

Düvell, F. and Jordan, B. (1999) 'Immigration, Asylum and Citizenship: Social Justice in a Global Context', *Imprints: Journal of Analytical Socialism*, 4 (1), pp. 15–36.

Düvell, F. and Jordan, B. (2000) '"How Low Can You Go?" Dilemmas of Social Work with Asylum Seekers in London', Exeter: Department of Social Work, Exeter University.

Düvell, F., Jordan, B. and Vogel, D. (2000) 'Police and Immigration Control: Patterns of Co-operation in the UK, Germany and the US', Bremen: Centre for Social Policy Research.

Dworkin, R. (1981) 'What is Equality? Part II: Equality of Resources', *Philosophy and Public Affairs*, 10, pp. 283–345.

Elster, J. (Ed.) (1986) *Rational Choice*, Oxford: Blackwell.

Elster, J. (1989) *The Cement of Society: A Study of Social Order*, Cambridge: Cambridge University Press.

England, H. (1986) *Social Work as Art: Making Sense of Good Practice*, London: Allen and Unwin.

Esping-Andersen, G. (1990) *The Three Worlds of Welfare Capitalism*, Cambridge: Polity.

Esping-Andersen, G. (1996) *Welfare States in Transition: National Adaptations in Global Economies*, London: Sage.

Esping-Andersen, G. (1999) 'The Jobs–Equality Trade-off', Paper presented at a summer school on Welfare States in Transition, European University Institute, Florence, 8 July.

Etzioni, A. (1969) *The Semi-Professions and their Organisation*, New York: Free Press.

Etzioni, A. (1988) *The Moral Dimension: Towards a New Economy*, New York: Free Press.

Etzioni, A. (1993) *The Spirit of Community: The Reinvention of American Society*, New York: Touchstone.

European Commission (1997) *The Member States of the EU and Immigration in 1994: Less Tolerance and Tighter Control Policies*, Luxembourg: European Commission.

European Commission (1999) 'Communication on a Concerted Strategy for Modernising Social Protection', *European Social Policy*, Supplement 100, Brussels: European Commission, October.

Eväsaari, R. (1995) 'Futures of Social Work: Everything in Human Hands – Handle with Care', in G. Jackson (Ed.), *Social Work in an International Perspective*, Helsingfors: SSKH/Helsingfors University.

Evason, E. and Woods, R. (1995) 'Poverty, Deregulation of Labour Markets and Benefit Fraud', *Social Policy and Administration*, 29 (1), pp. 40–54.

Fehér, F., Heller, A. and Márkus, G. (1983) *Dictatorship over Needs*, Oxford: Blackwell.

Fernandes, L.F. (1999) 'Re-regulation in the European Union', Paper presented at an ESRC Network meeting, University of Braga, Portugal, 17 November.

Field, F. (1997) *The Reform of Welfare*, London: Social Market Foundation.

Finch, J. (1989) *Family Obligations and Social Change*, Cambridge: Polity.

Finch, J. and Groves, D. (1984) *Labour of Love*, London: Allen and Unwin.

Finer, S.E. (1952) *The Life and Times of Sir Edwin Chadwick*, London: Methuen.

Fischer, J. (1993) 'Empirically Based Practice: the End of Ideology', in M. Bloom (Ed.), *System Design in the Social Services: Issues and Options for the 1990s*, New York: Haworth.

Fisher, M., Marsh, P. and Phillips, D. (1986) *In and Out of Care: The Experience of Children, Parents and Social Workers*, London: Batsford/British Agencies for Adoption and Fostering.

Fitzpatrick, T. (1999) *Freedom and Security: An Introduction to the Basic Income Debate*, London: Macmillan.

Flannery, M. and Glickman, M. (1996) *Fountain House: Portraits of Lives Reclaimed from Mental Illness*, Center City, MN: Hazelden Press.

Fook, J. (Ed.) (1996) *The Reflective Researcher: Social Workers' Theories of Practice Research*, Melbourne: Allen and Unwin.

Fook, J., Ryan, M. and Hawkins, L. (1997) 'Towards a Theory of Social Work Expertise', *British Journal of Social Work*, 27, pp. 399–417.

Franklin, B. and Petley, J. (1996) 'Killing the Age of Innocence: Newspaper Reporting of the Death of James Bulger', in S. Wagg and J. Pilcher (Eds), *Thatcher's Children: Politics, Childhood and Society in the 1990s*, London: Frances Pinter, pp. 134–55.

Freeden, M. (1989) *Rights*, Buckingham, Open University Press.

Fukuyama, F. (1994) *Trust: The Social Virtues and the Creation of Prosperity*, London: Hamish Hamilton.

Fuller, R. and Petch, A. (Eds) (1995) *Practitioner Research: the Reflexive Social Worker*, Buckingham: Open University Press.

Garbarino, J. and Kostelny, K. (1992) 'Child Maltreatment as a Community Problem', *Child Abuse and Neglect*, 16, pp. 445–64.

Garbarino, J. and Sherman, D. (1980) 'High-Risk Neighbourhoods and High-Risk Families: The Human Ecology of Child Maltreatment', *Child Development*, 15, pp. 188–98.

Garfinkel, H. (1967) *Studies in Ethnomethodology*, Englewood Cliffs, NJ: Prentice-Hall.

Genschell, P. (1999) *Tax Competition and Welfare States*, Cologne: Max-Planck Institute for the Study of Societies.

Gershuny, J.I. (1983) *Social Innovation and Division of Labour*, Oxford: Oxford University Press.

Gershuny, J.I. and Jones, S. (1987) The Changing Work/Leisure Balance in Great Britain, 1961–84, *Sociological Review Monograph*, 33, pp. 9–50.

Gibbons, J. Conroy, S. and Bell, C. (1995) *Operating the Child Protection System*, London: HMSO.

Giddens, A. (1998) *The Third Way: The Renewal of Social Democracy*, Cambridge: Polity.

Gill, O. and Jackson, B. (1983) *Adoption and Race*, London: Batsford.

Giller, H. and Morris, A. (1981) *Care and Discretion: Social Workers' Decisions with Delinquents*, London: Burnet Books.

Ginsburg, N. (1999) 'Putting the Social into Urban Regeneration Policy', *Local Economy*, May, pp. 17–28.

Ginsburg, N., Thake, S., Bieler, E., Ford, J., Foreman, J., Joyce, P., Lewis, J. and Ocloo, J. (1999) *Socio-Economic Assets in Poor Communities: Case Studies of Diversity; Interim Findings*, London: University of North London, School of Applied Social Sciences.

Goffman, E. (1968) *Stigma: Notes on the Management of Spoiled Identity*, London: Penguin.

Goffman, E. (1972) *Interaction Ritual: Essays on Face-to-Face Behaviour*, London: Penguin.

Goldberg, D. and Huxley, P. (1980) *Mental Illness in the Community: The Pathway to Psychiatric Care*, London: Tavistock.

Goodman, A. and Webb, S. (1995) *The Distribution of Expenditure in the United Kingdom*, London: Institute for Fiscal Studies.

Gosztonyi, G. (1993) 'Problems and Dilemmas in Organising Different Citizens' Groups towards Influencing Urban Renewal Plan in the City Centre of Budapest', Paper presented at an International Conference of Local Authorities (IULA), The Hague, Netherlands, 5 September.

Gould, N. and Taylor, I. (Eds) (1996) *Reflective Learning for Social Work: Research, Theory and Practice*, Aldershot: Ashgate.

Green, D. (1993) *Reinventing Civil Society. The Rediscovery of Welfare without Politics*, London: Institute for Economic Affairs.

Greene, J. (1994) 'Qualitative Program Evaluation: Practice and Promise', in N. Denzin and Y. Lincoln (Eds), *Handbook of Qualitative Research*, Thousand Oaks, CA: Sage, pp. 530–44.

Greer, G. (1970) *The Female Eunuch*, London: Paladin.

Grice, N. (1999), 'Shock for Blair over "Two-Nation Britain"', *Independent*, 8 September.

Habermas, J. (1987) *The Theory of Communicative Action*, Boston: Beacon Press.

Hadley, R. and Clough, R. (1995) *Care in Chaos: Frustration and Challenge in Community Care*, London: Cassell.

Hall, C. (1997) *Social Work as Narrative: Storytelling and Persuasion in Professional Texts*, Aldershot: Ashgate

Halverson, R. (1999) 'Paradoxes of Self-Organising among the Disenchanted in Welfare Society', Paper given at summer school on the Welfare State, European University Institute, Florence, 5 and 6 July.

Hardin, G. (1968) 'The Tragedy of the Commons', *Science*, 162, pp. 1243–8.

Hayek, F. (1976) *The Mirage of Social Justice*, London: Routledge and Kegan Paul.

Hayek, F. (1980) *Individualism and the Economic Order*, Chicago: University of Chicago Press.

Hazel, N. (1982) *A Bridge to Independence: The Kent Family Placement Project*, Oxford: Blackwell.

Held, D. (1980) *Introduction to Critical Theory*, London: Hutchinson.

Heron, J. (1996) *Co-operative Enquiry: Research into the Human Condition*, London: Sage.

Hilbert, R.A. (1992) *The Classical Roots of Ethnomethodology: Durkheim, Weber and Garfinkel*, Chapel Hill: North Carolina Press.

Hill, M. (1993) *The Policy Process in the Modern State*, Hemel Hempstead: Harvester.

Hill, M. (Ed.) (2000) *Local Authority Social Services*, Oxford: Blackwell.

Hill, M. and Laing, P. (1979) *Social Work and Money*, London: Allen and Unwin.

Hinks, N. (2000) *The Introduction of Knowledge-Based Practice and Learning within a Non-statutory Social Justice Organisation: Research on Action*, Exeter: Department of Social Work, Exeter University.

Hirsch, F. (1977) *Social Limits to Growth*, London: Routledge and Kegan Paul.

Hirst, M. and Baldwin, S. (1994) *Unequal Opportunities: Growing Up Disabled*, York: Social Policy Research Unit, University of York.

Hirst, P. (1994) *Associative Democracy: New Forms of Economic and Social Governance*, Cambridge: Polity.

Hobbes, T. (1651) *Leviathan*, ed. Michael Oakeshott (1966), Oxford: Blackwell.

Hoggett, P. and Burns, D. (1992) 'The Revenge of the Poor: The Anti-Poll Tax Campaign', *Critical Social Policy*, 33, pp. 95–101.

Hollis, F. (1960) *Casework: A Psychosocial Therapy*, New York: Random House.

Holman, B. (1981) *Kids at the Door: A Preventive Project in a Council Estate*, Oxford: Blackwell.

Holman, B. (1988) *Putting Families First: Prevention and Child Care*, Basingstoke: Macmillan.

Holman, B. (1998) *Faith in the Poor*, Oxford: Lion Books.

Home Office (1998) *Fairer, Faster and Firmer – A Modern Approach to Immigration and Asylum*, Cm. 4018, London: Stationery Office.
Home Office (1999) *Prison Statistics*, London: Stationery Office.
House of Commons Select Committee on Health (1994) *Community Care: the Way Forward*, London: Stationery Office.
House of Commons Select Committee on Health (1998) *Children Looked After by Local Authorities: Second Report from the Health Committee, Session 1997–8*, London: Stationery Office.
Howe, D. (1987) *An Introduction to Social Work Theory: Making Sense in Practice*, Aldershot: Wildwood House.
Howe, D. (1992) 'Child Abuse and the Bureaucratisation of Social Work', *Sociological Review*, 40 (3), pp. 491–508.
Howe, D. (1993) *On Being a Client: Understanding the Process of Counselling and Psychotherapy*, London: Sage.
Howe, D. (1996) 'Surface and Depth in Social Work Practice', in N. Parton (Ed.), *Social Theory, Social Change and Social Work*, London: Routledge.
Hudson, B. (2000) 'Adult Services', in M. Hill (Ed.), *Local Authority Social Services*, Oxford: Blackwell.
Hudson, B.A. (1993) *Penal Policy and Social Justice*, Basingstoke: Macmillan.
Hughes, G. and Little, A. (1998) 'New Labour, Communitarianism and the Public Sphere in the UK', Paper presented at 7th International Congress of Basic Income European Network, Amsterdam, 10–12 September.
Hughes, G. and Little, A. (1999) 'The Contradictions in Labour's New Communitarianism', *Imprints*, 4 (1), pp. 37–62.
Hughes, G. and Mooney, G. (1998) 'Community', in G. Hughes (Ed.), *Imagining Welfare Futures*, London: Routledge.
Hume, D. (1742) *Essays, Moral, Political and Literary*, Oxford: Oxford University Press (1985), pp. 309–52.
Hume, D. (1745) *A Treatise of Human Nature*, ed. L.A. Selby-Bigge (1988), Oxford: Clarendon Press.
Hume, L.J. (1981) *Bentham and Bureaucracy*, Cambridge: Cambridge University Press.
Iversen, T. and Wren, A. (1998) 'Equality, Employment and Budgetary Restraint: The Trilemma of the Service Economy', *World Politics*, 50, pp. 507–46.
Jack, G. and Jordan, B. (1999) 'Social Capital and Child Welfare', *Children and Society*, 13, pp. 242–56.
Jones, A. and May, J. (1992) *Working in Human Service Organisations: A Critical Introduction*, Melbourne: Longman Cheshire.
Jones, M. (1990) *Accomplishment in Adversity*, Exeter: Department of Social Work, University of Exeter.
Jones, M. and Jordan, B. (1996) 'Knowledge and Practice in Social Work', in S. Jackson and M. Preston-Shoot (Eds), *Educating Social Workers in a Changing Policy Context*, London: Whiting and Birch, pp. 254–68.
Jordan, B. (1970) *Client–Worker Transactions*, London: Routledge and Kegan Paul.
Jordan, B. (1972) *The Social Worker in Family Situations*, London: Routledge and Kegan Paul.
Jordan, B. (1973) *Paupers: The Making of the New Claiming Class*, London: Routledge and Kegan Paul.
Jordan, B. (1974) *Poor Parents: Social Policy and the Cycle of Deprivation*, London: Routledge and Kegan Paul.
Jordan, B. (1976) *Freedom and the Welfare State*, London: Routledge and Kegan Paul.
Jordan, B. (1978) 'Counselling, Advocacy and Negotiation', *British Journal of Social Work*, 17 (2), pp. 135–46.
Jordan, B. (1979) *Helping in Social Work*, London: Routledge and Kegan Paul.
Jordan, B. (1983) *Invitation to Social Work*, Oxford: Martin Robertson.
Jordan, B. (1985) *The State: Authority and Autonomy*, Oxford: Blackwell.

Jordan, B. (1987) *Rethinking Welfare*, Oxford: Blackwell.
Jordan, B. (1989) *The Common Good: Citizenship, Morality and Self-Interest*, Oxford: Blackwell.
Jordan, B. (1990) *Social Work in an Unjust Society*, Hemel Hempstead: Harvester.
Jordan, B. (1995) 'Are New Right Policies Sustainable? "Back to Basics" and Public Choice', *Journal of Social Policy*, 24 (3), pp. 363–84.
Jordan, B. (1996a) *A Theory of Poverty and Social Exclusion*, Cambridge: Polity.
Jordan, B. (1996b) 'Democratic Community and Public Choice', in E.O. Erikson and J. Loftager (Eds), *The Rationality of the Welfare State*, Oslo: Scandinavian University Press.
Jordan, B. (1997) 'Social Work in Society', in M. Davies (Ed.), *The Blackwell Companion to Social Work*, Oxford: Blackwell, pp. 8–24.
Jordan, B. (1998a) *The New Politics of Welfare: Social Justice in a Global Context*, London: Sage.
Jordan, B. (1998b) 'New Labour, New Community?', *Imprints: Journal of Analytical Socialism*, 3 (2), pp. 113–31.
Jordan, B. (1998c) 'Child Sexual Abuse and the Community', in N. Parton and C. Wattam (Eds), *Child Sexual Abuse: Responding to the Experiences of Children*, Chichester: Wiley, pp. 181–96.
Jordan, B. (1999a) 'Bulger, "Back to Basics" and the Rediscovery of Community', in B. Franklin (Ed.), *Social Policy, the Media and Misrepresentation*, London: Routledge, pp. 193–206.
Jordan, B. (1999b) 'Morality and Welfare', Paper presented at conference on 'The Morality of Welfare', St George's House, Windsor Castle, 28 June.
Jordan, B. (1999c) 'Undocumented Brazilian Workers in London: Identities, Decisions and Strategies', in E. Eichenhofer (Ed.), *Migration und Illegalität*, Osnabrück: Universitätsverlag Rasch, pp. 177–94.
Jordan, B. (1999d) 'Social Work in the Shadow of the Market Economy', Plenary address to the conference of the IFSW/ISSW, Helsinki, 20 June.
Jordan, B. (2000) *Improving Labour-Market Incentives in Recent UK Tax-Benefit Reforms*, Cologne: Max-Planck Institute for the Study of Societies.
Jordan, B., James, S., Kay, H. and Redley, M. (1992) *Trapped in Poverty? Labour-Market Decisions in Low-Income Households*, London: Routledge.
Jordan, B. and Jones, M. (1995) 'Association and Exclusion in the Organisation of Social Care', *Social Work and Social Sciences Review*, 6 (1), pp. 5–18.
Jordan, B. and Loftager, J. (1999) 'Labour-Market Activation in the UK and Denmark', Paper presented at a conference on unemployment, Graz, Austria.
Jordan, B. and Parton, N. (Eds) (1983) *The Political Dimension of Social Work*, Oxford: Blackwell.
Jordan, B. and Redley, M. (1994) 'Polarization, Underclass and the Welfare State', *Work, Employment and Society*, 8 (2), pp. 153–76.
Jordan, B. and Travers, A. (1998) 'The Informal Economy – A Case Study in Unrestrained Competition', *Social Policy and Administration*, 32 (3), pp. 292–306.
Jordan, B. and Vogel, D. (1997) *Which Policies Influence Migration Decisions? A Comparative Analysis of Qualitative Interviews with Undocumented Brazilian Immigrants in London and Berlin as a Contribution to Economic Reasoning*, Bremen: University of Bremen, Centre for Social Policy Research, Arbeitspapier 14/97.
Jordan, B., Redley, M. and James, S. (1994) *Putting the Family First: Decisions, Identities, Citizenship*, London: UCL Press.
Jordan, B., Vogel, D. and Estrella, K. (1997) 'Leben und Arbeiten ohne regulären Aufenthaltsstatus: Brazilianische Migrantinnen in London und Berlin', *Leviathan*, 17/97, pp. 215–31.
Jordan, B., Agulnik, P., Burbidge, D. and Duffin, S. (2000) *Stumbling towards a Basic Income: Tax-Benefit Reform in the UK*, London: Citizens Income Trust.

Karvinen, S., Pösö, T. and Satka, M. (Eds) (1999) *Reconstructing Social Work Research: Finnish Methodological Adaptations*, Jyväskylä: So Phil/University of Jyväskylä.

Kazi, M. (1998) 'Practice Research in England', Paper presented at International Conference on Research for Social Work Practice, Florida International University, North Miami, 24–26 January.

Keat, R. and Urry, J. (1975) *Social Theory as Science*, London: Routledge and Kegan Paul.

Kemshall, H. and Pritchard, J. (Eds) (1996) *Good Practice in Risk Assessment and Risk Management*, London: Jessica Kingsley.

Knijn, T. (1998) 'Social Care in the Netherlands', in J. Lewis (Ed.), *Gender, Social Care and Welfare State Restructuring*, Aldershot: Ashgate, pp. 85–110.

Kolankiewicz, G. (1996) 'Social Capital and Social Change', *British Journal of Sociology*, 47 (3), pp. 427–41.

Krempel, L. and Schnegg, M.N. (2000) 'Exposure, Networking and Mobilisation: The Petition Movement during the 1848/9 Revolution in a German Town', Cologne: Max-Planck Institute for the Study of Societies.

Kupperman, J.J. (1991) *Character*, New York: Oxford University Press.

Kusá, Z. (1997) 'Topics of Inequality and Exclusion in Poor People's Family History Narratives', Paper presented to 3rd ESA Conference, 'Twentieth Century Europe: Inclusions-Exclusions', University of Essex, 26–30 August.

Kymlicka, W. (1989) *Liberalism, Community and Culture*, Oxford: Clarendon Press.

Kymlicka, W. and Norman, W. (1994) 'Return of the Citizen: A Survey of Recent Work on Citizenship Theory', *Ethics*, 104 (2), pp. 352–8.

Lasch, S. (1994) 'The Making of an Underclass: Neo-liberalism versus Corporatism?', in P. Brown and R. Crompton (Eds), *Economic Restructuring and Social Exclusion*, London: UCL Press, pp. 157–74.

Leaper, R.A.B. (1968) *Community Work*, London: National Council of Social Service.

Lenaghan, J. (1999) 'Fit to Spend', *Guardian*, 20 December.

Leonard, M. (1994) *Informal Economic Activity in Belfast*, Aldershot: Avebury.

Leonard, M. (1998a) 'The Long-Term Unemployed, Economic Activity and the "Underclass" in Belfast', *International Journal of Urban and Regional Research*, 22 (1), pp. 42–59.

Leonard, M. (1998b) *Invisible Work, Invisible Workers: The Informal Economy in Europe and the USA*, London: Macmillan.

Leonard, M. (1999) 'Informal Economic Activity: Strategies of Households and Communities', Paper presented at 4th ESA Conference 'Will Europe Work?', Amsterdam, 18–21 August.

Leonardis, O. de (1993) 'New Patterns of Collective Action in "Post-Welfare Society"', in G. Drover and P. Kerans (Eds), *New Approaches to Welfare Theory*, Aldershot: Edward Elgar, pp. 177–89.

Lewis, J. (1992) 'Gender and the Development of Welfare Regimes', *Journal of European Social Policy*, 2 (3), pp. 159–71.

Lindblom, C. and Woodhouse, E.J. (1993) *The Policy Making Process*, Englewood Cliffs, NJ: Prentice-Hall.

Lisham, J. (Ed.) (1984) *Evaluation*, Recent Highlights in Social Work, 8, London: Jessica Kingsley.

Lister, R. (1998) 'From Equality to Social Inclusion: New Labour and the Welfare State', *Critical Social Policy*, 18 (55), pp. 217–29.

Lister, R. (1999) 'First Steps to a Fairer Society', *Guardian Society*, *The Guardian*, 9 June.

Locke, J. (1698) *Two Treatises of Government*, ed. P. Laslett (1967), Cambridge: Cambridge University Press.

Lorenz, W. (1995) *Social Work in a Changing Europe*, London: Routledge.

Macadam, E. (1945) *The Social Servant in the Making*, London: Allen and Unwin.

MacDonald, G. (1994) 'Developing Empirically-Based Practice in Probation', *British Journal of Social Work*, 24, pp. 405–27.

MacDonald, G. (1998) 'Promoting Evidence-Based Practice in Child Protection', *Clinical Child Psychiatry and Psychology*, 3 (1), pp. 71–85.

MacDonald, G. and Sheldon, B. (1992) 'Contemporary Studies in the Effectiveness of Social Work', *British Journal of Social Work*, 22, pp. 615–43.

MacDonald, R. (1997) 'Fiddly Jobs, Undeclared Work and the Something for Nothing Society', *Employment and Society*, 8 (4), pp. 507–30.

Macfarlane, R. (1996) *Unshackling the Poor: A Complementary Approach to Economic Development*, York: Joseph Rowntree Foundation.

Macias, C., Jackson, R., Schroeder, C. and Wang, Q. (1999) *What Is a Clubhouse? Report on the ICCD 1996 Survey of US Clubhouses*, New York: ICCD.

MacIntyre, A. (1981) *After Virtue: A Study in Moral Theory*, London: Duckworth.

MacNichol, J. and Smith, D. (1999) 'Social Insecurity and the Informal Economy: Survival Strategies on a South London Estate', Paper presented at the Annual Conference of the Social Policy Association, July.

Mandela, N. (1996) *Long Walk to Freedom*, London: Little, Brown.

Margalit, A. (1996) *The Decent Society*, Cambridge, MA: Harvard University Press.

Marquand, D. (1998) *The New Reckoning*, Cambridge: Polity.

Marshall, T.H. (1950) *Citizenship and Social Class*, Cambridge: Cambridge University Press.

Marske, C.E. (1991) *Communities of Fate: Readings in the Social Organisation of Risk*, Lanham, VA: University Press of America.

Marx, K. and Engels, F. (1848) 'Manifesto of the Communist Party', in K. Marx and F. Engels, *Collected Works*, London: Lawrence and Wishart, vol. 6.

Mattinson, J. (1975) *The Reflection Process in Casework Supervision*, London: Institute of Marital Studies, Tavistock Institute of Human Relations, Research Publications Services.

Mattinson, J. and Sinclair, I. (1979) *Mate and Stalemate: Marital Work in a Local Authority Social Services Department*, Oxford: Blackwell.

Mayo, M., (1998) 'Community work', in R. Adams, L. Dominelli and M. Payne (Eds), *Social Work: Themes, Issues and Critical Debates*, Basingstoke: Macmillan, pp. 160–72.

Mayo, M., Fisher, T., Connaty, P., Dolin, J. and Mollineux, A. (1998) *Small Is Bankable: Community Investment in the UK*, York: Joseph Rowntree Foundation.

Mazibuko, F. (1996) 'Social Work and Sustainable Development: The Challenges for Practice, Training and Policy in South Africa', Paper given at Joint World Congress of IFSW and IASSW, Hong Kong, July.

McCormick, J. (1994) *Citizens' Service*, London: Institute for Public Policy Research.

McGuire, J. (Ed.) (1995) *What Works? – Reducing Reoffending*, Chichester: Wiley.

Mead, L.M. (1986) *Beyond Entitlement: The Social Obligations of Citizenship*, New York: Free Press.

Mental Health Foundation (1996) *Building Expectations*, London: Mental Health Foundation.

Mezey, A. and Evans, E. (1971) 'Psychiatric In-Patients and Out-Patients in a London Borough', *British Journal of Psychiatry*, 118, pp. 609–16.

Middleton, H. and Shaw, I. (1999) 'Inequalities in Mental Health: Models and Explanations', *Policy and Politics*, 27 (1), pp. 43–56.

Midgley, J. (1995) *Social Development: The Developmental Perspective in Social Welfare*, London: Sage.

Midgley, J. (1997) 'Social Work in International Context: Challenges and Opportunities for the 21st Century', in M. Reisch and E. Gambrill (Eds), *Social Work in the 21st Century*, Thousand Oaks, CA: Pine Forge, pp. 59–67.

Milburn, A. (1999) Speech to Directors of Social Services, *Guardian*, 29 October.

Mill, J.S. (1889) 'On Liberty', in *Utilitarianism, Liberty and Representative Government* (1912), London: Dent.

Miller, E.J. and Gwynne, G.V. (1972) *A Life Apart*, London: Tavistock.

Miller, S. (1974) *Experimental Design and Statistics*, London: Methuen.

Millham, S., Bullock, R., Hosie, K. and Haak, M. (1986) *Lost in Care: The Problems of Maintaining Links between Children in Care and their Families*, London: Gower.

Mitchell, S. (2000) 'Future Organisation', in M. Hill (Ed.), *Local Authority Social Services*, Oxford: Blackwell.

Moroney, R.M. (1976) *The Family and the State: Considerations for Social Policy*, London: Longman.

Mueller, D.C. (1989) *Public Choice II*, Cambridge: Cambridge University Press.

Murgatroyd, L. and Neuburger, H. (1997) 'A Household Satellite Account for the UK', *Economic Trends*, 527, pp. 63–71.

Murray, C. (1983) *Losing Ground: American Social Policy, 1950–1980*, New York: Basic Books.

Murray, C. (1989) 'Underclass', *Sunday Times Magazine*, 26 November, pp. 26–45.

Niskanen, W.A. (1975) 'Bureaucrats and Politicians', *Journal of Law and Economics*, 18, pp. 617–43.

Nocon, A. and Qureshi, H. (1996) *Outcomes of Community Care for Users and Carers*, Buckingham: Open University Press.

NSPCC (National Society for the Prevention of Cruelty to Children) (1999) *Long-Term Strategy to End Cruelty to Children*, London: NSPCC.

Nuttall, C. (1999) 'Rising Optimism', *Guardian*, 13 October.

O'Brien, J. and Tyne, A. (1981) *The Principle of Normalisation: A Foundation for Effective Services*, London: Campaign for Mentally Handicapped People.

O'Hanlon, C. (1995) 'Breaking the Bad Trance', Paper given at a conference on Therapeutic Conversations, London.

Oliver, M. (1996) *Understanding Disability: From Theory to Practice*, Basingstoke: Macmillan.

Oliver, M. and Barnes, C. (1998) *Disabled People and Social Policy: From Exclusion to Inclusion*, London: Longman.

Olson, M. (1965) *The Logic of Collective Action: Public Goods and the Theory of Groups*, Cambridge, MA: Harvard University Press.

Olson, M. (1982) *The Rise and Decline of Nations: Economic Growth, Stagflation and Social Rigidities*, New Haven, CT: Yale University Press.

Ostner, I. (1998) 'The Politics of Care Policies in Germany', in J. Lewis (Ed.), *Gender, Social Care and Welfare State Restructuring*, Aldershot: Ashgate, pp. 111–37.

Ostrom, E. (1990) *Governing the Commons: The Evolution of Institutions for Collective Action*, Cambridge: Cambridge University Press.

Packman, J. (1975) *The Child's Generation*, Oxford: Blackwell.

Packman, J. and Hall, C. (1997) *From Care to Accommodation: Support, Protection and Control in Child Care Services*, London: Stationery Office.

Packman, J. and Jordan, B. (1991) 'The Children Act: Looking Forward, Looking Back', *English Journal of Social Work*, 21, pp. 315–27.

Packman, J., Randall, J. and Jacques, N. (1986) *Who Needs Care? Social Work Decisions about Children*, Oxford: Blackwell.

Pahl, R. (1984) *Divisions of Labour*, Oxford: Blackwell.

Parton, N. (1985) *The Politics of Child Abuse*, London: Macmillan.

Parton, N. (1991) *Governing the Family: Child Care, Child Protection and the State*, London: Macmillan.

Parton, N. (1994) 'The Nature of Social Work under Conditions of (Post) Modernity', *Social Work and Social Science Review*, 5 (2), pp. 93–112.

Parton, N. (1998) 'Risk, Advanced Liberalism and Child Welfare: The Need to Rediscover Uncertainty and Ambiguity', *British Journal of Social Work*, 28 (1), pp. 5–27.

Parton, N. and O'Byrne, P. (2000) *Constructive Social Work*, Basingstoke: Macmillan.

Parton, N., Thorpe, D. and Wattam, C. (1997) *Child Protection, Risk and the Social Order*, London: Macmillan.

Paugam, S. (1998) 'Poverty and Social Exclusion: A Sociological View', in M. Rhodes and Y. Mény (Eds), *The Future of European Welfare: A New Social Contract?* Basingstoke: Macmillan, pp. 41–62.

Payne, M. (1991) *Modern Social Work Theory*, London: Macmillan.

Peacock, A. (1979) *The Economic Analysis of Government*, Oxford: Martin Robertson.

Peile, C. and McCouat, M. (1997) 'The Rise of Relativism: The Future of Theory and Knowledge Development in Social Work', *British Journal of Social Work*, 27, pp. 343–60.

Phillips, M. (1993) 'Tough Love', *Observer*, 13 June.

Piirainen, T. (1997) *Towards a New Social Order in Russia: Transforming Structures of Everyday Life*, Aldershot: Dartmouth.

Pinchbeck, I. and Hewitt, M. (1973) *Children in English Society* (2 vols), London: Routledge and Kegan Paul.

Polanyi, K. (1944) *The Great Transformation: The Political and Economic Origins of Our Time*, Boston: Beacon Press.

Popkin, S. (1975) *The Rational Peasant: The Political Economy of Rural Vietnam*, Chicago: Chicago University Press.

Popper, K. (1950) *The Open Society and Its Enemies*, London: Routledge and Kegan Paul.

Power, A. (1997) *Estates on the Edge: The Social Consequences of Mass Housing in Europe since 1850*, London: Routledge.

Pressman, J. and Wildavsky, A. (1973) *Implementation*, Berkeley: University of California Press.

Pringle, K. (1998) *Children and Social Welfare in Europe*, Buckingham: Open University Press.

Pringle, K., Gray, S. and Higgs, M. (1997) 'User-Centred Responses to Child Sexual Abuse: The Way Forward', *Child and Family Social Work*, 2 (1), pp. 49–57.

Putnam, R.D. (1993) *Making Democracy Work: Civic Traditions in Modern Italy*, Princeton, NJ: Princeton University Press.

Rawls, A.W. (1989) 'Language, Self and Social Order: A Reformulation of Goffman and Sacks', *Human Studies*, 12, pp. 147–72.

Rawls, J. (1971) *A Theory of Justice*, Oxford: Oxford University Press.

Raynor, P. (1985) *Social Work, Justice and Control*, Oxford: Blackwell.

Redmond, G. and Sutherland, H. (1995) *The Proposed Earnings Top-Up: A Comment*, Cambridge: Microsimulation Unit, Department of Applied Economics.

Reid, W. (1994) 'The Empirical Practice Movement', *Social Services Review*, 68, pp. 165–84.

Reid, W. and Epstein, L. (1977) *Task-Centred Practice*, New York: Columbia University Press.

Revenko, A. (1997) 'Poor Strata of Population in Ukraine', Paper given at the 3rd International Conference on Social Problems, 'Social History of Poverty in Central Europe', Lodz, Poland, 3–6 December.

Rifkin, J. (1995) *The End of Work*, New York: G.P. Putnam's.

Rousseau, J.J. (1762) *The Social Contract*, ed. R. Smith (1952), London: Dent.

Rowe, J. (1989) *Child Care Now: A Survey of Placement Patterns*, London: British Agencies for Adoption and Fostering.

Rowlingson, K., Wiley, C. and Newburn, T. (1997) *Social Security Fraud*, London: Policy Studies Institute.

Rowntree Trust (1995) *The Joseph Rowntree Inquiry into Income and Wealth*, York: Joseph Rowntree Trust.

Ruggie, J.G. (1982) 'International Regimes, Transactions and Change: Embedded Liberalism and the Postwar Economic Order', *International Organisation*, 36 (2), pp. 379–415.

Ryan, A. (1983) 'Mill and Rousseau: Utility and Rights', in G. Duncan (Ed.), *Democratic Theory and Practice*, Cambridge: Cambridge University Press.

Ryburn, M. (Ed.) (1994) *Contested Adoptions: Research, Law, Policy and Practice*, Aldershot: Arena.

Sabel, B. (1983) 'Community and Social Services', in B. Jordan and N. Parton (Eds), *The Political Dimensions of Social Work*, Oxford: Blackwell, pp. 109–29.

Sackett, D.L., Rosenberg, W.M., Gray, J.H.M., Haynes, R.B. and Richardson, W.S. (1996) 'Evidence-Based Medicine: What it is and What it isn't', *British Medical Journal*, 312 (7203), pp. 71–2.

Sainsbury, E., Nixon, S. and Phillips, D. (1982) *Social Work in Focus: Clients and Social Workers' Perceptions of Long-Term Social Work*, London: Routledge and Kegan Paul.

Sandel, M. (1983) *Liberalism and the Limits of Justice*, Cambridge: Cambridge University Press.

Sassen, S. (1996) 'New Employment Regimes in Cities: the Impact on Immigrant Workers', *New Community*, 22, pp. 579–94.

Satka, M. (1999) 'Conceptual Practices in Theorising the Social Work Past for the Future', in S. Karvinen, T. Pösö and M. Satka, *Reconstructing Social Work Research*, pp. 17–53.

Satyamurti, C. (1980) *Occupational Survival: The Case of the Local Authority Social Worker*, Oxford: Blackwell.

Scharpf, F.W. (1999) *The Viability of Advanced Welfare States in the International Economy: Vulnerabilities and Options*, Working Paper 99–9, Cologne: Max-Planck Institute for the Study of Societies.

Schön, D. (1983) *The Reflective Practitioner*, New York: Basic Books.

Schumpeter, J. (1936) *The Theory of Economic Development* (1911), Cambridge, MA: Harvard University Press.

Scott, J.C. (1970) *The Moral Economy*, New Haven, CT: Yale University Press.

Scott, J.C. (1985) *Weapons of the Weak: Everyday Forms of Peasant Resistance*, New Haven, CT: Yale University Press.

Scott, J.C. (1990) *Domination and the Arts of Resistance: Hidden Transcripts*, New Haven, CT: Yale University Press.

Scriven, M. (1997) 'Truth and Objectivity in Evaluation', in E. Chelimsky and W. Shadik (Eds), *Evaluation for the 21st Century*, Thousand Oaks, CA: Sage.

Shaw, I. (1997) 'Social Work Evaluation: Emancipation or Evidence?', Paper given to IFSW/EASSW European Seminar, University College, Dublin, August.

Shaw, I. (2000) 'Mental Health', in M. Hill (Ed.), *Local Authority Social Services*, Oxford: Blackwell.

Shazer, S. de (1985) *Keys to Solutions in Brief Therapy*, New York: Norton.

Shazer, S. de (1988) *Clues: Investigating Solutions in Brief Therapy*, New York: Norton.

Shazer, S. de (1991) *Putting Difference to Work*, New York: Norton.

Shazer, S. de (1993) 'Creative Misunderstandings', in S. Gilligan and R. Price (Eds), *Therapeutic Conversations*, New York: Norton.

Shazer, S. de (1994) *Words Were Originally Magic*, New York: Norton.

Sheenan, M. and Tomlinson, M. (1996) 'Long-Term Unemployment and the Community Work Programme', in E. McLoughlin and P. Quirk (Eds), *Policing Aspects of Employment Equality in Northern Ireland*, Belfast: Standing Advisory Committee on Human Rights.

Sheldon, B. (1978) 'Theory and Practice in Social Work: A Re-examination of a Tenuous Relationship', *British Journal of Social Work*, 8 (1), pp. 1–22.

Sheldon, B. et al. (1999) *Prospects for Evidence-Based Social Care: An Empirical Study*, Exeter: Centre for Evidence-Based Social Services, University of Exeter.

Sheppard, M. (1998) 'Practice Validity, Reflexivity and Knowledge for Social Work', *British Journal of Social Work*, 28, pp. 763–81.

Simpkin, M. (1979) *Trapped in Welfare*, London: Edward Arnold.

Singleton, S. and Taylor, M. (1992) 'Common Property, Collective Action and Community', *Journal of Theoretical Politics*, 4 (3), pp. 309–24.

Skinner, B.F. (1973) *Beyond Freedom and Dignity*, New York: Knopf.

Smith, A. (1767) *The Theory of Moral Sentiments*, in H.W. Schneider (Ed.), *Adam Smith's Moral and Political Philosophy* (1948), New York: Harper.

Smith, A. (1776) *An Inquiry into the Nature and Causes of the Wealth of Nations*, ed. R.H. Campbell and A.S. Skinner (1976), Oxford: Clarendon Press.

Smith, S. (1986) *Britain's Shadow Economy*, Oxford: Clarendon Press.

Social Exclusion Unit (1998) *Rough Sleeping*, London: Stationery Office.

Specht, H. and Vickery, A. (Eds) (1977) *Integrating Social Work Methods*, London: Allen and Unwin.

Spragens, T. (1981) *The Irony of Liberal Reason*, Chicago: Chicago University Press.

SSI (Social Services Inspectorate) (1995) *Child Protection: Messages from Research*, London: Stationery Office.

SSI (Social Services Inspectorate) (1998) *Social Services Facing the Future: The Seventh Annual Report of the Chief Inspector*, London: Stationery Office.

SSI (1999) *Children's Services Planning: Planning to Deliver Change:* London: Stationary Office.

Standing, G. (1999) *Global Labour Flexibility: Seeking Distributive Justice*, Basingstoke: Macmillan.

Starrett, D.A. (1988) *Foundations of Public Economics*, Cambridge: Cambridge University Press.

Statham, D. (1978) *Radicals in Social Work*, London: Routledge and Kegan Paul.

Stevenson, O. (1998a) 'It Was More Difficult Than We Thought: Reflection on 50 Years of Child Welfare Practice', *Child and Family Social Work*, 3 (3), pp. 153–61.

Stevenson, O. (1998b) 'Social Work with Children and Families', in O. Stevenson (Ed.), *Child Welfare in the UK*, Oxford: Blackwell.

Straw, J. (1999a) Speech on asylum seekers, *Guardian*, 24 August.

Straw, J. (1999b) Speech on travellers, *Guardian*, 20 August.

Straw, J. (1999c) Speech on unruly child curfews, *Guardian*, 7 September.

Streeck, W. (1999) 'Comparative Solidarity: Rethinking the "European Social Model"', Working Paper 99/8, Cologne: Max-Planck Institute for the Study of Societies.

Sudnow, D. (1967) *Passing On: The Social Organisation of Dying*, Englewood Cliffs, NJ: Prentice-Hall.

Swaan, A. de (1988) *In Care of the State: Health Care, Education and Welfare in Europe and the USA in the Modern Era*, Cambridge: Polity.

Taylor, C. (1989) *Sources of Self*, Cambridge: Cambridge University Press.

Taylor, M. (1987) *The Possibility of Co-operation*, Cambridge: Cambridge University Press.

Thoburn, J. (1994) *Child Placement: Principles and Practice*, Aldershot: Wildwood House.

Thompson, N. (1997) *Anti-Discriminatory Practice*, London: Macmillan.

Thompson, N. (1998) *Promoting Equality: Challenging Discrimination and Oppression in Human Services*, London: Macmillan.

Thorpe, D. (1997) 'Policing Minority Child-Rearing Practices in Australia: The Consistency of "Child Abuse"', in N. Parton (Ed.), *Child Protection and Family Support: Tensions, Contradictions and Possibilities*, London: Routledge, pp. 59–77.

Thorpe, D., Smith, D. and Tutt, N. (1980) *Out of Care*, London: Allen and Unwin.

Thyer, B. (1989) 'First Principles of Practice Research', *British Journal of Social Work*, 19 (4), pp. 314–26.

Timms, N. (1964) *Social Casework*, London: Routledge and Kegan Paul.

Titmuss, R.M. (1968) *Commitment to Welfare*, London: Allen and Unwin.

Tocqueville, A. de (1836) *Democracy in America*, ed. J.P. Mayer and M. Lerner (1968), London: Collins.

Travers, A. (1999) 'The Face that Begs: Street Begging Scenes and Selves' Identity Work', in H. Dean (Ed.), *Begging Questions: Street-Level Economic Activity and Social Policy Failure*, Bristol: Policy Press, pp. 121–42.

Treasury (1999) 'Chancellor Announces Further Measures to Increase Employment Opportunities and Support Families', London: HM Treasury Press Office, 9 November.

Tunstill, J. (1996) 'Family Support: Past, Present and Future Challenges', *Child and Family Social Work*, 1 (3), pp. 151–8.

Ungerson, C. (1987) *Policy Is Personal: Gender and Informal Care*, London: Tavistock.

Valente, T. (1995) *Network Models of the Diffusion of Innovations*, Cresshill: Hampton Press.

Valente, T. (1996) 'Social Network Thresholds in the Diffusion of Innovations', *Social Networks*, 18, pp. 69–89.

Van Parijs, P. (1995) *Real Freedom for All: What (if Anything) is Wrong with Capitalism?*, Oxford: Oxford University Press.

Van Parijs, P. and Van der Veen, R. (1987) 'A Capitalist Road to Communism', *Theory and Society*, 15, pp. 635–55.

Van Trier, W. (1995) 'Every One A King', Doctoral Dissertation, University of Leuven, Department of Sociology.

Waddan, A. (1997) *The Politics of Social Welfare: The Collapse of the Centre and the Rise of the Right*, Cheltenham: Edward Elgar.

Walker, A. and Walker, C. (1998) *Uncertain Futures: People with Learning Difficulties and their Ageing Family Carers*, Brighton: Pavilion Publishing.

Walker, C. and Ryan, T. (1995) *Fair Shares for All?*, Brighton: Pavilion Publishing.

Walzer, M. (1983) *Spheres of Justice*, Oxford: Blackwell.

Weale, A. (1983) *Political Theory and Social Policy*, London: Macmillan.

Webb, S.A. (1999) *Some Considerations on the Validity of Evidence-Based Social Care*, Bradford: Department of Applied Social Studies, University of Bradford.

Weber, M. (1922) *Economy and Society*, ed. G. Roth and C. Wittick (1968), New York: Bedminster Press.

Weick, A. and Saleeby, D. (1998) 'Post-modern Perspectives for Social Work', *Social Thought*, 18 (3), pp. 21–40.

Weinstein, J. (1997) 'A Proper Haunting', *Journal of Grief Counselling*, 9 (2), pp. 101–19.

Weiss, L. (1987) 'Explaining the Underground Economy: State and Social Structure', *British Journal of Sociology*, 38, pp. 216–34.

White, M. (1993) 'Deconstruction and Therapy', in S. Gilligan and R. Price (Eds), *Therapeutic Conversations*, New York: Norton.

White, M. and Epston, D. (1990) *Narrative Means to Therapeutic Ends*, New York: Norton.

White, S. (1996) 'Reciprocity in the Defence of Basic Income', Paper given at Basic Income European Network Conference, Vicuna, 12–14 September.

Williams, A. (1994) *Contracting for Children*, Social Services Management Unit, Department of Social Policy and Social Work, Birmingham University.

Williams, B. (Ed.) (1996) *Probation Values*, Birmingham: Venture Press.

Williams, C.C. and Windebank, J. (1999) *Empowering People to Help Themselves: Tackling Social Exclusion in Deprived Neighbourhoods*, Department of Geography, Leicester University.

Williams, F. (Ed.) (1994) *Community Care: A Reader*, Basingstoke: Macmillan.

Williams, F. (1998) 'New Principles in a Good-Enough Welfare State in the Millennium', Paper delivered at World Congress of Sociology, Montreal, Canada, 26–31 July.

Wilson, W.J. (1989) *The Truly Disadvantaged: The Underclass, the Ghetto and Public Policy*, Chicago: Chicago University Press.

Wilson, W.J. (1997) *When Work Disappears: The World of the New Urban Poor*. London: Vintage.

Winnicott, D. (1958) 'Anxiety Associated with Insecurity', in D. Winnicott, *Collected Papers*, London: Tavistock.

Woodruffe, K. (1962) *From Charity to Social Work*, London: Routledge and Kegan Paul.

6, P. (1998) *The Future of Privacy, vol. 1: Private Life and Public Policy*, London: Demos.

6, P. (1999a) 'Tackling Social Exclusion and Unemployment: A Preliminary Assessment of New Labour's Approach in Britain', Paper presented at Foundaçion Sistema Conference, Madrid, 3 December.

6, P. (1999b) 'Welfare under Moral Scrutiny: Self-Reliance, Paternalism, Preventing Intrusion and Moral Character', Paper presented at consultation on 'The Morality of Welfare', St George's House, Windsor Castle, 27–29 June.

6, P. (2000) *The Politics of Moral Character: Cultural Change and Public Policy.*

6, P. and Randon, A. (1995) *Liberty, Charity and Politics: Non-Profit Law and Freedom of Speech*, Aldershot: Dartmouth.

6, P., Leat, D., Selzer, K. and Stoker, G. (1999) *Governing in the Round: Strategies for Holistic Government*, London: Demos.

Index

Lightning Source UK Ltd.
Milton Keynes UK
UKOW04f1803200314

228525UK00001B/55/P